TAKING MANHATTAN

ALSO BY RUSSELL SHORTO

Smalltime

Revolution Song

Amsterdam

Descartes' Bones

The Island at the Center of the World

Saints and Madmen

Gospel Truth

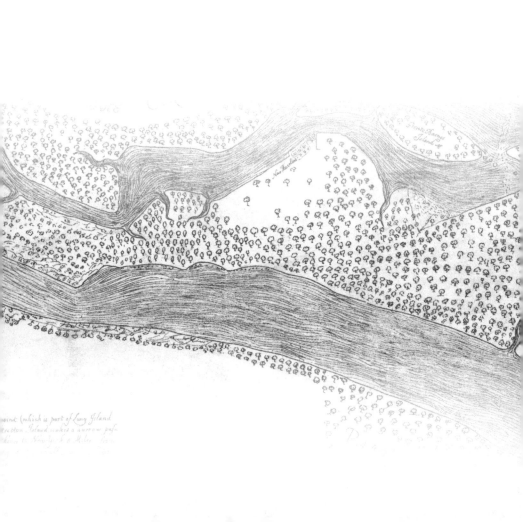

TAKING MANHATTAN

*The Extraordinary Events
That Created New York
and Shaped America*

Russell Shorto

W. W. NORTON & COMPANY
Independent Publishers Since 1923

For information about permission to reproduce selections from this book, write to
Permissions, W. W. Norton & Company, Inc., 500 Fifth Avenue, New York, NY 10110

For information about special discounts for bulk purchases, please contact
W. W. Norton Special Sales at specialsales@wwnorton.com or 800-233-4830

Manufacturing by Sheridan
Book design by Patrice Sheridan
Production manager: Anna Oler

ISBN 978-0-393-88116-5

W. W. Norton & Company, Inc., 500 Fifth Avenue, New York, NY 10110
www.wwnorton.com

W. W. Norton & Company Ltd., 15 Carlisle Street, London W1D 3BS

1 2 3 4 5 6 7 8 9 0

For Saul and Vienne

A peace is of the nature of a conquest;
For then both parties nobly are subdued,
And neither party loser.
—*HENRY IV, PART 2*, ACT IV, SCENE 2

We'll have Manhattan,
The Bronx and Staten
Island too . . .
—LORENZ HART AND RICHARD RODGERS

Contents

———

Part Three
A GAME OF CHESS

Part Four
THE INVENTION

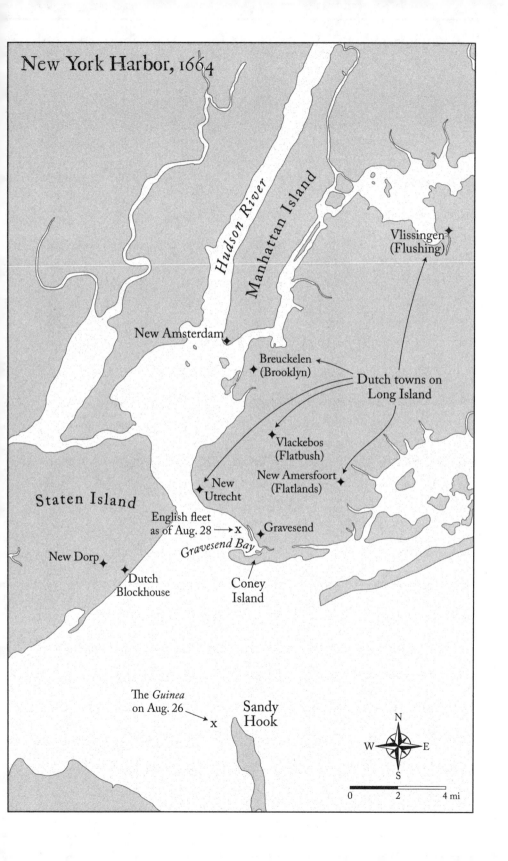

New York Harbor, 1664

Hudson River

Manhattan Island

Vlissingen
(Flushing)

New Amsterdam

Breuckelen
(Brooklyn)

Dutch towns on
Long Island

Vlackebos
(Flatbush)

New Amersfoort
(Flatlands)

New
Utrecht

English fleet
as of Aug. 28 → x

Gravesend

Staten Island

Gravesend Bay

New Dorp

Dutch
Blockhouse

Coney
Island

The Guinea
on Aug. 26
→ x

Sandy
Hook

N
W E
S

0   2   4 mi

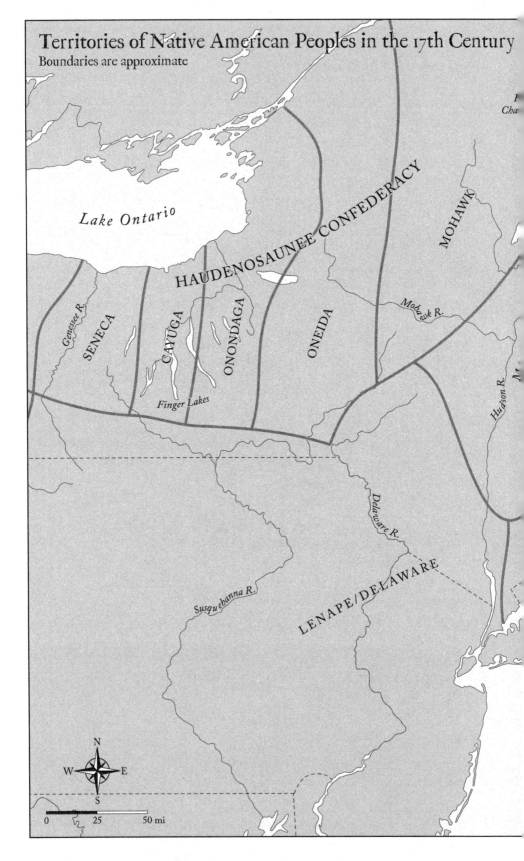

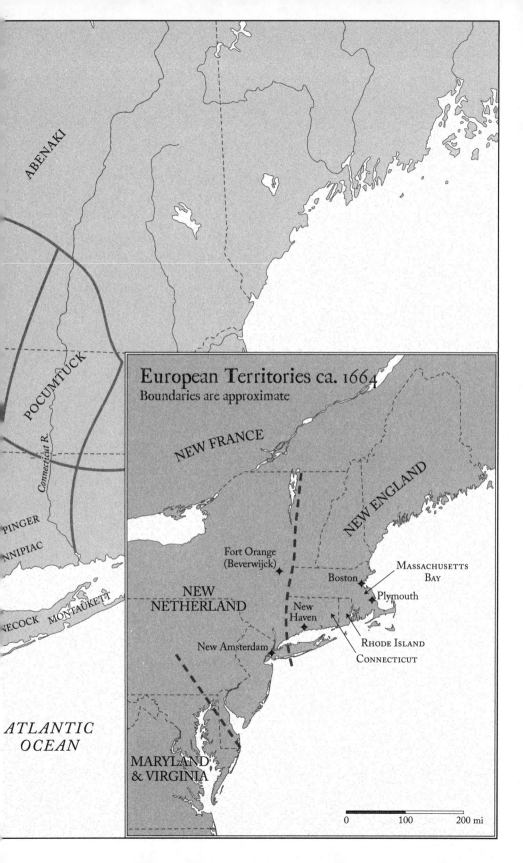

ABENAKI

POCUMTUCK

Connecticut R.

...PINGER

...NNIPIAC

...NECOCK   MONTAUKETT

ATLANTIC
OCEAN

European Territories ca. 1664
Boundaries are approximate

NEW FRANCE

NEW ENGLAND

Fort Orange
(Beverwijck)

Boston

MASSACHUSETTS
BAY

Plymouth

NEW
NETHERLAND

New
Haven

RHODE ISLAND

CONNECTICUT

New Amsterdam

MARYLAND
& VIRGINIA

0   100   200 mi

TAKING MANHATTAN

The Manhattan skyline seen from the
Ramapo Mountains, New Jersey.

Prologue

THE VIEW FROM
THE MOUNTAINTOP

---

*T*he building is so tiny I drive right past it on my first try, despite the GPS's meticulous instructions. Opening the door, I find myself in a CBD shop. One wall is lined with salves and essential oils, the other with jars of gummies. Unseen speakers pump out music at volume, Van Morrison informing the empty room that it's a marvelous night for a moon dance.

Behind the shop is a small space furnished with four weathered lounge chairs. Sprawling across two of these, staring into his cell phone, is Chief Vincent Mann, elected and hereditary leader of the Turtle Clan of the Ramapough Lunaape Nation, one of several groups of Lenape people, whose territory encompassed a wide swath of the East Coast of the United States for at least six centuries before Europeans arrived.* The Ramapough group's

---

* There are many names for the Indigenous people native to the region, including Lenape, Munsee, Munsee Lenape, Lenni Lenape, and Delaware. Though it was rarely employed during the seventeenth century, I will use Lenape in this book because that is the preference of many groups today.

ancestral land is gorgeously situated—from some spots in these rambling Ramapo Mountains of northern New Jersey you can see the skyline of Manhattan in the distance—but little of it remains in their possession.

Mann is fifty-five, built like a former fullback, wearing shorts and a T-shirt on this hot summer day, with a beaded choker around his neck. His silver hair is cropped short. I've come in hopes of getting some perspective that might help me connect the distant past with the present. He gestures for me to sit and starts speaking almost without prompting, in a gravelly murmur that can't compete with Van Morrison. He pauses, looks at the ceiling with a grimace. "Hey, Alexa—stop!"

He begins again and proceeds to talk for nearly three-and-a-half hours. It's a centuries-long litany of abuse that he regales me with. He names battles and broken treaties from the seventeenth century. He knows how many Lenape people were killed at a massacre at present-day Jersey City in 1643. You can see on his face and in his body that this history consumes him: over decades he has crafted himself into a being whose purpose is to call out injustice.

At some point his wife, Michaeline Picaro, knowledge bearer of the Turtle Clan, arrives. Together they run a farm that provides botanicals for the shop, and they work on environmental justice projects in their community of about five thousand people, many of whom live below the poverty line. She's also training to become a nurse. Generally speaking, both are involved in activities to promote healing among their people. The most recent abuse involves industrial pollution from the 1960s that flooded parts of their land with toxic waste. Mann and Picaro tell me they have been to dozens of funerals of friends and family members who have died from a variety of cancer types. A lawsuit netted a sizable payout, but the money only added insult to injury. "Two-thirds of it went to the law firm," Chief Mann said. "One-third got distributed among seven hundred or so people. The lawyers said if you don't sign, you're not getting anything."

I imagine most Americans would suppose that the Native people who famously "sold" the island of Manhattan to the Dutch centuries ago for twenty-four dollars' worth of knives and kettles are strictly of the distant past—that they were slaughtered, or died of diseases the Europeans brought, or were engulfed by waves of European immigration. All of those things happened, and yet the Indigenous groups native to the region survived. They were split apart through treaties and scams, and many were pushed out, bought out, or simply up and moved: to Oklahoma, Kansas, Delaware, and Ontario. Others, though, never went anywhere. "We're still here," Picaro told me, "only thirty miles away from where we were all those years ago."

It's an alluring notion for a writer of history to reach for in making a point about historic injustice: that descendants of the people who lost Manhattan—the people on the short end of what was arguably history's greatest and most iconic swindle—live on, precariously, four centuries later, almost literally within the shadows of the skyscrapers. In truth, nobody knows what Indigenous tribe participated in that event, let alone which, if any, of the present-day Lenape groups connect back to it. The US Bureau of Indian Affairs doesn't even recognize the Ramapough as a tribe, though the state of New Jersey does. The lack of federal recognition has something to do with their tangled lineage but also with a high-powered smear campaign that Donald Trump waged in the 1990s to protect his Atlantic City casinos from what he feared would be future tribal competition. In support of their claims to legitimacy the Ramapough have engaged researchers who created extensive family trees connecting them to the past, and they have their own oral tradition. Mann tells me he can trace his ancestry back to Katonah, a legendary sachem, or chief, of the seventeenth century.

My aim, though, isn't to try to identify current descendants of the Native people who bartered away Manhattan but to make a broader, perhaps obvious but nevertheless important point at the start of this book: that the people indigenous to the continent are still here. Native America is part of the fabric of the twenty-first-century United States. In fact, New York City has the largest American Indigenous population in the United States: 180,000 people spread across the five boroughs, far more than live in any of the approximately 326 reservations in the country.

Today we are coming to appreciate more keenly than ever before the injustice America has done to Native people. The taking of Manhattan Island by the Dutch in 1626 is the very emblem of that injustice. It was not quite the first act of European dispossession, but it's certainly one of the more outrageous examples.

That event is not the main subject of this book. The story I tell in these pages is of the second taking of Manhattan, which came thirty-eight years later when the English relieved the Dutch of it, resulting in the birth of New York. But the first taking of the island is very much a part of this story. The Native peoples of the region were a constant, vigorous presence throughout the Dutch period. They were crucial players in the faceoff between the English and the Dutch. And the injustice that the first taking of Manhattan represents remains a part of American reality in our time. The view from the New Jersey mountaintop—the contrast between the impoverished tribal community and the city of power and wealth—is a reminder of our failure to process the injustice that the American experiment is built on. As Michaeline Picaro said to me of her community, "We're still digging out from the rubble of what happened four centuries ago."

If the first taking of Manhattan represents a kind of original sin, the second, in 1664, is a richly meaningful event that has been curiously skipped over by the historical record, marginalized, though not exactly forgotten. It's an episode of American history that everybody knows about and nobody knows about.

That there was a Dutch presence—that New York was once called New Amsterdam—somehow holds a place in our collective awareness. But while we are stocked with histories and myths about the Pilgrims, the Puritans, and the Jamestown colonists, not to mention the Revolutionary era, who has any grasp of what that Dutch presence meant or of the struggle for control of this most consequential island? Of the players, what was at stake, and what it meant for the future? The end result of this struggle was far-reaching (the fact that I'm writing this book in English is but one aspect of it), and yet we've done this significant piece of our history a terrible disservice, treating it as though what happened was obvious and inevitable and thus not worthy of attention.

Most histories tell us that the story is a simple one. The Dutch had established a wobbly, inconsequential foothold in North America, with their capital, New Amsterdam, at the tip of Manhattan Island. The English engulfed it, renamed it, set up their own system, and thus began New York's rise.

This book offers a different perspective. It shows that the Dutch presence was substantial and that New York didn't come about as the result of a hostile takeover, with the English muscling their way in and the Dutch meekly retreating. It was an invention. Hundreds of people on both sides, representing a variety of nationalities, religions, and languages, took part in that act of invention. Thousands of miles away from their home governments, facing the likely prospect of cannon fire and bloodshed, they conceived of a remarkable solution to the problem confronting them. They would in effect disregard orders from their leaders in Europe and, rather than fight, join forces. They would create something wholly new.

If we think of New York as a child, we might see that the two European cultures involved in its birth were parents, each of which would contribute genetic material to the newborn. This is all the more remarkable when we consider that England and the Dutch Republic were rival powers in Europe, who fought a series of vicious wars against one another during this period. Their rivalry was intensified by the fact that they were at different stages in the process of building their history-changing empires. Through the early decades of the seventeenth century, England had been mired in civil turmoil while the Dutch Republic had created a global enterprise whose vastness is difficult to comprehend. The country had a weak central government, but connected to it were two very powerful multinational corporations, which did the work of colonizing and amassing wealth.

Over the course of the seventeenth century, the Dutch East India Company (Verenigde Oostindische Compagnie) shipped more than one million Europeans to work in its Asian outposts— more than all other European companies combined. It had twelve thousand sailors in its Asian fleet; in addition to fighters and seamen it employed armies of craftsmen, middlemen, administrators, clerks, translators, laborers, and accountants. It was a business enterprise, but its military tactics were unforgiving; its soldiers fought, tortured, burned, enslaved. One could argue that the East India Company has had a greater impact on the world than any other company in history. It revolutionized cartography and shipbuilding, reshaped whole cultures, brought untold misery to those it colonized and enslaved, and moved plants, animals, and insects around the globe, setting off the cycle of invasive species that we still live with. We can track its doings so well because it also pioneered corporate bureaucracy; its existing archives— scattered around the world, tucked in cabinets and file drawers throughout its former colonies—measures some four kilometers. The massive wealth generated by the East India Company was funneled back to the home country, giving rise to the so-called Dutch Golden Age.

The Dutch West India Company, meanwhile, which focused on the Atlantic region, could never match the might of its sibling, but thanks to its Africa trade, it did its part to change the world for the worse. From "incidental" efforts to buy human beings in the

1590s, it grew to eventually ship more than a half million people into lives of slavery. At the same time, the West India Company established the North American colony of New Netherland and the city of New Amsterdam, whose population, often in defiance of the parent company, went about constructing a novel, multi-ethnic society and a robust trading port that the English would come to covet.

Through these two companies the Dutch had been expanding their global reach for decades, fueling English envy and bitterness toward the little nation across the Channel to the point where hating the Dutch became a national pastime. As England grew and began to conceive of its own empire, including North American colonies, it became clear that the Dutch had to be dealt with.

What took place in and around Manhattan Island in the summer of 1664 began as a classic showdown of military forces in the age of rising European empires. Had you been part of it, it would have seemed like it was leading to death and horror, that it was an inevitable confrontation, fueled by mutual animosity, testosterone, historical forces, and orders from the respective home countries.

The outcome—the way those involved in the showdown decided the affair—shaped the contours of American history and echoes right down to the present. On the one hand, it ensured that the English would control much of the continent and would continue and accelerate the process of taking land from Indigenous people. Once it was under English rule, Manhattan would become an important piece in a geographical puzzle—others included Barbados, Jamaica, the New England colonies, and ports on the western coast of Africa—that, once assembled, would give rise to the British Empire. The annexation of New Netherland essentially fixed the "original" thirteen English colonies in place, ensuring that, for better and for worse, American history and American values would be tied to England's global push for power.

But if the resolution of the standoff over Manhattan resulted in an English city, it incorporated vital, world-changing elements that the Dutch had brought to North America. It helped to embed the concept of pluralism—and the notion of a society made up of a mix of different kinds of people as a core value—into New York's foundation and America's collective identity. It also ensured that the country would embrace capitalism, as both a rapacious and a liberating force, long before the word itself even existed. And the effervescent, messy society that resulted would become a countervailing influence throughout much of American history to the dour, self-righteous, theocratic Puritan sect centered in Boston.

In these and other ways the episode of our early history that gave New York its name helped set not only the city's but the country's destiny. It's all the more remarkable, then, that it has been so thoroughly ignored. One reason is that until relatively recently we lacked documentation of the Dutch presence—or, rather, we ignored it. This book relies on recently translated material, which deepens our understanding of this event. It builds on my 2004 book *The Island at the Center of the World*, though it is written to stand alone. That earlier book told the story of the Dutch founding of a North American colony. It detailed how the Dutch brought pluralism, free trade, and their brand of imperialism to the place. That story ended with the English takeover.

The present book zeroes in on the moment of transition from Dutch to English ownership, treating it like the world-changing event it was. The idea to write it slowly dawned on me as more volumes of Dutch records emerged from the capable hands of translators Charles Gehring and Janny Venema of the New Netherland Research Center at the New York State Library and Archives, giving details of what was at stake for the players in 1664.

Two questions hovered in my mind as I researched. First: Why does New York mesmerize people from all over the world? More than a few think it's pretty much the greatest city in the world. It seems to have something embedded in its core—an energy, a fecundity, a self-confidence—that no other city can quite match. This story suggests a partial answer.

Second: Who are we? Americans today feel their country is in a state of crisis. This connects to our sense of identity. How do we reconcile ugliness in our past with values we hope to live up to and with historical achievements we want to celebrate? New York's birth encompasses the roots of American pluralism and capitalism, things that most of us consider vital. It's also tied to the devastation of Native peoples and to the start of slavery in America. These too are elemental inheritances.

If reconciling these parts of our history feels impossible, maybe we are trying to do too much. Maybe for a start we simply need to unearth these pieces of the past like archaeologists digging up artifacts, brush them off, and see them in the clear light of day.

In 1664, someone in New Amsterdam made a sketch of the city from the East River. Amsterdam artist Johannes Vingboons used it as a model to paint this expressive watercolor—part of an effort to promote business in the Dutch colony.

Part One

SQUARING OFF

Chapter 1

THE INVADER

———

New York is all about water.

     Reasonable people may disagree with this assertion. Surely New York is about trade, finance, power. Fashion, food, art, media, design. Fusions and factions. Wall Street and Broadway. Skyscrapers and boroughs.

Yes, but water flows beneath and around all of these. If the coastline of the New York Harbor region were stretched out, it would be longer than the state of California. New York City's waterfront is bigger than those of Miami, San Francisco, Los Angeles, and Boston combined. As vast as it is, the area that is officially known as the New York–New Jersey Harbor Estuary is even more staggering in its complexity, encompassing such a concatenation of inlets, margins, banks, strands, runnels, rivers, reefs, rivulets, coves, creeks, and kills; of brooks, basins, bays, shoals, shores, islands, islets, and peninsulas; of jetties, bluffs, heights, scallops, spits, crags, beaches, reaches, bends, bights, channels, sandbars, sounds, and points, as to be virtually unmatched in the United States.

And yet, as varied as this shoreline is today, in past centuries, before hardscape and landfill, it was incomparably more jagged and meandering. The word *littoral* designates any space where land and water meet. Littoral zones are rich, fecund, life-fostering places. New York's harbor once supplied oysters around the world. It once produced single oysters the size of a dinner plate.

Bivalves aside, the harbor might well be considered the birth mother of America. Maybe that sounds like an exaggeration. Think, though, of some of the resonant names that were processed at Ellis Island or at Castle Garden before it—names like Einstein, Carnegie, Houdini, Frank Capra, Frida Kahlo, Bob Hope, Emma Goldman, Joseph Pulitzer, Lucky Luciano. Then consider that those names stand for tens of millions of others and that the effects of migration multiply over time. Consider that 40 percent of Americans alive today are Americans because New York Harbor beckoned their ancestors. Consider that the harbor became not just a nest for nurturing a city but a conduit for the peopling of a continent. When the Erie Canal was completed in 1825, it made a continuous sea journey possible from any port in the world into that harbor, up the Hudson River, and westward into the Great Lakes and the heart of North America. Buffalo, Erie, Cleveland, Detroit, Chicago, Milwaukee. You could call these cities the offspring of New York Harbor. Consider that for a portion of the nineteenth century more people and goods came through New York than through all of the country's other major ports combined.

Water was the reason for valuing this place before any Europeans arrived. Water was and is the primary element in Lenape culture. A version of the traditional water song, sung by Grandmother Clara Soaring Hawk of the Ramapough Lenape at an event I attended in 2024, goes like this:

We sing this song like a lullaby.
The song means the water is the life's blood of our mother
　　the earth.
Water is the life's blood of our own bodies.

The location of Manhattan Island—its relationship to the surrounding water and the continent it sits astride—is what drew both a French-speaking, teenaged girl from present-day Belgium in the 1620s and a young Jewish man from Lithuania in the 1650s, despite their awareness that life in such a place would be fantastically more primitive than back home. A woman from west-central Africa, who also arrived in the 1620s, probably in her teens, came unwillingly, but those who hauled her here did so because of the location. Another young woman, from a tribe at the eastern end of Long Island, knew the region from birth, above all in relation to the ocean: as a source of food, tools, and spirituality, of life and death.

This story is about these four people and several hundred others from a variety of backgrounds: their intertwined connections, what they made of this island and region, and how they pushed it forward into history.

———

So we begin on the water. It's August 26, 1664,* a Tuesday, late in the summer of what has already been a very busy year for a man named Richard Nicolls as he stands on the deck of a wooden vessel making its way into this broad, tree-bristling amphitheater of a harbor. He is faced with a dilemma. On the one hand, he's right where he wanted to be: hugging the coast of Long Island, approaching his objective. His problem is he's alone: it's just his

---

* For the most part, dates will be given in "New Style." At the time of these events, England still operated on the Julian calendar, while the Dutch Republic followed the newer Gregorian calendar (which we use to this day). The Julian calendar lagged ten days behind the Gregorian. To avoid confusion, people sometimes wrote dates as, for example, "June 5/15." Another source of confusion: the Julian calendar began the new year not on January 1 but on March 25. Hence, an event occurring on March 15, 1665, in the Dutch Republic or New Amsterdam would have been listed as taking place on March 5, 1664, in England and the English colonies. England switched to New Style dating in 1752.

one ship, gliding toward a vast, ornate waterscape that will soon become enemy territory. That isn't the case yet because his country, England, and the Dutch Republic, which has had a colony on this stretch of the eastern seaboard of North America for nearly a half century, are at peace. But tensions at home have been building—fueled largely by English jealousy toward the much tinier nation that within a short span has become Europe's economic powerhouse. This mission of his, as Nicolls knows perfectly well, will likely tip the two longtime rivals into war.

His full convoy, wherever the rest of it is, comprises 4 frigates, 450 men, and 92 cannons, "exceedingly well fitted with all the necessaries for warre," as a knowledgeable observer put it. The packing of the holds with powder and shot, not to mention firelocks, matchlocks, carabines, saddles and bridles, bandoliers and bells and halberds, flintstones and hatchets and nails, and the manning of the expedition with seasoned soldiers, was the result of careful planning six months earlier in England. But then came a hard ten weeks' crossing of the Atlantic, an eternity of puking and stinking soldiers pitching up and down with the swells, no doubt contemplating at times the likelihood, the mercy, of a watery grave. The ships became separated and continued to America one by one. Nicolls's flagship limped into port on the Maine coast; the others found their way to Nantucket. Nicolls and his lieutenants eventually regrouped in Boston. The convoy then set out south for the Dutch colony of New Netherland, but the ships became separated yet again. So here he is, sailing alone toward his future.

It's not giving much away to say that Nicolls will be the winner in the coming clash. He will set in motion a chain of historical events that will yield a landscape as familiar to us as the back of our collective hand: Coney Island, Central Park, Yankee Stadium, Saks Fifth Avenue, Katz's Deli, *Seinfeld*, the Dakota, the Statue of Liberty. Yet for all that, history has mostly forgotten him. The otherwise outstanding *Encyclopedia of New York City*, to give one instance of the oversight, doesn't even have an entry for Nicolls, never mind that he willed the city into being, named it, defined its original boundaries, and was the colony's first governor.

Declaring a winner suggests that the story will have a loser. But while Peter Stuyvesant, Nicolls's nemesis, is going to be beaten in the most obvious sense, it is possible to see that, in losing, he wins. And therein lies a major reason for New York's eventual success.

But we're getting ahead of ourselves.

It's a frigate, this ship of Nicolls's, the kind of high-decked, three-masted, cannon-studded wooden vessel that set about conquering the globe in what military historians call the age of fighting sail. Its very name—the *Guinea*, an homage to recent grim successes on the so-called Guinea Coast of West Africa—signals that we are already knee-deep in moral compromise.

Back home in Europe, the English scientist Robert Hooke has just identified Jupiter's Great Red Spot through his telescope. In the Dutch city of Delft, Johannes Vermeer is carefully positioning yet another of his costumed models at a table beneath a leaded glass window so that the light falls just so. People in London will soon begin filing insurance claims; Paris has started a public bus system; Amsterdam will shortly install street lighting. It's a sophisticated world, and Richard Nicolls—multilingual, up-to-date on scientific advances, a friend of earls and countesses as well as of soldiers and commoners—is a man of that world.

But he's not there. He's scanning the horizon of an utterly alien environment: the approximately nine million square miles that constitute the New World of North America. The continent has long been the stuff of lore for Englishmen, whose own native wildernesses were largely tamed centuries before. John Smith, for one, summarized the position of his fellow Jamestown settlers in Virginia: "The woods are so wide, the rivers so broad, and the beasts so wild, and wee so unskilled to catch them." A New Englander described the geography there as "a desart

Wildernesse." And those were the known landscapes. Farther west, rumor had it, were mountains and deserts of unimaginable, inhuman scope.

Englishmen of Nicolls's day typically refer to America as a wilderness, but they know perfectly well that it is anything but an empty landscape. It is intricately peopled. Europeans have interacted with the Indigenous people—fought, traded, sparred, married—for decades now. Some have learned their languages. Some have attached names to their tribes and lands, committed those names to print, doing their best to spell them out as they have heard them. Sanhican. Naraticon. Canomaker. Mahikan. Minnessinck. Wapanoo. Pequatoo. Waoraneck. Tockwogh. Konekotay. Tappan. Wappinges.

Richard Nicolls has no experience of these peoples, but he knows they are out there: in longhouse villages or wigwams, wandering into Dutch towns to buy bread or to barter for muskets, as wise and duplicitous, as capable of generosity or lethality as any European. If all goes well, he will have to deal with many of them before long.

Nicolls has some awareness too of the fact that this harbor and the island that is his objective give unique access to the continent that lies beyond. This awareness on the part of the English is fairly new. When the European settlement of the continent began six decades earlier, the English thought about little but what was right in front of them. The Jamestown colonizers brought few necessities for the long-term settlement of Virginia but lots of picks and shovels: they believed America to be a literal gold mine. They were going to dig and get rich. The infamous starvation that followed was partially a result of that lack of foresight. The Pilgrims showed up on the Massachusetts coast fired by religious zeal but without a map, a reliable guide, or a plan of action. The friendship they formed with the Pokanoket tribe, climaxing with the famous celebration of thanksgiving, had less to do with openness toward Native culture than with desperation. (Their first interaction with the local tribe involved the Pilgrims stealing the Natives' corn.)

The Dutch had come to the continent with a different sensibility. As a people whose very culture had been formed by water—the need to control it, to turn the problem of it to advantage—they approached their colony-building with a strategic awareness of geography. This stupendous harbor would be the heart of their New Netherland. The river that fed it was a broad highway into the interior. One hundred and fifty miles up it, another river valley fed into it. This one, the Mohawk, extended westward into the interior—toward vast bodies of water that the Haudenosaunee people told them of. The Great Lakes offered water access to an incomprehensibly vast region of possibility. At the time Nicolls's ship approaches the harbor, it is still mostly a dream, that exploitation of the heart of the continent, but it's one that lives in the minds of the Dutch who have made this region their home.

And now, belatedly, the English have cottoned onto this gem of geographic wisdom. That is one impetus for Nicolls's mission. The English have realized that they will never get anywhere with this continent if they allow their archrivals to hold this, the key to it.

———

Wind, water; the snaps and sighs of the shrouds overhead; the creaking of a wooden ship's bones.

Uncertainties surround Richard Nicolls. He has no idea what lies ahead in the harbor and even less of an idea how, should he accomplish his first task, to go about the second, which doesn't concern these Dutch at all but his fellow Englishmen. He dares not speak openly of this mission. Indeed, on his person are two sets of instructions, one public, to be shown to whoever may ask to see it, and the other private. While he is to "informe all men" about the mission to take the Dutch colony, the private instructions make clear that "the ground and foundation" of his venture is to bring the wayward New England colonies under the king's rule.

For all the precariousness about what lies ahead, he can take some comfort in certainties of the recent past: expressions of faith in him from the highest authority that came tricked out in pleasing fineries of expression echoing off palace walls:

> Our trusty and well beloved Colonel Richard Nicolls . . .
> imployed by us . . . You are to use great dilligence [in] . . . the
> possessing . . . and reduceing that people to an entyre sub-
> mission and obedience to us.

> —GIVEN AT OUR COURT AT WHITEHALL THE 23RD OF
> APRILL 1664, IN THE SIXTEENTH YEARE OF OUR REIGNE

It has been a long, slogging journey from England, and it's now nearing its end. Having ridden west along the beachy spit variously called Rechaweygh or Rockaway (probably from the Munsee for "sandy place"), Nicolls and his crew glide across a five-mile stretch of open water that separates two long, sandy peninsulas: skinny outstretched arms that function as gateposts, welcoming vessels into the harbor. It's a tricky passage, though. The eternal rush of water through the Narrows up ahead results in a continual buildup of silt around the more northerly of these two peninsulas, which snags the bottoms of unwary ships. But the ship's captain, Hugh Hyde, knows where he's going: he's making for the tip of the southern peninsula, which the Dutch here call Sant Punt and which the English call Sandy Hook. Captain Hyde is clear on his immediate destination because some of the men aboard the *Guinea* are New Englanders; they are well acquainted with these waters, as are their compatriots to the south in Virginia. By exploiting geography and their own business sense, the Dutch have made New Amsterdam a commercial hub, which draws trade and transport from the English colonies. This is another impetus for Nicolls's mission: to take this trade for England.

The ship rounds the sandy nub of the peninsula, tucking itself into this outer reach of the harbor, and the waters go calm. The sensation, relative to the exposed nature of life on the open ocean, might induce relief in a casual sailor, a welcome letting-down of one's guard, but Nicolls has no room for such luxury. In order to defend a trading empire that runs from Japan to the Caribbean, the tiny Dutch Republic has built one of the most fearsome naval forces in the world, with hundreds of warships. Nicolls knows too that the Dutch favor small vessels, which can more easily maneuver: they are well suited to spaces such as this waterscape of coves and crannies. So while the waters here in the outer harbor are dazzling in the summer sun, changing with the light minute by minute, from milky coffee to cobalt to gunmetal glinting with diamonds, Nicolls isn't enchanted. His spies have told him that Dutch spies have tracked his progress: very shortly they will know that he is here. His intelligence also informs him that this harbor in which the Dutch capital lies is lightly fortified, but intelligence can be wrong. He could be sailing into a trap.

———

If Richard Nicolls is cautious, it is not because he's the sort who shies from conflict. He gave himself over to a military life as a youth. He was leading a cavalry troop into battle at the age of eighteen. Eleven years before entering this harbor, he was part of an army laying siege to the French town of Mousson, for three nights enduring barrages of "hand grenades, fire works, and fire itself" raining down on them as they tried to erect a defensive wall. In the same action, an enemy cannon shot came whizzing through their encampment, piercing three barrels of gunpowder but failing to ignite them: an amazing occurrence that many who witnessed felt showed the hand of God. These were campaigns of mud and rain, of horses and men competing to out-shriek one another in their agonized cries. In a battle at Étampes, 1,400 men were killed in a span of hours, not mowed down with merciful efficiency but hacked, gouged, stabbed with pikes, shot at close range, some even hammered to death by stones when a wall gave way and men on both sides took up pieces of it, lunged at one another, and began bashing in skulls.

Such experience was part of the reason Richard Nicolls was selected for this mission.

Hugh Hyde, Nicolls's skipper, has chosen a good place both to wait for the other vessels and to keep an eye out for trouble. But the very primeness of the location likely leads Hyde to order the gunners to their stations. The Dutch of New Netherland have been known to post lookouts here, for it commands a view of the entrance to the harbor and thus of all approaches to Manhattan.*

A sail appears, and sure enough, it's Dutch. Fears of an attack, however, are quickly allayed. It's only a sloop—single-masted, probably hauling cargo locally. But though it poses no instant threat to them, Nicolls does not want it alerting the Dutch capital of his presence. Captain Hyde orders his men into action. They run the ship down, presumably fire a warning shot, and before long its captain is aboard. He coughs up his name: Claes Verbraech. He has been in the Dutch colony for several years, is based at what they call the South River—the Delaware—and was en route from there to Manhattan. No doubt he was startled to find the guns of an English warship pointed at him.

With Captain Verbraech on ice and his vessel impounded, things go quiet again. The *Guinea* drops anchor and sets a watch. From this vantage Nicolls has a long, straight line of sight north-

---

*Smugglers were a regular presence in the Dutch colony. They were known to steal into the harbor and sneak through the Arthur Kill, behind Staten Island. By doing so, smugglers could attempt to slip past Manhattan, make for the western shore of the river, and sail northward.

ward. Eight miles across the harbor, the body of water called the Narrows acts like a scope, focusing attention on what lies beyond: the inner portion of the harbor and the southern end of the island the Lenape long ago named after a type of wood that grew there, wood they favored for making bows. Manna-hatta.

The encounter with the sloop will surely have heightened Nicolls's senses, set him on high alert. At his disposal at present are thirty-six cannons and a crack team of gunners. He has inflicted mountains of harm in the past and will do so again if need be. The world into which he was born was largely devoured by war and theologically fueled hatred during his youth and coming of age. He has spent much of his life since on horseback, a sword in his hand, doing his part to hack a new world into being. He is forty-one years old, has never been married, has no children. Most of the wealth he possesses is in cash or jewelry: light, transferable, a soldier's savings. All he really has, at least as far as the records of history tell us, is an unwavering, lifelong commitment to a man named York.

Chapter 2

THE DEFENDER

———

R ichard Nicolls may be stuck for the moment off Sandy Hook, left to guess what fury the Dutch might have lurking in one of the harbor's coves, but we know what lies ahead of him. Leaving the *Guinea* behind, we can zip northward in our mind's eye, past the sandy tip of the peninsula, and cross over the waters of the Lower Bay. The view here is of an immensity of blue-brown tidal chop backed by strips of low-lying land rimmed in places with reed beds. To the right is another stretch of sand—Brighton Beach it will be called two centuries later, in imitation of the town of that name in England (an attempt at branding a nascent seaside resort for New Yorkers)—and, straight ahead, the channel that separates Long Island (so named by the Dutch: *Lange Eylandt*) from Staten Island (ditto, after the *Staten Generaal*, or States General, the governing body). Passing the site of the future Verrazzano-Narrows Bridge, we see down below a stretch of water moving in the other direction, making for the open ocean.

Rounding the southern tip of Long Island, we enter another wide bay, this one more estuarial, fed by the fecund waters of surrounding rivers and streams, principally the one the Mohicans call

Muh-he-kun-ne-tuk, or River That Flows Both Ways, which the Dutch refer to as the North River. It will eventually take the name of the explorer Henry Hudson. Crossing this inner bay, we catch a glimpse of what the Dutch call Oyster Island, which exactly 222 years later will become the home of the Statue of Liberty.

And so we come to the southern tip of Manhattan Island and find ourselves hovering above a thriving little patch of civilization. Indeed, New Amsterdam is in a way its own world, a place not quite like any other. Later, American history will decide that it, and the colony of which it has been the capital these forty-odd years, was inconsequential. Washington Irving will almost singlehandedly achieve this feat of dehistoricization by recasting the period as faux-historical slapstick in the book *A History of New York: From the Beginning of the World to the End of the Dutch Dynasty*, more commonly known as *Knickerbocker's History of New York*. Thanks to this satire generations will see the Dutch presence as a somewhat silly prelude to history. Irving's cartoon image of the place would be amplified when political cartoonists in New York's nineteenth-century newspapers picked up his comic stock characters—Peg-Leg Pete and Anthony the Trumpeter and Wouter the Doubter—and use them to illustrate political arguments of their day. Mostly, though, the judgment that this period was inconsequential will be recorded by not recording it: it will be ignored.

The reason for that neglect has everything to do with what will transpire here over the next two weeks. It has to do with the fact that the English will win the island and its colony, and as a result later American history will come to see this period through English eyes. And the English of the 1600s want nothing more than to will the Dutch into oblivion or, failing that, into irrelevance. They have it in for the Dutch in the worst way. They curse them casually to let off steam. They make them into bogeymen with which they scare their children. A particularly memorable anti-Dutch screed of the period, a pamphlet entitled "The Dutchmens Pedigree," purported to show interested readers "How They

Were First Bred and Descended from a Horse-Turd Which Was Enclosed in a Butter-Box." The litany of derogatory expressions in the English language that have the word *Dutch* in them—Dutch treat, Dutch uncle, Dutch courage, going Dutch—dates to this era of rising, rival empires and the bitter jealousy of the English.

The sense that what the Dutch brought to Manhattan Island is inconsequential, that the history of this place only truly began once the English took the reins, can begin to be dispelled by looking around New Amsterdam.

What we see looks like a cross between a stately little Old World city that Vermeer might paint in the manner of his *View of Delft* and a backlot set for a Wild West town. There's a tidy collection of red-tiled rooftops—about three hundred of them, according to a census conducted four years earlier. The city is shaped like a triangle, following the contour of the island's southern tip, crisscrossed by approximately sixteen streets (depending on what you consider a street). The houses look much like those in Amsterdam, the parent city of this New World outpost: gabled, some of them crammed side by side as if the price of Manhattan real estate were already a thing, each facing the street and giving onto a garden behind. As if to announce the governing nationality of the place, there's a windmill positioned on the southwestern shore. (There's also a Dutch flag flying from a nearby pole.) Belying the tidiness, there are scraggly wooden fences, a higgledy-piggledy character to the layout, and farm animals—pigs, cows, sheep—roaming free on the unpaved streets.

And there are the people: about 1,500 live here, a respectable number for a rough-and-ready outpost on the edge of the continent. Sailors, soldiers, farmers, traders, tailors. Investors in voyages, teachers of Latin, bookkeepers, ministers of the Dutch Reformed Church. Dealers in wine and brandy, brewers of beer, bakers of bread, sellers of peas and rye seed. Magistrates and midwives. Thieves, whores, adulterers, libelers, smugglers, murderers, and purveyors of "liquor to the Indians" in defiance

Johannes Vermeer, *View of Delft,* 1660–1661.

of the law. Honest millers, wheelwrights, carpenters, and build-ers. Tavernkeepers. Landlords and tenants. Wives and husbands, babies and youths. Humble supplicants cowering beneath the moody gaze of a capricious God. People from a panoply of back-grounds: Portuguese, Germans, French, Swedes, a Bohemian from Prague, the odd Italian. Ashkenazim and Frisians, Walloons and Angolans. Enslaved Africans as well as some who were formerly enslaved. Owners of enslaved people too, of course.

The mix of backgrounds among this collection of humanity points to the city's true identity. Despite its sleepy appearance, it was set up to be an entrepôt, a global trading port. And that mix is perhaps its most distinguishing feature. Keep in mind that this is the seventeenth century, an era in which intolerance (that is, religious intolerance) is official policy in most of Europe, with Louis XIV visiting soldiers upon Protestant households in France to beat and abuse them into returning to Catholicism, with England imposing persecution on religious outliers via an official "witchcraft act," and with England's Connecticut colony, just to the north, having tried no fewer than thirty-four people as witches in recent years. In an age in which bloodletting and "animalculism"—the belief that sperm consists of microscopic, fully formed human beings—are considered common sense, so is intolerance. Life is fraught; people die early, horribly, and suddenly, not only from little-understood diseases and foreign invasions but from civil strife. Nothing is more likely to lead people to hate their neighbors than religious differences. People need government for their survival, and government needs to enforce cohesion, which entails weeding out alien forces. Otherwise, as the Englishman Thomas Hobbes memorably penned in *Leviathan* thirteen years before these events, life would be "nasty, brutish, and short." For the most part, it is anyway. Variety of opinion is dangerous. Ergo, official intolerance is the norm in most places.

But New Amsterdam—following the home country, which is known for its relative toleration of religious and other differences—seems to tack in the other direction. Twenty-one years prior to Nicolls's arrival, a visiting Jesuit priest* learned that eighteen languages were being spoken in the little town, and that at a time when the population wasn't much more than five hundred. In fact, if you count the Native and African languages, which the priest almost certainly did not—Munsee and Unami, Mohawk and Mahican, Popo, Akan, Kimbundu, and Kikongo—there must have been at least twenty-five languages heard in and around the

---

* To be precise, he was less a visitor than an escapee. Father Isaac Jogues had been a missionary to the Indigenous people of New France (that is, Canada), when he was captured by a Mohawk raiding party, tortured extravagantly (fingernails pulled out, thumb chopped off), and imprisoned. A leader of the Dutch town of Beverwijck helped him escape and eventually brought the bedraggled but still ardent (and observant) priest to Manhattan, where for a time he was something like a tourist.

place. And since the time of the priest's visit, the city has tripled in size. Its complexity and robustness provide vigorous evidence to counter the notion that pluralism begets weakness. We can jot down a preliminary hypothesis here: New York was New York even before it was New York.

The city of New Amsterdam is at this moment on high alert. Voices sound in the hot summer air, guttural syllables, cursing and huffing. Dozens of men are ranged around the triangular perimeter of the town, digging to heap up defenses. Some are Black ("resolved by the Court to demand twenty five negroes from the Rt Hon. Director General and Council for the Space of eight days to labour at the City's works"), others, white ("At this conjuncture of time and current rumors, the Board . . . decrees and resolves . . . that one third of the inhabitants . . . without any exception shall appear in person or put another in his place furnished with a shovel, spade or wheel-barrow"). A civic guard, armed with pikes and muskets, is parading around the same perimeter. We might picture the guardsmen decked out as in Rembrandt's *Nightwatch*, with floppy hats and high leather boots, though it's probably wise to mentally clothe them more humbly than the artist did his self-important Old World subjects. They march past the diggers, along the waterfront below the fort, across the tip of the island, up the strand astride the East River, across the recently erected plank wall that defines the northern border of the city (the future Wall Street), and back down along the Hudson River shore.

The fort is swarming with men in military uniform. Whereas those marching around the perimeter of the town are lay militia, made up of regular burghers, or citizens, these—about 150 in total—are actual soldiers, in the employ of the West India Company, the for-profit entity that four decades earlier put up the money to launch this colony in the wilderness. Cuirassed and helmeted, with muskets nearby, they are sitting, stewing, waiting for orders.

We can imagine at some point a disturbance among the soldiers, a hasty backpedaling to get out of the way of a man who suddenly bursts from a doorway and stomps with a determined, irregular clip-clop gait through their midst, heading out of the fort with authority. We may imagine some such clumsy deference because Peter Stuyvesant—Petrus, to give him his true first name—has a personality that demands as much. He is a man of somewhat ponderous middle age—about fifty-four at this moment (we don't know the exact date of his birth)—with a round face, tight mouth, furrowed brow, high forehead, and swooping, angular nose. Wisps of chestnut hair trail down onto his shoulders, which are probably clad in metal sheathing, the political leader having shifted to military mode.

But the eyes are what draw you: he has an ice-cold gaze, packed with intelligence and experience and will. Yet deep down there's a discernible layer of what must be sadness. It's the gaze of an impossible-to-please commander, or father, a gaze suggesting an endlessly calculating mind and a naturally impetuous temperament that has belatedly and begrudgingly succumbed to the necessity of patience.

He has been running this colony in the wilderness for seventeen years. His job description has included managing relations with the growing and increasingly pushy English colonies to the north and south; doing likewise with many groups of Native Americans, all of whom have as well their own complex relations with one another; dealing with incursions by other European colonizers in the New World, including from France and Sweden; and trying for every one of those seventeen years to strike a balance between his superiors in the home country, the gentlemen leaders of the West India Company whose dictates and expectations of profits are perennially at odds with their awareness of North American realities, and his often unruly and defiant local population.

Petrus Stuyvesant.

He is tough, disciplined, smart, dogmatic, at times dictatorial. He has become a leader of men in his time on this island. He has learned to leaven ideology with compromise. He has become a father here, twice over, and he and his wife have raised their sons, bought land, improved it, tended it with care. He has sent men to their death. He has become a dealer in human beings. He is the stern son of a Calvinist minister, who laces his speech with both biblical pieties and streaks of blue cursing.

A key to Stuyvesant's personality might be found in his past—in what happened after he was grievously wounded in battle against the Spanish on the Caribbean island of St. Maarten twenty years earlier, resulting in the horror of having a leg sawed off at the knee without anesthetic. After beating the odds by surviving that ordeal, he elected not to opt for early retirement and a life of convalescent ease amid his country's Golden Age, as might have been expected, but, once he had learned to manage the wooden substitute appendage, requested a new appointment to another hard-bitten West India Company outpost. He requested, that is, another go at the true enemy—the Anti-Christ.

That would have been Spain, the arch-Catholic empire, against which the Dutch Republic fought a bitter, eighty-year war of independence. Jaap Jacobs, one of the leading scholars of New Netherland, who as I write this book is at work on a biography of the man, thinks Stuyvesant originally came to Manhattan to fight a holy war. "He believed he was chosen for that fight," Jacobs told me. "He probably believed his recovery from the loss of his leg was a sign of God's favor." But the war against the Spanish ended in 1648, a year after Peter Stuyvesant arrived on Manhattan, so almost immediately on arrival he had to shift his focus to the colony itself: making it work, defending it not from the Evil One but from an array of less grandiose threats.

At this moment, Stuyvesant is probably seething. All in all, he has done a remarkable job of creating a thriving port city. He has known for years that this day might come, repeatedly warned his superiors in Amsterdam about it, told them that if they valued the place, saw its potential for exploiting the continent, they needed to send more soldiers. Nobody was more aware of the looming nature of the English threat in the preceding months.

But his anger isn't only at the company that employs him. He is also annoyed at himself, for he now realizes that he made a strategic error.

Three months earlier, a man named Seweckenamo strode through the gate and into this same fort, the nerve center of New Netherland, and stood before Stuyvesant. The two knew each other. Like Stuyvesant, Seweckenamo had over the years both fought for and negotiated on behalf of his people. He was a sachem of the Esopus tribe, whose territory lay a hundred miles to the north. Twice in recent years brief but ugly wars had broken out between the Esopus and the Dutch: the first arguably started by Dutch settlers, the second, arguably, by Esopus villagers. Stuyvesant invited Seweckenamo and seven other sachems from area tribes to discuss terms. The sachems brought twenty men with them, who took positions among the Dutch: besides Stuyvesant there were ten men from New Amsterdam and one woman, Sara Kierstede, who served as a translator. Tensions were surely high because the last time the Dutch had invited Native Americans into a settlement on a peace mission—less than a year before, at the village of Wiltwijck, in the Esopus region— the Native people had tricked them, launching a surprise attack, burning down houses and kidnapping women.

Now, though, the mood was different. Sara Kierstede—a gifted linguist who had learned the Mohawk and Mahican languages as a child in the northern part of New Netherland and later picked up the very different Munsee spoken closer to Manhattan, in the process becoming the colony's most important interpreter— recorded that Seweckenamo "prayed to his God (whom he called Bachtamo) . . . that he might conclude something good with the Dutch in the presence of all the chiefs now here and that the conclusion might remain as solid as a stick," an example of which he held up. Seweckenamo promised that all tribes of the region would respect this new peace. Stuyvesant asked why, if the Esopus were bent on peace, the other three sachems of their tribe, whom he referred to by name—Keercop, Pamyrawech, and Niskahewan—were not present. Seweckenamo replied that one was old and blind and the other two had given him their assurances that they wanted peace and would abide by the treaty.

In the end, all present swore a vow—"All that has happened formerly shall be forgotten and forgiven and not remembered again"—and each leader inscribed the accompanying document with a signature or mark.

Meanwhile, 150 miles to the north, at nearly the same time that this treaty was being concluded, two Dutchmen serving as Stuyvesant's emissaries, Jan Dareth and Jacob Loockermans, along with three Mohawks and three Mahicans, left the Dutch outpost of Fort Orange and hiked, sweated, grunted, and plodded for five days, traveling east up a steep mountainside, battling a May snowstorm,* and came at last to a remote English settlement in what would later become western Massachusetts. The next day others arrived: Englishmen from the region, then Native people representing an array of tribes—Abenaki, Agawam, Pajassuck, Nalwetog, Pocumtuck, Wissatinnewag.

Around a council fire they discussed their interlocking interests: land, farms, cattle, furs, wampum, firearms, gunpowder. They brought up wars going back thirty years: family members slaughtered, villages burned, alliances forged and broken, the need to forget past grievances, the weariness of all parties, the benefits of peace. One group, the Soquackick, were absent from the negotiation. They had launched the most recent attacks and didn't feel safe among so many who likely still considered them enemies. In the end, though, a Pocumtuck negotiator said of the Soquackick, "Let them send us a present, then we will release their prisoners and bring a present back to their land, to thus renew our old friendship." The other parties eventually signaled their agreement with this, and the council ended. Everyone smoked a pipe. On the way back to Fort Orange, the Dutchmen and their Mohawk allies camped on the banks of the Connecticut River, where fish "jumped up in great quantities." The Mohawks pulled out nets and caught some as big as twenty-eight inches.

---

* Such occurrences were not uncommon during the so-called Little Ice Age. The Hudson River, which rarely freezes over today, did so for much of the winter in the seventeenth century.

To seal the peace treaty all agreed that the Mohawks, after returning with the Dutch to Fort Orange, would venture to the village of the Pocumtuck, a tribe central to the negotiations, to present wampum. The Mohawk leader, a man named Saheda— "much beloved" by both Native peoples and the Dutch, according to a prominent New Netherlander—would take on this important mission himself.

It may be worth pausing to note how many groups were involved in these interlocking treaties, how small in size each of the groups was, and how complicated the alliances were. It is useful to hold a couple of different notions concerning European-Indigenous relations in the mind at the same time. Taking the long view, and applying our own sense of morality to the past, it's appropriate to note that the only reason there were European-Indigenous relations was because the Europeans had migrated to North America and began imposing their will on the people they found there. From our perspective that is a historic injustice.

But we can also zoom in on the players on the ground. We might try to erase from our minds the notion of Europeans versus Native Americans or of Dutch versus English. It might be constructive instead to envision dozens of tribes in the northeastern portion of the future United States, speaking a variety of languages, worshipping a panoply of gods, and holding various beliefs about their people, the creation of the world, the meaning of life. Some of these tribes had names like Canarsee, Montauk, and Massapequa. Others called themselves English, or Puritan, and had given their villages names like Boston and New Haven. Their interests may or may not have aligned with those of the mother country, England. Those who were Dutch called their colony New Netherland, its capital New Amsterdam, and its secondary village Beverwijck (the future Albany, New York). They too saw themselves as connected yet distinct from their home country in Europe. Yet another category of tribe was the French who had colonized portions of this New World. We tend to look at historical events in terms of national interests. Shift your perspective instead to the ground level, and, as the historian Daniel Richter has written, "The neat picture breaks down into a kaleidoscope of local and supralocal leaders working at cross-purposes, struggles and alliances among competing interest groups, and tangled family quarrels—the stuff of small town life."

We might go even further in this leveling exercise and qualify the land claims of the various tribes. Certainly the Europeans were recent arrivals, most of whose settlements in North America were no more than a few decades old. And it's incontestable that, for example, the Haudenosaunee, or Iroquois, of whom the Mohawk were a constituent nation, occupied a portion of this region long before the arrival of the Dutch, English, or French tribes. But it's worth keeping in mind that the Iroquois in their turn had taken portions of that land from the Huron-Wendat peoples, that archaeological evidence points to patterns of warfare and land grabs going back centuries beyond the horizon of the historical record.

The point of this exercise is not to diminish the brutality of the eventual European conquest but to tease out the individuals of a given time from the whole sweep of history. Each of us may have a burden of culpability for past deeds, whether our own or our ancestors', but surely we can't as individuals be shouldered with the whole weight of past history. It can be useful in studying the people of a given time and place to try to see all as simply human, in this case to bring all of these tribes—of North American and European origin—onto the same plane. People today often hold an unexamined supposition that the Indigenous tribes were morally superior to the Europeans and to assume that Europeans were more technologically advanced than the Indigenous people and thus more clever. But the so-called noble savage myth and its counterpart don't fit reality. Humans are humans. Europeans were not smarter than the Native Americans nor were Native Americans morally superior to Europeans. Once European colonization was under way, all were caught up in the consequences, joined in a network of desires—for furs, kettles, knives, muskets, gunpowder, access to fertile meadows and good ports. All wanted to protect their families and their honor—a powerful concept in the seventeenth century that was equally elemental to European and Native American cultures. Changes in the network—the introduction of smallpox into the region, a massive drop in the beaver supply due to overtrapping, the increasing dependence of Native Americans on muskets and other supplies from the European tribes—repeatedly disrupted alliances and altered the balance of power, making peace elusive.

From the moment of his arrival on Manhattan in 1647, Peter Stuyvesant had been part of this struggle. He engaged in complex business agreements with the Lenape peoples around Manhattan and with the Mohawk to the north, trading guns and food for furs or land rights. He negotiated boundaries with the New Englanders and assisted Dutch traders who sought deals over land and tobacco with Englishmen to the south in Virginia. He sat in councils himself and sent emissaries to Boston and Hartford, to the Esopus and Tappan and Wappinger. Increasingly, he had insinuated himself in the trade in human beings, which further connected his tribe to these others.

The present treaties, of which Stuyvesant was a central instigator, were the most complex yet, involving months of work on the part of hundreds of people, linking the tribes—Native and European—of the southern portion of the Hudson River with those of the river's northern reaches and beyond. Dutch, English, and Native Americans alike were signatories. Years of strife, he hoped, were behind them. There was a way forward, a future of peace, the hope of mutual trade and prosperity.

It would all come down to one final meeting, with Saheda, the highly respected Mohawk sachem, bringing ceremonial offerings to the Pocumtuck. He never arrived. In June 1664, two months before Richard Nicolls's arrival in the harbor, Saheda and several companions were on their way to fulfilling that mission, traveling through the forest somewhere near the future Deerfield, Massachusetts. On the outskirts of the main settlement of the Pocumtuck, the party was waylaid. Saheda and his comrades were murdered. No one knew who the killers were, but soon Mahicans began a wave of attacks on Mohawk villages and, since the Dutch were allies of the Mohawk, on Dutch settlements around Fort Orange. Abraham Staets, a ship's captain who in the past had advised Stuyvesant on relations with the Native people, had his house burned to the ground and with it a young man who was staying with him. Mohawks launched counterattacks. Panic swept through the Dutch settlements around Fort Orange. Suddenly it was happening all over again: flames, bloody murder.

The harrowing news reached Stuyvesant in New Amsterdam. He had spent considerable energy on this treaty. His colony depended on trade, which could only flourish with peace. He had become aware meanwhile—this was in early August, three weeks before Nicolls's *Guinea* sailed into the harbor—that a convoy of English frigates had crossed the Atlantic. He'd heard rumors of an English takeover attempt off and on for the past several years. Was this it?

It was a classic leader's dilemma. Two emergencies demanded his attention. The crisis zones were 150 miles apart: several days' travel by ship. What should he do?

He talked. Seated nearby, pen poised above a broad sheet of rag paper, was Cornelis van Ruyven, secretary to the provincial council, who served as Stuyvesant's scribe.[*]

---

[*] Very occasionally, Stuyvesant wrote letters himself, in a heavy, slashing hand; most of his correspondence, however, was in the careful, tightly looped penmanship of a professional scribe.

This was going to be a long session, so we might imagine Stuyvesant dictated from a chair in his office in the fort. Perhaps at times during the course of the session, he felt the need to get up and pace, stumping up and down the room, the wooden leg clopping rhythmically. We can picture his office ornamented with the heavy, dark furniture of the period, an oak table, probably covered by a "Turkey carpet." The office seems to have been located above the gate into the fort perhaps so that he could look down and see who was coming in and out. Probably the door and windows were open to allow the summer breeze in: it was always windy down here at the tip of the island.

Over the course of writing this letter, Stuyvesant was going to think, to weigh the options. He would use the process more as therapy than an appeal for help. After all, the recipients—his superiors, the directors of the West India Company—wouldn't receive it for six or eight weeks, by which time the consequences of his decision would have long been fixed.

His people were dying up north; trade, the very reason for the colony's existence, was in danger of collapsing under the threat of all-out war. And ships from England were headed this way, their sails fat with wind.

He began to speak, ceremonially addressing the gentlemen in Europe as if they were in front of him: "Esteemed, Wise, Prudent, and Right Honorable Lords . . ."

Stuyvesant chose to devote the beginning of his letter to the complexities of long-distance communication: "Our last letters not yet received by your honors and consequently unanswered were under the date of 26 April, sent by the ship *Stattijn*, and sent under the date of 10 June, which left with the *Vos*, the first duplicated with the last, and going hereby is the duplicate of the last letter together with the accompanying enclosures . . ."

In addition to the fact that in his era getting your message across the ocean took forever, there was the distinct possibility that it might not get there at all. Thus everything was sent in duplicate, or even triplicate, on different ships. People were therefore constantly checking and rechecking their questions and replies to one another and reminding one another of where they were in the chain of communication.

Eventually he homed in on two topics: "the dangerous troubles with the *Barbaren*," i.e., Native people, and "the immediate agony" regarding the situation with the English.

He was highly conscious of his role as leader. He had to protect his charge: the colony and the people who made it their home. His ranking of dangers was not necessarily what future historians would see looking back. He didn't have their ability to pinpoint the most salient ones any more than someone can determine whether the greater threat to their health might be the cancer their doctors have managed to keep in remission or the car coming toward them on the highway.

A concern was the fact that the English residents of some villages in his colony had recently declared independence from Dutch rule and proclaimed allegiance to England. In a sense there was nothing new in this. Stuyvesant had been struggling against his New England neighbors for seventeen years. In 1650, three years after his arrival, he negotiated what he hoped would be a permanent boundary between the Dutch colony and its English neighbors to the north. That line had remained more or less fixed—in fact, the line drawn by Stuyvesant and his English counterpart is still reflected in the boundary between the states of New York and Connecticut—but the civil strife in England led to an influx of settlers to the English colonies, while the so-called Golden Age in the Dutch Republic made his colony, where life was a constant struggle, a hard sell in the homeland. English settlers, hungry for land, kept spilling into his territory.

But the latest threats were more serious than in the past.

Were they part of a concerted effort? Were the ships that were headed toward America from England a related threat? He tried to reason it out. He noted that he had heard—"from skippers and passengers coming over"—that the English ships were headed for his colony. Such reports, he avowed, "make us very circumspect, anxious, and watchful."

On the other hand, his bosses, the directors of the West India Company, the very men he was writing to, had themselves urged him not to be swayed by rumors. The English ships, they had informed him, were being sent not to Manhattan but to the New England colonies, where their mission was to "introduce bishops."

That seems a quaint, innocuous phrase to us today. To Stuyvesant it would have resonated powerfully. England, he knew perfectly well, had been engulfed in civil unrest for decades, with religion at the heart of the matter. Where we might think of "the English" of the seventeenth century as a single bloc, he knew better. Many of the New England colonists to his north, with whom he had dealt all these years, considered themselves the bitter enemies of the Stuart monarchy. The leaders of the Massachusetts Bay Colony were part of the same Puritan faction that had rebelled against the corruption and decay of the Church of England, fought a war against King Charles I, captured and beheaded him, and installed a nonroyal Protestant ruler—Oliver Cromwell, the "Lord Protector"—at the head of the country.

Cromwell lasted five years. Then the Royalists fought their way back into power, and Charles II, son of the beheaded king, assumed the throne. The Restoration had occurred only four years prior to the moment when Stuyvesant sat considering his situation. With the return of the monarchy, many Englishmen promptly switched their allegiance from Puritanism to the king's party and did their best to make it look like they had always been loyal subjects. But the New Englanders, protected by the buffer of the Atlantic Ocean, had remained mostly defiant.

It had taken a while for the new Stuart government to get around to dealing with these colonial holdouts. But now Stuyvesant's bosses were telling him, based on their sources, the English king was asserting authority, and in a way that would surely provoke outrage in New England. If there was one element of England's pre-Cromwellian era that drove the Puritans out of their minds with fury, it was the bishops of the Church of England, who had been the main persecutors of their sect. If "introducing bishops" was the mission of these English frigates, then this was the next volley in the power struggle that continued to engulf the English.

Stuyvesant wasn't at all certain that was the case, but his bosses had advised him to trust that it was. And if it was, it would be a positive development from his perspective. Civil unrest among his pushy neighbors to the north meant they would expend less energy threatening him.

And if English ships were headed to New England (so many ifs!), then he could devote himself to the situation in the north of his own colony. He described for the gentlemen in Amsterdam the "new and worrisome troubles" with the Native people. He mused on a report being pushed by his Mohawk allies that the English of New England were behind the murder of the beloved Mohawk diplomat Saheda. Stuyvesant didn't buy this, believing the Mohawks had fabricated the story "in order to make us join them in the war." Whether this was true or not, the situation was urgent.

He pondered. What was best for his colony? He saw it very much as *his* colony. He had watched it mature: more sails on the horizon each year, the streets filling with people, children growing into adults, the elderly passing into memory. It was throbbing, alive with commerce, the babble of languages, a cosmopolitan chinking of coins—doubloons, florins, pieces of eight. True, the beaver trade was falling off: to feed demand in Europe, the Mohawk had nearly trapped out the population in their territory.

But there was so much opportunity here. The business leaders of New Amsterdam were actively developing other markets: tobacco for one. And just now, not two weeks ago, a new initiative had begun to bear fruit. Indeed, the *Gideon*, the ship that had delivered the cargo, was still out there in the harbor, at anchor alongside two other recently arrived vessels.

Slavery had existed in the colony almost from the start, but it had been an ad hoc affair. For much of New Netherland's existence the enslaved population had numbered in the mere dozens. It had only been five years earlier that the directors of the West India Company had written Stuyvesant from Amsterdam instructing him to develop slavery into an income stream by setting up "an experiment with a consignment of Negroes."

There are few indications in the records that Stuyvesant or any of the other leaders of New Netherland harbored moral objections to developing such a trade. The tolerance for which the Dutch have been praised, while real, was mostly for white European Christians and to a lesser extent Jews. It certainly didn't apply to Africans or Native Americans. In the early days of the trade, there seems to have been some unease in the home country regarding the morality of slavery, since religious leaders took the trouble to outline when it was justified. Race was less of a factor in these justifications than circumstance. One prominent minister instructed that "Turks and Heathens who were captured in a just war" were fair game, as were people who had been "purchased from their masters for a fair price as reportedly is the common practice in Angola." Statements like these gave the church's blessing to the enterprise.

Starting up a slaving industry on Manhattan turned out to be easier said than done. Stuyvesant's authority extended to the Caribbean, to the island of Curaçao, which had been involved with slavery for some time, putting captured Africans to brutal and often fatal work on sugar plantations. This venture had not yet been profitable, but the directors in Amsterdam decided it was the logical place from which to draw shipments of human beings. But the logistics of bringing that business to Manhattan were formidable. Developing an entirely new trade on the island, not to mention one involving human cargo, required significant cooperation and organization.

This had been a central activity over the past five years, and Stuyvesant might have looked at the sizable shipment that had just arrived—290 men, women, and children—as a sign of progress. But there were complications. Nine of the captives had died on the trip from the Caribbean, and the quality-control officer who processed those that reached New Amsterdam pronounced them "a very poor lot." They were hungry too, and there was already a food shortage in New Amsterdam. As much as slavery represented an opportunity to advance the economic interests of the colony and the West India Company, at this moment it was simply one of many headaches for Stuyvesant.

Meanwhile, up north, his people were suffering and dying. Stuyvesant felt responsible for each of them. Perhaps he was thinking right now of the young man before him, head bent over the quill, dipping it into the pot of iron gall ink, scratching out the words as Stuyvesant spoke them. Cornelis van Ruyven had arrived on Manhattan eleven years earlier from Amsterdam and got busy at once: wooing and then marrying the daughter of the town's influential Dutch Reformed minister, buying a five-acre plot in Flatbush, and taking up the position of secretary to the provincial council. The secretary and his wife had children now and owned a house just beyond the gate of the fort: he and Stuyvesant could probably see it from the window. This young man represented the future of this place. But what future was there if relations with the Native people dissolved into bloody murder?

Stuyvesant made up his mind. He would assume that the English ships were heading for Boston. He would leave Manhattan and go to Fort Orange. Remarkably, he didn't include this information in the letter. There was logic behind the omission. He was a company man, ambitious, always conscious in official correspondence of his own position. There was no sense in giving his superiors cause for later making a case against him. After all, it was possible that he had made the wrong decision.

Chapter 3

ENEMY WATERS

———

*A*t about the time Stuyvesant was thinking aloud in his letter to his superiors in Amsterdam, trying to suss out which crisis to apply himself to, Richard Nicolls was sailing the *Guinea* into enemy territory. It wasn't Dutch territory: that was still some weeks in the future. After having become separated from their convoy during the Atlantic crossing, he and his shipmates had reached Cape Cod and found their way from there to Boston Harbor, which, just as Stuyvesant's bosses had told him, was their intended destination.

Two New Englanders, a Captain Oliver and a Captain Davis, were at the dock to meet him. He was expected. Nicolls, royal official in a hurry (never mind the past ten weeks of being banged around by the Atlantic), stepped ashore, presented documents from the king, and requested an immediate meeting with the provincial council.

Yes, certainly, the captains replied. Right away. Except, of course, this was Saturday, evening was approaching, and tomorrow was the Sabbath. An "immediate" council could be arranged—in about three days.

It must have been a moody march from quayside to their quarters, the conversation speckled with brittle niceties. The greeting at the dock set a tone for the stay that Nicolls had surely anticipated. He was not welcome here.

Boston had existed for thirty-four years, was home to about three thousand people, making it twice the size of New Amsterdam, yet it had a more rural look. Houses were spread out, separated from one another by farmland and orchards, the city having not yet exhausted the confines of its peninsula. Otherwise there were two churches, a statehouse, and a little downtown stretch, "full of good shopps," according to one resident.

It was a place where religion ruled. As such, it was a place of hypocrisy. Two contradictions in particular governed Boston as it grew. It was founded on Christian notions of peace and piety, yet thirty years earlier the Puritans had all but annihilated the Pequot tribe and then set up an income stream by extorting other Indigenous peoples, making them pay "tribute" in exchange for not murdering them. The city was also founded on—and remains associated with to this day—the principle of freedom: its leaders' desire for religious freedom and, later, the political and economic freedom epitomized by the Boston Tea Party. Yet once they had escaped persecution in the old country, the city fathers quickly established a theocratic regime that punished anyone whose faith veered much beyond the limits of their own.

Eventually, the general court and council of the Massachusetts Bay Colony "courteously enterteyned" Nicolls, according to their record of the event. It may have been courteous, but it wasn't friendly. With Nicolls was one of his three fellow commissioners, the other ships of his convoy having arrived by this time. These men were Nicolls's deputies for the complicated mission he was to undertake in America. George Cartwright, who stood beside Nicolls in the state house, and Robert Carr were Royalists who had served both the present king and his father. Like Nicolls, they had no previous experience with North America.

The fourth commissioner gave the game away. As far as the leaders of the Massachusetts Bay Colony were concerned, Samuel Maverick was hell on earth. He wasn't present with Nicolls this day, probably in an effort by Nicolls to soften the objective of his commission as it related to Massachusetts, but Maverick had already made his presence known to the Puritan leaders. The moment he disembarked from his Atlantic crossing, he had graced those who were at the dock to meet him with, as they put it, "words and carriages that were distasteful." Apparently, he caused enough of a fuss that he needed to be restrained; he responded by "menacing the constable."

The Puritan leaders knew Maverick, who was sixty-two years old but full of vigor, self-righteousness, and bile; they had lived alongside him, endured him, and tangled with him for decades. And Maverick knew the colony—more intimately perhaps than any of its council members or any other inhabitant. We are inclined to think of New England as having been settled by Puritans from the start, but that isn't the case. Maverick had been among the first English to come to Massachusetts, arriving in about 1623, before the Puritans. He had lived and prospered here and built a fortresslike residence on Noddle's Island, a short boat ride from Boston's mainland. (Today, Maverick Square, in East Boston, marks the site of his estate.) From there he had watched in dismay as the religious cult took over the city and the colony. Many other early settlers who refused to subscribe to Puritan dogma had left or been forced out over the years. Maverick, however, was not the quitting sort.[*] As a committed Royalist and member of the Church of England, Maverick had spent half a lifetime clashing with the colony's hard-line leadership.

There hadn't been much Maverick could do to combat the

---

[*] The stubbornness may have been in the blood: the Samuel Maverick who was a hard-bitten Texas rancher and politician in the nineteenth century, a signer of that state's declaration of independence, after whom *maverick* came to mean *rebel*, considered himself a descendant.

Puritans as long as their compatriots ruled in England, but the moment the Stuarts retook the throne, he hopped on a ship and showed up in London with a petition to King Charles in which he persuasively demonstrated how the leaders in Boston, out of their hatred of the Church of England and of the Stuart monarchy, had set up in effect an independent fiefdom. Knowing how tenuous the king's grip on power was, and thus how vital the support of the colonies was, he laid out evidence of the Puritans' treachery. They had maligned the red cross flag, emblem of the monarchy, "terming it a badge of the Whore of Babelon," he informed the king, treated royal emissaries as the "Enemie," and went so far as to mint their own money, "melting downe all the English Coyne they can gett" and converting it into shillings of their own stamp. The colony had been established with a royal charter, according to which officeholders would be chosen by a majority vote of the inhabitants, but the only way a resident could take part in elections, Maverick noted, was by joining the Puritan congregation and declaring "the discipline of the Church of England to be erroneous and to renounce it." The sect, Maverick informed the king with righteous indignation, having based its colony around the principle of religious freedom, not only then "denied it to others" but whipped, imprisoned, hanged, or banished any Protestants to whose beliefs they objected. (Maverick added, quite accurately, that many of those who were banished by the Puritans of New England ended up in the Dutch colony, where they "found more favour and respect.")

On top of all this, he observed, the Puritans of Boston had steadily pushed beyond the ascribed boundaries of their patent, swallowing up portions of Maine that had been granted to Royalists. In sum, Massachusetts, over the period of the civil wars and while the Stuarts were off the throne, had become a rogue state.

Maverick wasn't alone in his critique. More than a dozen people filed complaints against the Massachusetts Bay Colony in London following the restoration of the monarchy. What's more, Maverick was perfectly correct in this view. The Puritans of Massachusetts had done their best to fight what they viewed as the two elements of corruption in the Old World: a debased religion and a monarchy pocked by decadence and excess. They had ridden a reformist wave for decades and had built their colony into the powerhouse of New England. But in England, times had changed.

Maverick was rewarded by the king's advisers for his information by being given a place on Nicolls's commission. And, as Charles's men must have known would be the case, his name listed among those of the other commissioners told the Puritans that Richard Nicolls had not only been assigned the task of wresting Manhattan Island and the surrounding territory from the Dutch. Nicolls's other job—perhaps the more pressing one in terms of the stability of the monarchy—was to rein in the Puritans.

Nicolls held out a letter. It was sealed in wax and bore the inimitable royal stamp. The members of the assembly settled themselves as one of their number broke the seal and prepared to read it aloud.

The letter from King Charles did not state outright that Nicolls had been assigned the job of dismantling their theocratic regime, but it bristled with subtext. With Samuel Maverick off in some inn or tavern biding his time, Nicolls, Carr, and Cartwright sat in the council chamber as the king's words echoed around the chamber. They were surely able to register its various effects as they flickered on the dour Puritan faces.

While praising the New England colonists for having "given a good example of industrje & sobriety," His Majesty was forced to admit that he had heard rumors that certain of "our subjects in those parts doe not submit to our gouernment, but looke vpon themselues as independent vpon vs & our lawes." Surely— *surely*—these rumors were baseless, so the king felt certain the Massachusetts representatives would not mind his commissioners looking into things. His Majesty promised to uphold the colony's precious charter, which had been granted by—but wait, *who* had signed the charter, back in 1629? Ah, yes, the king noted, as if he had just remembered: it was "granted by our royall father, of blessed memory." The same who had had his head sliced from his shoulders by Puritan zealots. But never mind that. All was forgotten. Meanwhile, though, His Majesty needed hardly remind the council that regarding the commissioners who were there to do his bidding, "wee doe looke vpon any injury done to them as done to ourselfe."

The king felt sure that looking into rumors of an errant American colony would be pro forma, mere housekeeping. After all, were they not all English—all on the same side? Of course they were. Thus, this was a mere side issue. Charles's main point was to make the Puritan leaders aware of a vital task that Richard Nicolls had been assigned, one with global import. And they, the leaders of Massachusetts, had a role in it. They were to assist the commissioners in going after the common enemy: "vigorously in recouering our right in those parts now possessed by the Dutch & reducing them to an entire obedjence & submission to our gouernment."

There must have been a robust silence when the reading of the letter reached its end. These were intensely delicate matters. Today we may think of a king of that era as close to all-powerful, but Charles was only recently installed on his throne after a civil war that had split the country apart. The fissures had run through towns, families, institutions, the nation's very soul, and they were slow to heal. Charles had many enemies at home. He relied on a wobbly coalition, on skillful compromise, on stout partisans like Richard Nicolls, and on slippery words. What did his letter actually command? Very little, because Charles—or rather his advisers, the king himself not being a great one for nuance—understood the power that the leaders of Boston had amassed. They had bullied the surrounding colonies, stolen land from them, made their city and its colony all but independent of England. A long-standing thesis in American colonial history holds that the Puritans of Boston were intellectual precursors of the American Revolution: that both the notion of America's independence from England and of religious liberty have their origins in the Massachusetts Bay Colony of the previous century. There are problems with this reasoning. The Puritans were aggressively intolerant of other faiths, and their yearning for political independence was not in the name of "life, liberty, and the pursuit of happiness" but for the sake of "godly rule," of which they were to be the arbiters.

But if the letter didn't overtly command, it conveyed a great deal. It hinted, backed away, coddled, seemed to threaten. It left the truly hard work up to the king's representatives, to Richard Nicolls in particular. There is no surviving portrait of Nicolls, though one account describes him as "a little above the medium height; of fine, stately presence, with a fair, open face, a pleasant, magnetic gray eye, somewhat deeply set, and the hair slightly curled at the ends." He was also strong, loyal, temperate, steadfast, and smart. Some called him "Honest Dick Nicolls." All of that had to have shown on his features as he stood surrounded by these powerful Puritans who were both his countrymen, who represented a vital piece in the future expansion of England's power, and his enemies.

He had an opposite in the room: a generation older, a lifelong religious warrior, an indefatigable politician and colonizer, a zealous murderer of Natives. When he was in his prime, John Endecott had been barrel-chested and had the sharp eyes of a ferret. He sported a ridge of moustache and a beard that jutted down his chin like a spike. Endecott, the governor of the colony, was an Ur-Puritan. He had come to America thirty-six years earlier, leading the original group of Puritan settlers of what would become the Massachusetts Bay Colony, and set about displacing Samuel Maverick and others who had made homes in the area a few years earlier. His naming of their original settlement Salem, after *Shalom*, the Hebrew word for "peace," belied his lifelong tendency to violence in the name of religion. He had banished settlers for failing to conform to the Puritan brand of nonconformity. As head of the military, he had frightened other settlers with his fervor. He turned a mission of revenge against the Pequots, over the murder of a Puritan, into a bloody war that nearly wiped out the tribe and became a defining event in relations between Europeans and Native Americans.

Endecott's fearsome aspect, as he faced Richard Nicolls, must have been substantially worn down: he was in his sixties and had less than a year to live. But the spiritual rage still burned in him, and his lifelong detestation of the Stuart rulers was undiminished. Near the conclusion of the meeting Nicolls formally proposed that the governor and his council "make an act to furnish us with such a number of men, armed, as they can spare," so as to assist in their conquest of Manhattan Island.

The council deliberated and decided that rather than "make an act," they would put the matter to the General Court.

Nicolls was displeased; he saw this as a stalling tactic. In his annoyance he revealed more, telling Endecott and the council that there were "many more things" that the king wanted from Massachusetts and that he would be back once he dealt with the Dutch. He marched out of the council chamber and shortly afterward his forces sailed from Boston.

Chapter 4

STUYVESANT'S ERROR

---

*I*f you were a European adventurer in search of the "American frontier" circa 1664, you would not have recourse to follow the likes of Daniel Boone, Davy Crockett, or Lewis and Clark, none of whom would be born until the next century. You wouldn't head for Dodge City or Cheyenne, which didn't exist. But you might make for Beverwijck, the second city of the Dutch colony of New Netherland. It consisted of a cluster of dusty streets lined with small wooden dwellings interspersed with patches of farmland, a stream running down the middle, and a stockaded fort just to the south. Enclosing these elements of human civilization, serving as borders of the community, were two natural features. On one side towering forests loomed above the town, rising not only with the height of the treetops but with the sloping elevation. The forest continued onward, westward, mile after dark and impenetrable mile. It would be an exaggeration to say that it extended unbroken all the way to the Pacific Ocean, but not too great a one, at least in the European imagination.

The other boundary, a few feet on the opposite side of Beverwijck, was the river that the English explorer Henry Hudson

had charted on behalf of the Dutch fifty-five years earlier: a
supreme, broad-bellied mirror onto the endless sky above the
wilderness of the region. It was the reason for the town's existence, its source of communication not only with Manhattan 150
miles to the south but, via that island's harbor, with the rest of
the world.

Like frontier settlements in old movies, Beverwijck was a
place where Indigenous and European cultures mingled. Native
people strolled into town, bought bread and supplies, had muskets repaired. Some stayed in local people's homes. Friendships
formed, sometimes love affairs (or less consensual relationships),
which occasionally resulted in children, who became natural liai-
sons between the two worlds.

Four decades after the start of the community, members of
its second and third generations were tough backcountry folk—
rougher than people on Manhattan, bred to the bone-cracking
cold and isolation of northern winters. New Amsterdam, for all
its remoteness from Europe, was cosmopolitan in comparison. Up
here was big sky country.

Stuyvesant's ship sailed up to the riverside dock on or about
August 22, five or so days after leaving Manhattan following
his determination that problems here were more pressing than
rumors of an English invasion. The man he wanted most immediately to see was probably waiting at the dock to receive him.
Johannes La Montagne, Stuyvesant's second in command in the
colony, ran the place.

La Montagne was an old hand—he'd been in the colony since
1637 and was close to seventy by this time—and a fascinating
fellow. He was born and raised in France and educated at Leiden
University in the Dutch Republic, receiving a medical degree,
a rarity at the time. In his early years he had ventured up the
Amazon River, then lived for a time on the Caribbean island of
Tobago. He was from a Protestant family, which was problematic
in France at the time, and his wanderings had been partly in

search of religious freedom. That was what brought him, along with his wife and their four children (the last of whom was born during the crossing), to New Netherland. On arrival in the colony he impressed Willem Kieft, Stuyvesant's predecessor. Among other skills he spoke at least four languages: useful in a polyglot and often raucous settlement. He signed on as a colonial councilor. When Stuyvesant arrived, he and La Montagne developed a bond. In 1656, at Stuyvesant's request, he moved his family to Beverwijck to manage the development of this wilderness town that was the center of the fur trade. By now he was a fixture to people in the settlement akin to the sheriff of an Old West town: the keeper of the peace. All through his tenure he had managed the difficult task of staying in government—which often meant enforcing unpopular rulings—and yet remaining trusted and liked by most.

The two men probably had a routine they followed on Stuyvesant's arrival. The director sailed up north at least a couple of times a year, beginning in the spring as soon as the ice on the river broke. They would likely have started each visit walking from the dock into the town, the doctor showing Stuyvesant the latest improvements: a new bakery, a brewery changing hands, renovations to the poorhouse, a new sawmill.

This time it would have been a hasty tour, partly because of the urgency of the situation but also because Stuyvesant had recently been suffering from an "indisposition" of some kind. He was hurting. Perhaps he availed himself of Dr. La Montagne's medical services.

Fairly quickly, then, they would have gotten down to business. But the point of the visit—discussing how to deal with the breaking of the momentous peace treaty that was now in shambles, which had been signed by so many parties, Indigenous and European alike, and the subsequent cascade of violence—was cut short. Stuyvesant hardly had time to acclimate himself before, like an apparition, a messenger from Manhattan appeared. The man had been dispatched by the city council in New Amsterdam shortly after Stuyvesant himself had left. His vessel tracked right behind Stuyvesant's all the way up the Hudson River. We can picture him drenched in sweat, having run from the river in the summer sun at full speed to the fort, where he delivered the most urgent message of Stuyvesant's long tenure.

The English were heading for New Amsterdam. In all likelihood they were already there.

———

Stuyvesant's decision to go upriver to Fort Orange was actually his second mistake in dealing with the impending English attack. In January—seven months earlier, even before the English flotilla had left home—he had gotten a clear warning that it would be coming and chose to ignore the warning as well as the offer of cooperation that had come with it, which might have averted what he was now facing.

It's possible he dismissed the warning because of its source. It came from one of the *wilden*, literally "wild people"—and a woman to boot. That January, Stuyvesant had sent envoys to meet with two sachems from Long Island tribes that were having problems with English settlers near their land. The sachems seemed to be the emissaries of a female chief, known as a sunk-squaw. She isn't named in the record of the meeting, but she was likely Quashawam, the daughter of a powerful Montaukett sachem called Wyandanch.

Quashawam, who appears in tantalizing snippets in Dutch and English records, would seem to be one of the more remarkable figures of the period. Europeans referred to her as "the great Sunk squa Quashawam." Her father had died five years earlier; when his wife and son died shortly after, during a smallpox outbreak, Quashawam ascended to the leadership. She was in her early twenties and her people were facing an existential crisis, but she had experience to draw on. Her childhood had been a time of unending strife for the Montaukett, against not only the English and Dutch but Shinnecock neighbors on Long Island and the Niantic people of what would become Rhode Island. She had grown up observing her father as he maintained power by making alliances and playing the groups off of one another. When she was thirteen, she was taken prisoner in a Niantic raid; Wyandanch paid ransom to get her back. She had watched and learned.

Now, with the English and the Dutch encroaching, she decided to try to join forces with one of the European powers against the other. She chose the Dutch.

The Native envoys told Stuyvesant's agents that they wanted their help in dealing with the English settlers in their vicinity. They cast it as an opportunity for the Dutch to strengthen their tenuous hold on Long Island. As a token of friendship, the envoys offered information, which they had gotten from the English: "Three ships would come from England," they had been told, "to drive out the Dutch and Stuyvesant." Further, they had heard that "if Stuyvesant tried to do anything," the English were going to "tie his hands behind his back and send him out of the country or kill him."

It was a moment around which history potentially turned. As it happened, it turned against New Netherland. Stuyvesant dismissed the warning and the offer to collaborate with the Native coalition that Quashawam was building. A month later she approached the Shinnecock and the English settlers, who agreed to join forces with her.

Had Stuyvesant acted differently, he might have avoided the position he found himself in now. Four days after leaving Beverwijck, he was back on Manhattan, arduously making his way out of the little boat that rowed him ashore from the river-going vessel.

Right in front of him as he hit land was city hall.* There was a buzz inside, which probably spilled out into the street. Stuyvesant likely made straight for it.

The members of the city council—men he'd known a long time, worked with, tangled with—were all here. Tymotheus Gabry, the clerk of the council. Pieter Tonneman, the *schout*, or sheriff: the city's legal officer. Jacob Backer, who happened to be married to Stuyvesant's sister, Margriet. Most prominent among them was Cornelis Steenwijck, one of the pair of *burgemeesters* (mayors) and one of the wealthy traders with whom Stuyvesant had worked to develop the city's economy.

It's likely that a fair portion of New Amsterdam's residents were crowded in and around the little building. The summer air was hot with tension and fear, but the men reached swift decisions on immediate steps to take to fortify the town against attack.

Stuyvesant had no role here. There was a division of power in the colony. This group represented the city of New Amsterdam. Stuyvesant was director general—akin to governor—of the colony as a whole. His office was located a few minutes' walk away, inside the fort. But at this moment the town's and the colony's interests were one and the same.

Propriety, and the fact that Stuyvesant was out of town when they began their day's session, required the council to put a formal request to him concerning the situation in writing, and that was what they were in the process of doing before he arrived. They prefaced it with the latest intelligence. "Whereas we are of a certainty informed, that four frigates have arrived from Old England at Boston or thereabouts in N. England, provided with a considerable number of soldiers with intention, as reports run, to attack and invade this place," they asked him to please "favour this place with eight pieces of good and heavy cannon provided

---

* Today an outline of gray stones on the sidewalk near the corner of Pearl Street and Coenties Slip marks the location.

with their carriages, balls, swabs, brushes, picks and spoons." That is, they wanted him to move the cannons from the fort to positions around the town, reasoning that the English would attack the town itself first, "it being considered that this place being lost, the fort is not tenable or very little so."

Stuyvesant gave his answer. The requested aid was "not only granted" but "absolutely necessary." There could be no distinction between the city and the colony or the people and the fort. In short, he would do all he could, as he expected they would. Commands and orders were shouted, passed down the line. Muskets, bullets, powder, shovels: the town began shifting onto a war footing.

By the day's end there was still no sign of the English.

Picture Stuyvesant then, as the light fades, stumping off homeward, walking south toward the tip of the island, with the East River on his left, crossing the little bridge over the canal, past the very first row of houses to be constructed when the city was brand new, and coming to the fine home he had built for his family. He is in pain and exhausted. His wife, Judith, stands waiting to greet him. They had met nineteen years earlier, in the home country. She had been his nurse, helping him recuperate from the loss of his leg, and as she tended him, they fell in love. She was steely and steadfast enough not only to get him through that ordeal but to go along with his remarkable decision, once he was sufficiently recovered, to venture across the sea and into the unknown. To boot, she was pregnant with their first child during the voyage to Manhattan. They arrived together—and together took in the wild and semi-lawless place that Manhattan was in those days. They had been through worlds, nurturing a thriving community on a wilderness island, raising two sons. Was it all about to end?

In the morning came news that a ship had been sighted, anchored off Sandy Point. Then another report: "the English general" was aboard. Stuyvesant read his name on yet another intelligence report that was handed to him: "Niccles."

On Thursday, August 28, after two long days of waiting and no doubt with huge relief, Richard Nicolls spotted three sails riding along the Rockaway Peninsula making for the harbor. His convoy had at last arrived. The vessels reached the tip of the peninsula, then tracked southwest to join the *Guinea*.

He wasted no time. Within hours the four ships sailed due north, toward Manhattan.

Standing at the tip of Manhattan Island today, strain as you might, you won't be able to see the Verrazzano-Narrows Bridge connecting Brooklyn and Staten Island, which marks the channel through which the English ships were expected to sail. But the entire city of New Amsterdam was now trying to do just that: trying to see what was coming.

Dorothea Angola was trying. As her name suggests, she had been born in Africa but had lived most of her life in New Amsterdam. And while she was African, she was enslaved to no one but was, in fact, a property owner, a woman who commanded respect.

Catalina Trico was trying too. She had come from Europe, a free but poor white woman, and had been here even longer than Dorothea. Both women had experienced the whole sweep of the city's development. Both had children and grandchildren; each was a matriarch of the colony.

Asser Levy was also trying. He had arrived in New Amsterdam ten years earlier, searching for opportunity and fleeing oppression. From his native city of Vilnius, in present-day Lithuania, he had made his way to Amsterdam, which was known for its relative toleration of Jews. Soon after arrival he learned of the wide-open spaces in the Dutch settlement in America. He'd assumed the role of leader of New Amsterdam's Jewish community, defending it against the sneers—"a deceitful race," Stuyvesant called them—and intolerance that belied official stances, and had become an established man of affairs.

Margriet Hardenbroek was also trying. She was a recent arrival in New Amsterdam: young, churning with ambition, and, thanks to the unusual latitude women had in the Dutch system, was quickly building one of the island's fastest-growing trading companies.

All of these people had a stake in this place and its future. So did hundreds of others: people with houses, debts, families, years of building a life here.

Of all the townspeople who were straining to see what was coming, nobody was trying harder than Stuyvesant himself. He might at this moment have been up on the ramparts of the fort to get a better view, peering out into the clean brightness of the bay, listening to the sounds below of his city scrambling to defend itself, running scenarios through his mind.

There were three ships in plain view, sitting at anchor—not the would-be English invaders, however. One of them, the *Gideon*, having arrived two weeks earlier, still hadn't left. It was refitting, scheduled to sail for Amsterdam shortly. Standing right before his eyes, as bold as brass in the sun, it must have brought to mind all that he was in the middle of doing as he built his island of commerce and opportunity. What would become of its cargo: those 290 men, women, and children who had been offloaded from her, the beginnings of the "experiment with a consignment of Negroes"? Some had already been sold off to work in tobacco fields. The rest? Here, in the city, on the island. They, too, were a part of what would happen.

The execution of King Charles I, in 1649, was a defining moment in England's long struggle involving monarchy and religious extremism.

Part Two

SETTLEMENT AND EXILE

Chapter 5

RABBITS ON AN ANTHILL

———

*A*ccounts of early New York tend to use the same few recycled facts and phrases in bringing Richard Nicolls, the leader of the English expedition that would menace New Amsterdam, briefly into their narratives. He is that alluring combination of a highly influential yet seriously neglected figure. Who was he before coming to Manhattan to stare down Peter Stuyvesant?

On inspection it seems almost as if the forces of his era propelled him toward the climax of his life. And the same forces that guided him would in time shape not only New York's but America's development.

Nicolls grew up surrounded by rabbits. The town of Ampthill, in the county of Bedfordshire, sits forty-five miles north of London, and for centuries before Nicolls was born here, its main industry was breeding "coneys" that were shipped to the vast meat market at Newgate and wound up in the stewpots of the capital. By one estimate Ampthill was nearly three-quarters surrounded by warrens. Its warreners, empowered with authority to guard against poachers, served as the local constabulary. A German traveler who showed up a few decades before Nicolls came on the scene characterized Ampthill succinctly: "We saw an immense number of rabbits." The business continued to expand long beyond Nicolls's time. In the nineteenth century an authority on the "Breeding, Rearing, and Fattening all kinds of Domestic Poultry, Pheasants, Pigeons, and Rabbits" noted that the town "may well be styled our grand NATIONAL RABBIT BAZAAR."

Rabbits aside, Ampthill was a classic, no-nonsense English town, with the straightforward nomenclature to match. The central stream was called Running Waters; the high ground where cattle were sold was Cow Fair Hill; the barren patch beyond was the Waste. The mill stood on Mill Street and the church on Church Street. The three inns in the town center, offering ale and beds to travelers, had archetypal English pub names: the Swan, the Crown, and the Hart. The road just beyond them, perhaps a location for another kind of service, was known as Slutts End.

The Anglican church, St. Andrew's, is a picturesque little building, nicely set off by the tilted, lichen-crusted tombstones in the yard. There was a church on the site in the twelfth century. The present building owes its origins to Sir John Cornwall, a fifteenth-century hellraiser who returned from the Battle of Agincourt rich with the spoils of war, bought up much of the town, organized its wild outskirts into a great park (which became known as the Great Park), built a castle at the top of it, and had the church completely redone.

For an unassuming town, Ampthill has managed to ensnare itself in a good many historical events over the centuries, several of which are reflected in the church. Cornwall, the rebuilder, is memorialized in stained glass. So is one of the most dramatic domestic tales in English history: the effort by Henry VIII to cast aside his wife, Catherine of Aragon, so that he could marry her lady-in-waiting Anne Boleyn. It happened that on visiting Ampthill, Henry decided to make its Great Park into a royal hunting ground. Thereafter his court regularly spent part of the year in the town. (In Shakespeare's *Henry VIII*, the playwright makes reference to the town in association with the king.) Henry loved the place—he called it "Anthill," which is in fact the Anglo-Saxon origin of its name—and as part of his courtship of Anne Boleyn he would give her a bow and arrow, position her in a special stand in the park, and have his gamesmen drive a herd of deer past so that he could manfully wrap his arms around her and assist her in taking shots at the beasts. The long-suffering queen, meanwhile, was placed under house arrest in the nearby castle while Henry pressed for an annulment of their marriage. From Ampthill, Catherine wrote to her daughter, "To the Kingdom of Heaven we never come but through many troubles." The words are preserved on a stained-glass panel in the church, along with a stylized image of her at prayer.

Richard Nicolls may not have gotten his due in the larger world of history, but he has pride of place in this church. His tomb stands prominently right next to the altar, bearing a large stone plaque on which, in Latin, his achievements are inscribed. The town's unofficial historian, Kevan Fadden, told me Nicolls is still remembered in these parts, at least by some. Indeed, his tomb, when I visited, was festooned with recently placed American and British flags.

The tomb provides a good deal of information. The church has no record of when it was constructed, but Mr. Fadden and I surmised that it must have been shortly after Nicolls's death, based on the fact that it is written in Latin and because it identifies Nicolls's primary accomplishment as winning for the English not Manhattan Island but "the well-known Long Island." The information would likely have been inscribed by someone who knew and was close to Nicolls at a time before New York City rose to prominence.

Nicolls's life story—including how and why he was chosen to take Manhattan—flows directly from his childhood and the involvement of the English monarchy in Ampthill.

Despite Henry VIII's many wives and his lifelong quest for a son to succeed him, he died without a male heir, and his daughter Elizabeth took the throne in 1558. Queen Elizabeth apparently had little interest in Ampthill, so the palace and Great Park fell into ruin during her forty-four-year reign. When she died child-less in 1603, the crown of England passed to the king of Scotland, James Stuart. Although he had had years of practice at being a king and had schemed to win the English crown, once he got it, he didn't take much to the details of his job, spending a good deal of his time on philosophy, theology (including the commis-sioning of what became the King James Bible), and, apparently, young men. (Some biographers of James say that historians who claim he had a sexual interest in boys and young men have mis-read seventeenth-century sources, but not all of those sources are circumspect. A contemporary French poet penned the fairly straightforward lines, "And it is well known that the King of England / Fucks the Duke of Buckingham.") Hunting was another favorite pastime, and when James got a look at the rolling 650 acres of Ampthill's Great Park that his predecessor had adored, he ordered it to be cleaned up and its woods restocked with deer.

A great many noble Scots moved from Edinburgh to London with James. One, who had been James's envoy to Queen Elizabeth and thus helped to ease the transition, was an accomplished law-yer named Sir Edward Bruce. Several Bruces followed him, join-ing the migration and setting up home in England in the new regime. In 1613 one of these, Thomas Bruce, was named by the king to the office of steward of Ampthill's Great Park, where his duties included making it fit "for the exercise of falconry and ven-ery [i.e., hunting] and fishing."

The Bruces thus became the town's noble family. Thomas Bruce—Lord Bruce, who was subsequently created Earl of Elgin (one of his descendants became infamous for pilfering the so-called Elgin Marbles from the Parthenon in Athens)—took up residence in an Ampthill estate thought to be designed in part by the famed architect Inigo Jones.

In 1609 a local barrister with upwardly mobile ambitions, by the name of Francis Nicolls, married Margaret Bruce, the niece of Sir Edward Bruce, and in short order found himself in possession of the coveted job of keeper of the Ampthill Parks. The couple moved into the Great Lodge, which sat in the middle of the Great Park (there was also a Little Park), set off from the rest of the town by hundreds of acres of forest, meadow, and rabbit warrens.

Here, in 1625, Richard Nicolls, the last of their six children, was born. A great deal of tragedy surrounded the period of his birth. Two of the couple's children died before Richard was born and another died shortly after, as did the boy's father. Richard grew up in a family that consisted of his mother, himself, and two older brothers. His mother retained her late husband's position, which allowed her family to remain at the Great Lodge. They had endured suffering, but no more than most families of the time. And they had many advantages to help them overcome their pains. They were not nobility, but they were high-level gentry. Their house was one of the grandest in the area, and it came with a fleet of servants.

But their greatest advantage—which would eventually prove to be problematic—was their close connection to the royal family. When King James died, in the year that Richard Nicolls was born, the crown passed to his son, Charles, who maintained the tradition of visiting Ampthill. And whenever he did, he and his family stayed at the Great Lodge.

The king's eldest son, the future Charles II, was five years younger than Richard, and James, the second son, was eight years younger. "From the cradle," we are told by Richard Nicolls's anonymous epitaph writer, he was intimately connected to the Stuarts. The indications are that as the boys grew, a particular fondness developed between Richard Nicolls and James Stuart. Both were youngest sons of their families. Factoring in the difference in age and status, Nicolls seems to have behaved like a protective older cousin. He grew up, then, not as an aristocrat exactly, but with an insider's view of the royal family and a boy's sensory awareness of royalty: its rich stews and fabrics, its prized horses and rude jokes.

What might young Richard and the even younger Duke of York (as James was styled from birth) aka the Lord High Admiral (a title James was given at age five) have gotten into in their times together at Ampthill? Both boys were described as full of zeal (Nicolls was called "a bold and intrepid youth"), and the place was rich with possibilities to explore, starting with the house itself, which had ten grand bedrooms, each with wood paneling and its own "Convenient Clossett." The entrance hall was palatial: twenty-six feet long by fourteen feet wide. There were two enormous parlors, walls lined with dark wood wainscoting, and a stately dining hall. Perhaps more intriguing to explore were the attached buildings that served the household: the bakery, brewhouse, stables, granary, and two kitchens.

And just outside the door lay the Great Park. You could lose yourself in the meadows, shoot arrows on the archery course, play on the bowling alley, wander among one of England's finest expanses of mature oak trees, roam the ruins of the castle on the hilltop that Sir John Cornwall had built two centuries before, and, of course, explore the two hundred acres of rabbit warrens. The boys would certainly have hunted from an early age. And there was tennis. An illustration exists of James at about five years old thwacking a ball before appreciative spectators, and it seems that as an adult Richard Nicolls was a crack tennis player, so they may well have squared off on the courts at the Great Lodge.

In October 1642 childhood came to an abrupt end for both boys but especially for James Stuart. There would be no more romping in Ampthill or at the palaces of Hampton Court, Richmond, and Greenwich. Instead, there would be war. He had just turned nine.

The king, his father, had been in power for seventeen years. After a rocky start Charles for a time seemed to have righted the ship of state. He was meticulous, orderly, smart, and detail oriented. He was one of the greatest art collectors of all time. He was a family man who doted on his French wife, Henrietta Maria, and their children.

If he had a fatal flaw, it was an inability to appreciate that compromise is the essence of politics. One of his most oft-repeated quotes—"princes are not bound to give account of their actions, but to God alone"—is remembered not because it prefaced a statement in which he tried to do just that but because its inherent dogmatism seemed to capture his true nature.

Unfortunately for him, he ruled in an age when a competing dogma was ascendant. The roots of English Puritanism went back to Henry VIII and his break with Catholicism to form the Church of England. The early leaders of that church considered that they had begun a process of purifying Christianity, ridding it of many of the gaudy rituals, abuses, and theologically problematic trappings that successive popes had built up. But from the start people disagreed about how far the purification should go.

This process was well under way when Charles came to power. Puritanism was, to him, a fundamentally destabilizing force. Everyone knew that the king's power derived from divine authority (among his titles were Defender of the Faith and Supreme Governor of the Church). A radical reformation of the church taking place outside the king's sphere was inherently sacrilegious, heretical, and treasonous. He had no choice but to fight back.

Charles's father had resisted the Puritans before him to some extent, but in the main James had compromised with the growing movement. Charles believed he could not afford that luxury, especially since the Puritan movement was rapidly growing in Parliament. A dangerous battle of words began. In 1628, Parliament proposed to do away with a tax that directly benefited the monarchy, on the grounds that there was no basis in law for it. Charles—elegant, fine-boned, with a steely gaze and the archetypal Van Dyke beard—stood before these men who were fast becoming his enemies and declared that he was shutting down Parliament before it could act, arguing that "only under me belongs the interpretation of laws, for none of the House of Commons . . . have any power either to make or declare a law without my consent."

The Puritans wanted to give individual churches autonomy. They called for the abolition of bishops. Again, Charles saw these steps as attacks on him since the bishops represented a vital rung in a church government that had him at the top and individual parishes at the bottom. He struck back, vowing to "conserve and maintain the Church committed to our charge," and decreeing that the existing "Articles of the Church of England . . . do contain the true doctrine," that bishops would remain and would retain their power as "assented unto by us," and that, concerning all matters of doctrine, "we will not endure any varying or departing in the least degree."

So no compromise.

Shortly after this utterance, large numbers of Puritans followed the example of earlier settlers and departed for New England. There, they would live according to their principles, basing their faith not on the man-made institution of the church but on the Bible and the words and deeds of Jesus.

Others, however, chose to stay. They ramped up the fight. They protested a relaxation of laws against Catholicism and "Popish superstition" and complained about "the suppressing and restraint of the orthodox doctrine." They were outraged at "sundry new ceremonies" in the Church of England, such as setting the altar at the upper end of the chancel and adorning it with candlesticks, in imitation of Catholic practice, and "the publishing and defending points of Popery in sermons and books, without punishment." All of this amounted to, in their estimation, a danger for the nation that was "very great and imminent."

Charles dismissed Parliament for the second and last time in 1629, and for the next eleven years—the period known as the

Personal Rule—he essentially governed alone. Charles's troubles were economic as well as religious, and if the Puritans imposed harshness from the pulpit—tamping down dancing, plays, and other forms of wickedness—the king made things even worse, spreading a blanket of financial misery over the course of the 1630s by increasing taxes and in other ways squeezing every level of society. He was distant enough as a ruler that he failed to notice the growing discontent, or failed to see the danger in it.

It's a fool's game to try to identify a single event that touches off mass conflict, but that often happens seemingly spontaneously as a society attempts to put its past in perspective. In this case the story that people later pointed to centers on a woman named Jenny Geddes. The place was St. Giles Cathedral in Edinburgh, Scotland; the date was July 23, 1637. It was Sunday morning, and James Hannay, dean of the cathedral, had taken the pulpit. As he began to read from the newly reissued *Book of Common Prayer*, Jenny Geddes, about whom we know nothing else, picked up the stool she had been sitting on and hurled it at his head. She is supposed to have cried, *"Deil colic the wame o' ye, fause thief; daur ye say Mass in my lug?"* which can be roughly translated as, "Devil give you colic, false thief: dare you say the Mass in my ear?"

Over the preceding decades, the Scots had taken to Puritanism and Presbyterianism. Charles had pushed back steadily. The new edition of *The Book of Common Prayer*, which was based on the Anglican liturgy, was the culmination of what many Scots felt to be a program of encroaching re-Catholicism. People in the congregation had known this was coming—that this was to be the first reading of an insupportably offensive text. They were ready for a fight.

The church erupted. The rioting spread—across Scotland. Scottish authorities requested that the book be removed from their churches. Charles rejected the appeal. By this time his enemies weren't confined to one class of society. Commoners,

gentry, nobles: the combination of perceived financial and religious oppression cut across the spectrum.

By 1642, Parliament had raised an army. So had Charles. The
two sides—thirty thousand men in all—met on an open plain
near Edgehill, a hamlet in Warwickshire, eighty-five miles northwest of London. The first battle of the English Civil War* was
not a tentative affair, with each side feeling the other out. Both
armies were stocked with veterans of the Thirty Years' War. They
went at it murderously, each hoping that a crushing victory would
bring the polarization that had characterized English society for
decades to a climactic conclusion.

Not only did Charles ride into battle himself; he thought it fit
that his two boys—Charles, the heir to the throne, was twelve;
James was nine—observe the action. Their minder for the day
was no less a personage than William Harvey, discoverer of the
circulation of the blood, who was Charles's personal physician.
The elderly gentleman—Harvey was sixty-four—was not a fan of
warfare and parked himself and the boys under a hedge out of the
way of the fight, where he proceeded to read aloud to them as a
distraction. But then a "bullet of a great gun grazed on the ground
near him," according to Harvey's biographer, and the great man
scampered farther away from the scene, bringing the boys in tow.
Nevertheless, James Stuart got a schooling in carnage.

Richard Nicolls went off to Oxford at about this time, with a
mind to follow his father in the study of law. Some scholars have
asserted that Nicolls never did go to Oxford, based on the fact
that there is no record of his enrolling. But records from that
time are highly imperfect, and his tomb states that he went there.
Besides that, in later life he maintained a lively correspondence
with members of the Royal Society, which showed him involved in

---

* Some historians formally divide the conflict taking place in the British Isles between 1642 and 1651 into three civil wars. This book will treat the unrest as one
conflict and refer to it as the English Civil War.

natural philosophy (what we would call science), and the paperwork he generated once in his post in New York indicates a familiarity with the law. All of which points to his having gotten a
grounding in higher learning.

But his education was cut short. Nicolls's first battlefield experience came soon after that of the young princes. While Ampthill,
like the rest of Bedfordshire, was Puritan country, given the family's connection to the monarchy, there was no question which
side they would take. The moment the standoff became violent,
the Nicolls family found themselves living in enemy territory.
There were, however, other Royalists around. A pocket of them,
perhaps including Richard Nicolls, gathered one evening around
the hearth of one of the local taverns, where a wall painting hon-
oring young Charles, the Prince of Wales, was unveiled. Then, for
safety's sake, it was plastered over, presumably to be revered in
secret in the ensuing years of turmoil. Over time, it was forgotten, until restoration of the tavern in 1975 revealed the image: a
design incorporating a fleur-de-lis, English roses, thistles representing Scotland, and the motto of the prince: "I serve." It is still
viewable today in the tavern in the center of Ampthill, which is
now called the White Hart.

Nicolls entered the field of battle in 1643, at the age of eighteen. His first action may have been in Ampthill itself. In October
of that year a group of Royalist cavalry, four hundred strong,
stormed into town and broke up a Puritan gathering whose purpose was to seize property throughout the county owned by families loyal to the king. We are told that in the Civil War, Nicolls
was given the rank of colonel and that he "commanded a troop
of horse." It's a sprightly sounding expression; the reality, in this
era poised midway between the medieval and the modern, was
grim and fierce. During the course of the English Civil War there
were more than six hundred battles between Roundheads, as the
Parliamentary supporters were called, and Cavaliers, as Royalists
came to be known. A typical battle saw the two armies facing one

another with infantry troops in the center and cavalry units at the ends. A troop such as Nicolls commanded involved somewhere between thirty and a hundred riders, each armed with swords and either a brace of pistols or a short musket called a carbine; they were helmeted and probably partly sheathed in armor. Nicolls and his fellow riders trotted toward the opposing cavalry three abreast, blasted away with their firearms, then, since guns could only fire a single shot before having to be laboriously reloaded, switched to slashing with swords—all, of course, while facing the same tactics from the enemy. Mounted soldiers who survived the first encounter might then turn and ride into the infantry, where pikemen planted their twelve- to eighteen-foot steel-tipped pikes, angling them so as to impale horses, and where ranks of musketeers took aim at the riders.

As the war began to go badly, Charles decided to keep his young children apart from him, reasoning that if all should die together, his line would end and the monarchy fall into chaos. Yet he also determined that it was time to "unboy" his eldest son. The Prince of Wales, at fourteen, was named a general and fought in his first battle. James spent the next three years in Oxford, where the court, after being chased out of London, had set up temporary quarters. Richard Nicolls may have been with him for part of the time. Otherwise, Nicolls fought, though we don't know where.

After being routed in the Battle of Naseby in 1645, King Charles gave himself up to Scottish forces, who in turn sold him to Parliamentary forces, from whom the so-called New Model Army of Oliver Cromwell wrested him. He was moved from place to place. At one point, en route to Hampton Court, he asked his captors if they could make a detour to Ampthill. There, he stayed one last time at Richard Nicolls's family home, the Great Lodge, and presumably allowed himself a moment to daydream of happier times. Back in London he was tried for treason. He would not speak in his defense but only declared that the court had no jurisdiction over him. On January 30, 1649, in front of the Banqueting

House in London, in what is surely the single most shocking act in the history of the English monarchy, he was beheaded. It was simultaneously the apex and nadir of English Puritanism.

James Stuart was not there to witness the spectacle. The year before, at the king's urging, the boy undertook a daring escape—which involved a barber, a maid, a coach, and a sympathetic barge owner—and, disguised as a girl, made his way across the English Channel to the Dutch Republic. His brother escaped to France. Eventually, the brothers reunited in The Hague. While the Dutch were on-and-off enemies of the English, the intermarrying of European royal families created a system that transcended ordinary politics. Charles and James's older sister, Mary, was now the Princess of Orange, wife of Willem II, the Stadtholder of the United Provinces of the Netherlands, and at her court Charles and James found a safe haven.

But they could not just sit there. After the execution of King Charles, the brothers were not only fatherless exiles and hunted men; they were also poor. Cut off from all their sources of income, James, still a teenager, decided that he would work for a living and at the same time advance his political interests on the Continent by becoming a soldier for hire.

He was not alone. He had companionship in what would become a quest for survival, manhood, legitimacy, and identity, as hundreds of Englishmen who remained loyal to the Stuarts sailed across the Channel to share their fate, whatever it might be. Among them was the twenty-three-year-old Richard Nicolls.

Chapter 6

THE TRAILBLAZER

———

*W*hile England was tearing itself apart, the Dutch Republic was coming together in the most remarkable way. Few countries have ever experienced such a rapid rise. In the late 1500s the Dutch provinces—Holland, Zeeland, Utrecht, Groningen, Friesland, Overijssel, and Gelderland—were flat, windswept, bucolic outliers in Europe, vassal states under the control of the Spanish Empire. Within a generation they had banded together into a nation that became quite possibly the most consequential on the planet.

The colony of New Netherland was founded in 1624, a year before Richard Nicolls was born. It was established as a trading post and evolved into a settlement colony. In time its West India Company overlords hoped it would become a vehicle for extending the success the Dutch had had in Asia into the Americas.

If we can use Richard Nicolls's life to help us understand the turmoil in England through the middle decades of the seventeenth century, we might likewise focus on one of New Amsterdam's oldest residents to help us appreciate what the Dutch created on Manhattan. Among the hundreds waiting anxiously in August 1664 for the English ships under Nicolls to come into view, she had arguably more at stake in what was to come than any other. Catalijntje Trico, then age fifty-nine, was probably the longest-residing inhabitant of New Netherland. Catalina, as she is often referred to, had devoted her life to this place. She had raised eleven children here. Skittering among the nervous crowds watching for the English sails were her grandchildren, numbering in the dozens.

She had arrived in 1624—forty years before Nicolls sailed into the harbor—on one of the very first ships of settlers, long before Stuyvesant appeared and before the city of New Amsterdam was even imagined. She was a double émigrée, having first left her home, a small village in present-day Belgium, for Amsterdam. The city was then in the throes of its world-changing growth. In the previous decade, heady on profits from their early experiments with capitalism, exuberant city planners had drawn out on a piece of paper a massively ambitious plan for expansion: a wide semicircle around the medieval center, incised by canals, increasing the city's size by a factor of five. Then everyone got to work to realize it. When Catalina arrived, and for decades to come, the place was a giant construction site: six miles of canals were dug, twelve miles of roads laid down, three thousand houses and more than a hundred bridges erected, all of it more or less by hand. The stupendous urban expansion project and the need for workers drew immigrants from all over Europe.

Catalina Trico traveled to Amsterdam together with her sister Margriet. The two girls had followed another sister. Marie was ten years older than Catalina, married, and lived with her husband in a street called the Nes. Catalina and Margriet moved in with them. Whether she came intending to put down roots we don't know, but within a short time Catalina had met a young man named Joris Rapalje, a cloth worker who was only a year older and had emigrated from the same region. They would not participate in Amsterdam's Golden Age rise after all but together would set out in a wholly new direction.

Three years earlier, in 1621, the Dutch West India Company had come into being. Its goal was to emulate the runaway success of the East India Company, whose vessels, laden with cinnamon, pepper, nutmeg, and other rare commodities from Asia, touched off a period of unprecedented economic and cultural growth.

The West India Company hoped to do the same by exploiting the so-called West Indies—the Atlantic coasts of North and South America as well as the Caribbean islands. It took three years to raise capital, build a fleet of vessels, and get them manned. The Dutch were at this time still in the midst of what would eventually become known as the Eighty Years' War against Spain and its ally, Portugal. Those two nations controlled much of South America and the Caribbean. One part of the West India Company's mission was military: to do battle against the country's enemies and wrest control of their trade routes.

But the company's directors also had their eye on some intriguing real estate in North America. Back in 1609 the English mariner Henry Hudson, sailing on behalf of the Dutch, had charted the region from present-day Delaware northward up the coast to New York Harbor and the river that would come to bear his name. Based on his voyage, the Dutch had laid claim to that whole swath. The exact boundaries of the Dutch colony—or for that matter of Virginia to the south or Massachusetts Bay and the other New England colonies to the north—were never entirely settled in the period. As far as the Dutch were concerned, New Netherland encompassed much of the territory described by the future states of New York and New Jersey as well as parts of Connecticut, Delaware, and Pennsylvania.

By 1624, shortly after Catalina and Joris arrived in Amsterdam and found one another, the call went out: the company was looking for settlers. It proved difficult to find them. Life was good in Amsterdam, Rotterdam, Utrecht, and other Dutch cities. Young men were launching business ventures. A hundred paths to employment had opened up. Bricklayers, glaziers, thread winders, wool washers, nap shearers, brass smiths, shipwrights, rope walkers, sugar refiners, wig makers, hatters, tanners, printers, mirror makers, diamond cutters—all of these professions were booming. Ships filled the harbors, their holds increasingly stocked with everything the wider world had to offer that humans might want to buy, from Indian tea to Chinese porcelain to printed books to live jungle cats. At around the time Trico arrived, the Amsterdam warehouses of the East India Company contained nearly four million pounds of pepper. Street kiosks groaned with their wares; whole markets were devoted to individual products: butter, poultry, vegetables, fish. Who would cast such plenty aside and choose to spend ten or more weeks on a perilous sea voyage, only to begin a life of danger and uncertainty in a place nobody had ever heard of?

She would, and he would. It was mostly recent immigrants like Catalina and Joris who filled the first ship bound for Manhattan, the *Eendracht*, or *Unity*: people with nothing to lose, who were willing to become trailblazers. In fact, those first settlers were mostly from the same region Joris and Catalina hailed from. They were nearly all Walloons: French-speaking Protestants from northern France or what is today Belgium, who had previously fled religious persecution in their homeland and sought refuge in the Dutch Republic.

The organizers of the voyage had been in search of couples; they wanted Adams and Eves for their New World Eden. The initial numbers were remarkably small. Trico herself tells us that there were five women on the voyage, including her. All had come with partners. The other four couples married at sea. Joris and Catalina apparently didn't fancy those conditions for their honeymoon. Instead, four days before they sailed, they went to the Walloon Church in Amsterdam—a pretty little building set back from the Oudezijds Achterburgwal, one of the city's oldest canals, which stands to this day and still holds services in French—and exchanged their vows. He was nineteen; she was eighteen. Her sister served as witness. Neither could read or write: they made marks in place of signatures in the betrothal registry.

Many hard weeks later the couple sailed into the harbor of their new North American homeland, marveling at its expanse and feeling thankful to have reached it alive. In the following weeks the dazzled newcomers took the measure of what was to them unadulterated wilderness: a landscape of wide rivers, high cliffs, thick forests, and natural abundance, of wild grapevines and walnuts, of deer and turkey, of rivers and bays wriggling with salmon and sturgeon.

The few dozen raw and inexperienced Walloons were instructed to begin settling the land at once. Aside from the practicality, this was deemed necessary to support a legal claim to the territory. According to the European doctrine the Dutch were following, the right to ownership of "wild" lands was based on 1) first discovery (by Europeans) and 2) settlement. Trico and her few shipmates had the outsized job of establishing a credible case for European settlement of a geography that is today home to tens of millions of people. Survival and common sense might

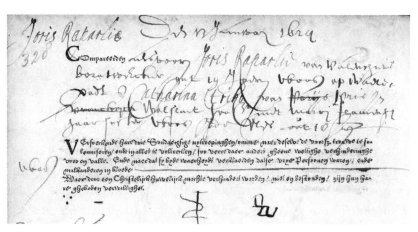

Amsterdam's betrothal registry shows that Catalina Trico and Joris Rapalje got married just before their ship departed for New Netherland in 1624. As neither could read or write, they made their marks at the bottom.

have dictated they stay together in one place, but to support the legal claim it was decided that they had to spread out. So two couples and six men were sent off north to what they dubbed the Fresh River (now the Connecticut River); two couples and eight single men went south to the Delaware River; eight men stayed at Manhattan; and the last group, including Catalina and Joris, shipped 150 miles up the Hudson River to a place they called Fort Orange.

The first task was to fashion shelter. No sooner did they finish cobbling together "some huts of Bark" than they received their first visitors. Standing up from their labors, bathed in sweat, they gazed dumbstruck as groups of Native people approached. Settlers found them pleasing in appearance. They were about the same size as the Europeans, their hair "jet black, quite sleek and uncurled," as one wrote; they had "fine faces with black brown eyes and snow white teeth," and both men and women were "broad shouldered and slim waisted."

What we know of the first encounters comes from Catalina herself. In the year 1688, when she was eighty-three and living a peaceable life on Long Island surrounded by family, she was sought out by English authorities in the region who were sorting through competing boundary claims and asked to swear a deposition as to the particulars of the earliest European settlement. She described the beginnings of what would later become Albany, New York. With the knowledge that she would gain in later decades regarding the different Native peoples of the area, she looked back at those early weeks and specified which nations paid a visit in these first encounters: Mohawk, Oneida, Onondaga, Cayuga, and Seneca, all members of the Haudenosaunee, or Iroquois, confederacy, as well as Mahican. Probably they didn't all come at once, as the Mahican were not on friendly terms with the others. Further, she made clear that whatever initial fears the Europeans may have felt were quickly allayed. The Natives, she declared, "came & made Covenants of friendship" with their captain, a man named Arien Jorise. They gave him beaver pelts, she went on to say, and "desyred that they might come & have a Constant free Trade."

Exploratory missions of Dutch traders had been coming here starting a decade or so earlier, so that by the time Trico and her party arrived, the Native people of the region were ready for them—ready to do business. Indeed, one impetus for the settlement of the colony was to supply the European market with furs. Beavers were particularly prized because beneath their fur was another layer, which, when processed, resulted in a material—felt—that was water-resistant, light and thin, yet warm. For decades Europeans had traded for such furs from Russia. Beavers there had mostly been trapped out, so the North American market was prized. The Indigenous people knew this.

Over the next two years Catalina and Joris, together with other families, carved out an extraordinarily rough but steady life: clearing trees; planting wheat, rye, barley, and oats; laboring under blazing sunshine and amid winters colder and snowier than they could ever have imagined back home. They felt alone in this vastness, yet they knew where they were. They had a good sense of the Haudenosaunee peoples to their west and of the Mahican to the east. They knew that the English Pilgrims had planted their own colony to their north. (Massachusetts Bay would not come into being for several more years.) The pact with the local tribes held, and for these two years, as the government officials later recorded Catalina's remembrance, "yᵉ sᵈ Indians were all as quiet as Lambs & came & Traded with all yᵉ freedom Imaginable."

For Catalina two events stood out in this period. The first was joyous: in June 1625 she gave birth. She and Joris called the baby Sarah. The girl would become famous throughout the colony as its first American-born settler, and she seems to have spent her life wearing the designation as a badge of honor. It was a time of hardship and wonder: of wild, productive days, impossibly full, the sky endless, the river on whose shores they labored all-encompassing, and of nurturing this new life she had been given. Trico must have wondered at times if it was like this for Eve, the first woman.

The second event brought this idyllic period to an abrupt and violent end. The West India Company had appointed a man named Willem Verhulst as provisional director of the colony, and Verhulst posted a contingent of company soldiers to the settlement for protection. The company had a standing rule: the soldiers were not to interfere in intertribal affairs. In the summer of 1626, Daniel van Crieckenbeeck, the leader of the squadron, broke that rule. The two nearby nations, the Mohawk and Mahican, had been at war for some time, which had increased tension in the settlement since the colonists traded with both. A Mahican chief—possibly a man by the name of Monemin—asked for Van Crieckenbeeck's aid. He must have been persuasive because Van Crieckenbeeck agreed to join their side in the fight. Together with several of his men he set off with the Mahicans into dense woods. Three miles from the settlement Mohawks ambushed them, killing several men, including Van Crieckenbeeck and three of his soldiers.

The event had outsized ramifications—for Catalina Trico, for the colony, and for the future United States. As word of the first bloodshed trickled across the hundreds of square miles that made up the Dutch territory, it focused attention on their leadership. Verhulst, barely a year into his job, was voted out. A new man, Pieter Minuit, who had come on the mission as a volunteer, was chosen to replace him. Minuit proved to be a smart and strategic thinker. Spreading so few people out across such a vast landscape, he concluded, was madness. He recalled everyone to the harbor—150 miles to the south of Catalina and Joris's settlement—into which they had first sailed. Up to now there had been no capital chosen for their colony. Here, the original site for a settlement had been on what the Dutch called Nut Island—later to become Governors Island. Minuit made the determination that he needed a capital, that Nut was too small, but that the tip of Manhattan Island, two thousand feet away, was an admirable location.

And so Joris and Catalina moved south and started all over again. They helped lay out roads, build houses, mound up earth into the walls of a crude fort—all while Catalina was pregnant with their second child. And they presumably participated in the event referenced at the start of this book, a ceremony that has entered popular myth and echoes to this day, in which Minuit, on behalf of the West India Company, "bought" the island, probably from a branch of the Lenape.

We don't know the name of Minuit's counterpart, but he presumably entered willingly into this ceremony whose purpose, as far as he understood it, was to forge an alliance. He would not likely have been coerced into it because in this era the Lenape, like other nations of the wider region, were stronger and more numerous than the Europeans. Before getting to this point, the Lenape leader would have held a council with his community, at which the matter of entering into such a relationship would have been debated at length. Colonist Adriaen van der Donck, who made a thoughtful study of the Indigenous tribes of the region, wrote, "Peace or war with neighbors and surrounding nations are not decided in haste or by the few, but debated in all their councils, where anyone who has any authority is free to state their opinions at such length and as amply as they please without anyone interrupting them, no matter how long the speech or whether it goes against the mood of the many." Only once the group had gone through this lengthy process and achieved a consensus would their leader have called for this ceremony, which would have involved eating, drinking, dancing, smoking, and speeches and would likely have included all the Dutch settlers as well as the members of the tribe.

It also involved a European custom: a paper, the words of which were read aloud and onto which men on both sides scratched signatures or marks. There is a widely held but mistaken view today that Native Americans prior to contact with Europeans had no notion of property rights—that to them land was as free and universal as the air. It's more accurate to say that the Lenape and other groups had a different idea of property rights. They had no sense of individual ownership of land, but they had a concept of territory over which a particular tribe or nation had authority. They fought territorial wars with one another. And a tribe could choose to grant others access to their land or to a portion of it. But such a grant wasn't exclusive: it didn't mean that they themselves wouldn't continue to use it. And it wasn't permanent. The deal could be revised later. It's also wrong to think the Native people had no way of recording such agreements. They didn't use a system of writing, but they marked important events with wampum—strings of beads—or on notched sticks.

So there was some common ground between the Europeans and the Native Americans. Both had a sense of territorial rights, both were capable of fighting over territory, but both also had traditions whereby they could change who was entitled to that possession. Hence this ceremony.

But of course there were vast cultural differences. The Dutch knew more or less how the Lenape viewed land and ownership of it. They knew the Native people didn't think in terms of a permanent giving-away of rights to land. They knew the Lenape looked upon the ceremony as a pact by which the newcomers were being given permission to use the place on the understanding that the Lenape would continue to do so as well and that if either was attacked, the other would come to their aid.

But the Dutch also saw the ceremony through their own, European eyes. Even though they were knowingly entering the cultural space of the Lenape, this was also, when seen through the Dutch cultural prism, a purchase, a legally binding transaction. It would give them a document to show others: French, English, other Dutchmen, for whom a deed of sale held concrete meaning. Of course the Dutch had no idea how the future would pan out, but it's fair to say they were playing two cultural games at once.

Robert Grumet, an authority on the Munsee-Lenape, has argued that the Dutch likely only began issuing deeds in New Netherland three years later, after a 1629 decision by the West India Company to establish patroonships—private estates within the colony of New Netherland. If true, then the "sale" of Manhattan in 1626 would have involved only a verbal agreement. I find that unlikely because if they had initially settled for a verbal agreement, the Dutch, being highly conscious of such administrative matters, would have gone back to the Lenape later to put it in writing, and there is no mention of such a later event. After Grumet's book was published, Charles Gehring of the New Netherland Research Center found proof of a sort that there was a deed, buried in the *Minutes of the Executive Council of the Province of New York*. In 1670 a group of sachems appeared before Francis Lovelace, then the English governor of New York, maintaining that they had rights to land around Harlem. The English produced "all the Old Dutch Records," which showed that the island "was bought & paid for 44 yeares agoe."

So there was a deed between the Dutch and the Lenape in 1626. Like most documents from New Netherland's early years, it has vanished. We do, however, have a record of the event, for when the next ship from Manhattan arrived in the home country, the government official who logged it in, a man named Pieter Schagen, noted the purchase. He recorded of the colonies that "they had all their grain sowed by the middle of May, and reaped by the middle of August," and to indicate that, the ship carried "samples of these summer grains: wheat, rye, barley, oats, buckwheat, canary seed, beans and flax." Those on the ship who had come from the colony, Schagen wrote to his superiors, reported that "our people are in good spirits and live in peace. The women also have borne some children there."

Such details went toward the territorial claim. Crops in the ground and babies in laps sent a message to others: *You see? This land is ours.*

To this same end Pieter Schagen added the kicker, the sentence that has stuck in the craw of America's dominant culture and remains undigestible four hundred years later: "They have purchased the Island Manhattes from the Indians for the value of 60 guilders."

The 60 guilders, which a nineteenth-century translator infamously calculated at $24, was neither a payment nor was it made in cash. It was customary for the Indigenous peoples to seal treaties with token offerings. In this case "the value of" 60 guilders would have meant useful objects: knives, kettles, cloth. These were not intended as payment in exchange for ownership of what

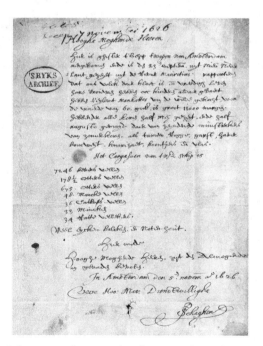

Pieter Schagen's letter—indicating that "our people . . . have purchased the Island Manhattes from the Indians"—is both the foundation on which New York would be built and a prime artifact of colonialism.

is today some of the most valuable real estate on earth. They were gifts, ritualized tokens of alliance.

Within a short time the Dutch would find it convenient to forget the Lenape reading of the event, according to which they would share the land. They would see the deal strictly in European terms. They, and then the English, would go on to negotiate hundreds of real estate deals with Lenape chiefs, which, as time went by, became more coercion than negotiation. Among the last and most infamous was the so-called Walking Purchase of 1737, in which the sons of William Penn pressured the Lenape

More than a century after the "purchase" of Manhattan Island by the Dutch, the Lenape chief Lapowinsa was among the last of his people's leaders to be coerced into giving up their land. While he was in Philadelphia trying to block what he considered to be a fraudulent land grab, he sat for a portrait.

chief Lapowinsa and others to sell them 1.2 million acres of Pennsylvania, supposedly an area that a man could walk in a day and a half. Lapowinsa protested, but English settlement persisted. (In 2004 the Delaware Nation, a branch of the Lenape, took the state of Pennsylvania to court over what it claimed was an underlying fraud but lost the case.)

And so the ceremony at the tip of the wooded and marshy island of Manhattan would eventually be seen as an archetype of western colonialism, a template to be repeated over and over in what would be a long, ugly saga of dispossession, which would see Europeans sweep the Native peoples of the continent out of their homelands, scatter them, pen them, murder them, rob them of everything. From the long perspective of history, it's certainly correct to say that the Lenape were swindled. Catalina Trico— holding little Sarah in her arms as people from both communities took part in the ceremony, exchanging wampum and other tokens by firelight—was likely an eyewitness to what from our vantage looks to be the single most emblematic act of European injustice toward Indigenous peoples in all of American history.

Having reached their agreement, both sides, following the Native custom, would have eaten huge amounts of food—"Nothing must be left over," Van der Donck said of such ceremonies. And after the meal "the old and staid have a smoke to round off the feast, while the young and not-so-young take to singing, skipping, and dancing, often the whole night through."

Not long after the event that marked the first taking of Manhattan, Catalina and Joris engaged in a land deal of their own, for a plot on what is today Pearl Street. It was prime real estate—at the very tip of the island, facing toward the harbor and the ships at anchor. Here, in the coming years, they built two houses, side by side. They raised their family in one and probably rented out the other. When Sarah was grown and married, her family lived there, next door to her parents.

Though they occupied a choice location and had done well for themselves, the family was surrounded by chaos. New Amsterdam was rudderless in its early years. Sarah grew up with the colony; her early life in New Amsterdam's mean streets was spent dodging prostitutes and drunken sailors. When she was thirteen, a gunner was stabbed during a fight in front of the fort, just around the corner from her house—the town's first murder. On the other hand, that same year the first official school opened, providing some structure for her and the several dozen other children now in the community.

A new director arrived at about this time. Willem Kieft seems not to have had any experience to qualify him for the position but rather got it through family ties to the West India Company. He hit town in 1638 with a determination to clean the place up. The

t' Fort nieuw Amsterdam op de Manhatans

The earliest view of New Amsterdam, circa 1628, shows houses and a windmill clustered around the fort at the tip of Manhattan Island. Sailing vessels and Native people in canoes show the prominence of trade.

fort was so tumbledown, he noted on arrival, that you could walk in and out of it on all sides. The West India Company farms (to the north, in today's East Village) were overgrown. The director's house inside the fort was falling down. Kieft issued edicts against public drunkenness and smuggling.

The root cause of the drunkenness—and of the general state of things—was the smuggling. The company directors had tried to run the colony as a trading post, where they would exercise control over what was shipped in and out. That didn't work. New Amsterdam was too far away from Europe, and in the absence of a strong military garrison and with so many furs coming in from their Native American partners, smuggling became so commonplace that officials complained that illegal furs crowded out the licensed product on West India Company ships. In Amsterdam a faction on the board decided the place needed to develop into a colony, with settlers who had a personal stake in it. But such a plan required long-term investment, which other members of the board refused to support. Without a clear direction from the bosses across the ocean, the place languished.

The situation improved at about the time Kieft arrived, though no thanks to him. Under pressure from the States General, the Dutch governing body, which liked the idea of an overseas settlement colony, the company was forced to abandon its monopoly on the fur trade. As a result, the owners of small trading companies located on the canals in Amsterdam began sending sons to open branch offices in New Amsterdam. Business increased. In the early years New Amsterdam sent five thousand or so pelts annually to Europe. By 1635 it was nearly fifteen thousand; we don't have figures for the post-monopoly years, but the numbers kept going up. A smuggler's haven turned into a free trading port.

Joris and Catalina had stuck it out through the chaotic early years and now began to reap the rewards of what turned out to be an investment in a New World manifestation of Dutch capitalism. Like many other people in town, Joris became a trader, putting down money on shipments of furs. He reinvested his prof-its, opening a tavern nearby. It's hard to imagine how Catalina managed through these years. She had eleven children over a twenty-five-year period (all but Sarah were born on Manhattan); she farmed; she probably helped run the tavern. She had Sarah to help with the younger children, and as soon as they were old enough, everyone would have taken part in chores. I imagine their household as a New World version of a Jan Steen interior: chaotic, brimming with life, with children darting back and forth between the two houses.

Similar stories played out in the streets around them—people of humble status, from a variety of backgrounds, finding a way for-ward. Anthony van Salee was apparently born in Spain to a Dutch pirate father and a Moorish mother. Griet Reyniers was a German or Dutch prostitute. They met and married in Amsterdam, then emigrated to Manhattan, where between the two of them they racked up fifteen court appearances in a two-year period, for drunkenness, fighting, slander, and the time a group of sailors called Griet a whore and she responded by baring her bottom and crying, "Blaes mij daer achterin!" which could loosely translate to "Kiss me back there!" But just when we might expect to see the couple fall through the cracks of the records and into oblivion, they find their footing in society. They become prominent land-holders. Their children married into the elite, and their progeny stayed there, with descendants who would include Warren G. Harding and Cornelius Vanderbilt.

What was happening in New Amsterdam relates back to old Amsterdam and to Dutch history. Two forces were at work: one financial, the other cultural. A case can be made (I've made it elsewhere) that both have their origins in the very beginnings of Dutch society, when in the Middle Ages migrants from other parts of Europe traveled to what was essentially a vast river delta and found they needed to build dams and dikes to control the water so that their homes and fields didn't flood. They created polders—land reclaimed from the sea—eventually nearly doubling the size of the country. Where in much of the rest of Europe land ownership was tied to the feudal system—a manor, or estate, was controlled by a nobleman, under whom were peasants and craftspeople and above whom were the hierarchies of church and crown—here things developed differently. Newly created land was divided up among individuals in a locality; people used their plot to raise crops or cattle, sold their products, and built up wealth. Instead of a society of serfs and nobles, it became one of entrepreneurs. People looked for more opportunities, and innovation followed upon innovation. Dutch businessmen cornered the European markets on everything from herring to soap.

The climax of this activity came in 1602, with the founding of the Dutch East India Company. In addition to fueling the so-called Golden Age, spawning fabulous growth and wreaking untold havoc and misery in the lands it colonized, the company spurred the development of many of the basic elements of capitalism: shares of stock, a stock exchange, the very idea of a permanent company that individuals could own and sell pieces of. Under its sibling, the West India Company, New Amsterdam was launched as an outpost for the exploitation of the western hemisphere. When the West India Company gave up its trading monopoly, things on Manhattan began to get interesting, as an experiment got under way in which an overarching multinational corporation attempted to make money by permitting other, smaller companies to do business within its protective framework.

The other force at play in New Amsterdam, which likewise relates back to the home country, was toleration. The idea that there ever was such a thing as a Dutch policy of toleration in the seventeenth century has been called into question in recent years. How can we call a society tolerant that was responsible for

a large share of European colonialism, including mass enslavement and the enduring legacy of systemic racism? If there even
was such a thing, the toleration that came into being in the Dutch
Republic was surely quite narrow.

These are valid points. We need to cast a cold eye on the
mindset of our ancestors. At the same time, we ought to appreciate historical moments that spawned the values we hold. In an
age in which Europe was awash in religious warfare—when intolerance was official policy in Spain, France, and England; when
European armies were slaughtering one another over doctrinal religious disputes—the Dutch determined that they should
tolerate those who believed differently. The toleration that the
Dutch pioneered didn't include everyone. Limited though it was,
however, it was real. It was enshrined in the Union of Utrecht
of 1579, the agreement that brought the disparate provinces
together into one nation. This text decreed "that each person
shall remain free in his religion and that no one shall be inves-
tigated or persecuted because of his religion." This was a water-
shed. It was also grudging. There were whole sectors of society
that thought it was a bad idea to tolerate even other forms of
Christianity. Yet throughout the course of the 1600s religious
toleration—pushed by a group of reformist Calvinists called the
Remonstrants—became a feature of the Dutch system. By the
latter decades of the century, foreign visitors to Dutch cities
remarked on it. Often they did so in the negative, believing that
accepting other forms of religious expression weakened a society
and went against God's will.

The origins of Dutch tolerance may also relate to geography.
Without mountainous borders the Low Countries were relatively
easy to run to for those fleeing religious persecution. And a
country poised for oceangoing trade would be naturally inclined
toward tolerating a variety of peoples and cultures.

So the concept of tolerance of others—of evolving a society
out of a mix of peoples from varying backgrounds—seems to have

developed as a feature of Dutch culture. But did it transfer to the New World?

Yes, but again in a limited way. On the one hand, there were indeed people in New Amsterdam who highlighted religious toleration as part of the community's makeup. Adriaen van der Donck, in his *Description of New Netherland*, which was written to entice Europeans to migrate there, underscored the mixed character of the population and considered it a good thing. And Willem Kieft, as director, beckoned people who had fled from old England to New England only to face persecution at the hands of the Puritans there, inviting them to join his colony and touting the Dutch policy of freedom of religion. Van der Donck wrote of one of those persecuted New Englanders who answered Kieft's call that he "betook himself . . . under the protection of the Netherlanders, in order that he may, according to the Dutch reformation, enjoy freedom of conscience, which he unexpectedly missed in New England." Two of the most famous residents of New Netherland— Lady Deborah Moody and Anne Hutchinson—fled New England Puritanism and became beneficiaries of the Dutch policy of religious toleration.

So the colonists themselves were aware of Dutch tolerance, and at least some championed it and considered it part of their makeup. On the other hand, Peter Stuyvesant, once he replaced Kieft, did his level best to bar Lutherans, Quakers, and Jews from settling in New Netherland. And the attitude toward Native Americans and Africans argues pretty decisively against any broad underlying ethos of tolerance.

How much should these failures matter to us? We don't need to judge people of the past according to our standards so much as we need to recognize patterns and milestones in history. Whether or not New Amsterdammers felt they were exponents of an ideology of toleration, the city reflected both the unusually multiethnic character of the home country and the vigorous Dutch approach to trade and business. It was three years after the breakup of the West India Company's monopoly that Willem Kieft gave the French Jesuit priest Isaac Jogues his estimate that eighteen languages were being spoken in the little city. Ethnically Dutch people made up only about half of its population. That pluralism was a radical thing for the time, which makes it all the more remarkable that it was a defining feature of New Amsterdam. New York would become what it became thanks in part to the makeup of New Amsterdam and to the history behind it.

The way Dutch toleration played out in both Old and New Netherland, and how it contrasted with other parts of Europe, is illustrated by the case of Asser Levy. As mentioned earlier, Levy, a Jew, had left his home in present-day Lithuania as a young man, probably fleeing potentially lethal antisemitism in his home country. He made for Amsterdam, then hopped on a ship bound for Manhattan. It arrived in August 1654, bringing him and one or two other Jews: the first in the colony. Just two weeks later, another ship anchored with twenty-three Jews seeking refuge. These newcomers arrived under very different circumstances from Levy. They were Sephardim—Jews whose ancestors had lived for centuries in Spain and Portugal—whereas Levy was an Ashkenazi, of Eastern European heritage. There was a cultural divide: the former mostly spoke Spanish, whereas Yiddish would likely have been Levy's mother tongue. Their common faith bound them together, but Levy remained distinct.

The ancestors of the Sephardic group had fled from Portugal to Brazil, then a Portuguese colony, more than a century earlier, after the Portuguese Inquisition had expelled them. They were able to live under Portuguese rule there by becoming "conversos," i.e., pretend Christians. Then, in 1624, the Dutch took Brazil from Portugal, and the Dutch policy of toleration of religion came into effect: the Jews came out of hiding and began practicing their faith openly. A generation later, however, in 1654, Portugal retook Brazil, and, faced with persecution, many in the community— which may by this time have numbered about 1,500—fled.

Sixteen ships left the South American colony headed for the Dutch Republic.

One of those ships was waylaid by pirates, then recaptured by a French vessel. The captives managed to convince the captain that if he took them to the nearest Dutch-controlled port, they would find a way to pay him for his trouble. He made for New Amsterdam, marched into the fort, and told Stuyvesant he expected to be paid. Stuyvesant considered Jews "a deceitful race" and believed that if they stayed, they would "infect" the colony. He wanted nothing to do with them. His soldiers gathered up the few possessions they had with them and sold them to raise money to pay the French captain. This wasn't enough to cover the debt, so Stuyvesant had two of the Jews imprisoned as security. The money wasn't the real point. A policy of tolerating religious differences might be fine in theory, but Stuyvesant had a colony to run. In his mind such differences weakened a society. A young city perched on the edge of a wilderness couldn't afford such niceties. He wanted them gone.

While this story unfolded, some of the Jews managed to write letters to relatives in Amsterdam explaining their plight. These contacts were people of wealth and substance who appealed to the West India Company directors, noting that Jews had rights within the Dutch system and arguing that those should apply in Dutch colonies as well. Eventually, the company agreed and ordered Stuyvesant to allow the Jews to remain.

And so they did, but they had to put up with official badgering. Levy seems to have been treated differently from the others, possibly because he had come with money and was able to support himself. He decided to take on the mantle of spokesperson for the Jewish community and appeared regularly in court on their behalf as well as on his own business. After failing in his effort to evict them from the colony, Stuyvesant tried to restrict them in other ways. He denied them the "burgher right"—essentially, city citizenship, which would allow certain privileges—in light of what he said was the "disgust and unwillingness" of the guard officers to serve alongside Jews. He then decided that since they were not burghers, the Jews could not participate in the burgher guard, which protected the city. Then the government taxed them for failing to serve in the guard.

Levy and a colleague, Jacob Barsimon, took this blatant unfairness to court, arguing that they should either be given burgher status or made exempt from the tax. Stuyvesant denied the petition with gusto, saying that if they didn't like his terms, they were free to "depart whenever and wherever it may please them."

Levy persisted and won the burgher right. He bought a house in New Amsterdam, lent money, backed ventures, and developed a business that dealt in tobacco and grain. He returned to Europe in 1660, met and married a woman named Miriam, and brought her back to Manhattan. In becoming a New Amsterdammer, and a prominent one at that, he forced the Dutch to reveal both the extent and limits of their policy of toleration.

Economically speaking, New Netherland got a restart in the year 1640, with the decision by the West India Company to drop its monopoly on trade. Sails appeared on the horizon, bringing new settlers and with holds crammed with goods. The place would survive, thrive, grow. The future was full of promise.

A year later horror descended: murder, screams, homes set ablaze, crops destroyed. In a sense it was all self-inflicted. If the taking of Manhattan from the Lenape was a kind of original sin, the nightmare that began in 1641 might be considered retribution.

In the fifteen years since the Dutch had laid claim to the island, the Lenape and other tribes in the region had endured incalculable suffering. The unnamed chiefs who put their marks to a deed concerning Manhattan in 1626 had done so from a position of relative strength. They had the numbers on their side.

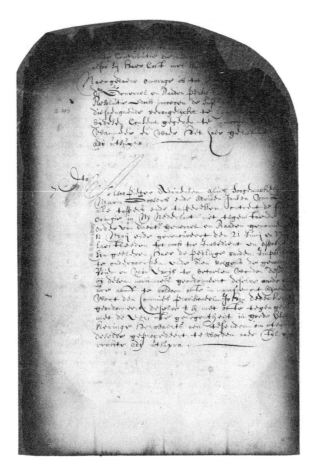

As a leader of New Amsterdam's Jewish community, Asser Levy asked that Jews be admitted as burghers or be exempt from taxation. In this document, the council ruled against them and said that the Jews were free to "depart whenever or wherever it may please them." Levy appealed and eventually won the burgher right.

Scholarly estimates of the Native population in the region at the moment of European contact range as high as thirty thousand, while the Dutch at the time probably numbered no more than a few hundred. But the balance was already turning. Waves of infectious diseases had swept through Europe in the preceding centuries—smallpox, typhus, measles, cholera, scarlet fever—

killing a sizable percentage of the population. Those who survived had built up immunity but could still transmit to others. The Native people of the Northeast were defenseless.

We can scarcely imagine the suffering that took place in long-houses and Native villages through the late 1620s and the 1630s. Venturing among the Mohawks in 1634, a Dutch colonist noted that "none of the chiefs was at home . . . because many Indians here in the castle had died of smallpox." By 1655, Adriaen van der Donck estimated of the Natives that their "numbers have dwindled owing to smallpox and other causes to the extent that there is now barely one for every ten." Twenty-five years later a missionary reported hearing from longtime settlers that "there is now not 1/10th part of the Indians there once were, indeed, not 1/20th or 1/30th; and that now the Europeans are 20 and 30 times as many." Referring in particular to the Lenape, Robert Grumet notes that the losses "were nothing short of catastrophic. Entire clans . . . almost certainly were wiped out."

Put these horrific details alongside the rapid pace of land deals that the Dutch made with Lenape and other groups in this period, as well as those the English were making at the same time in contested areas between New Netherland and New England—the Lenape alone put their marks to no fewer than six hundred deeds with Europeans in the colonial period—and you begin to sense the vise the Lenape felt themselves in the grips of. Loved ones had vanished. Their very culture was on the brink of collapse. In desperate attempts to maintain a foothold, they agreed to land deals that came with promises of protection. They would give up some of their territory and move to adjacent land with the under-standing that they were entering alliances with the Europeans. But the proliferation of newcomers and the cheek-by-jowl living arrangements brought new tensions.

Let's back up to 1626. The Lenape and the Dutch have just made their deal for Manhattan Island. The Dutch begin building a fort at the place they will call New Amsterdam. One day two

Lenape men and a boy show up at a pond to the north of the future city, where Europeans and Natives alike go to collect fresh water. They have some beaver pelts they are hoping to trade. A party of Dutchmen arrive, attack the Lenape, take the furs, and kill one of the men. The boy escapes, and for the next fifteen years lives with the memory of the murder of the man, who was his uncle. Now, in 1641, a grown man known to and liked by the Dutch, he shows up at a tavern outside New Amsterdam, recognizes the old man who runs the place as one of the party who killed his uncle, picks up an axe, and cuts his head off.

Not surprisingly, settlers were enraged by the murder. Willem Kieft ordered West India Company soldiers to attack Native villages in reprisal. Two attacks in particular—one at Pavonia, across the river from New Amsterdam, and another at Corlears Hook, in the present-day Lower East Side—were massacres, with soldiers hacking men, women, and children while they slept. This in turn brought disparate Lenape tribes together into a counterattack. For four years each side inflicted devastation on the other. Dutch farms in outlying lands were burned to the ground. Settlers retreated into Fort Amsterdam for safety. Many were killed, including Anne Hutchinson, the Puritan Englishwoman who had fled from persecution in New England, along with five of her children.

Finally, in August 1645, five sachems—Oratany, Sesekemu, Willem, Mayauwetinnemin, and Aepjen—representing ten different tribes, made their way into Fort Amsterdam and, "in the presence of the entire community" of New Amsterdam, signed a peace agreement with Kieft.

The Dutch apparently didn't see the horror of Kieft's War as a result of any kind of hubris on their part—didn't feel that the nightmare stemmed from their having forced themselves into the ancestral lands of the Lenape, first taking Manhattan Island and then stitching together a patchwork of properties up and down the Hudson River and on Long Island. Many of those in

In 1644, two Dutch soldiers took a Lenape man they had captured during Kieft's War to Amsterdam, where they exhibited him for money. Some scholars believe this engraving is of that man, whom the soldiers identified as "Jaques."

the colony circa 1640 had only recently arrived; to them this was simply their new home, which suddenly and bewilderingly became engulfed in war.

Some residents gave up and left during the time of trouble, but most of the survivors stayed and rebuilt. The war and its conclusion brought a new conviction to forge a more stable society. A group of townsmen Kieft had called together to rubber-stamp his initial decision to attack the Lenape evolved to his dismay into an opposition party, which represented the interests of the community and began a campaign to oust Kieft. They argued that Kieft had gone against the wishes and interests of the colonists in waging war against the Lenape, that the Natives were in fact their trading partners. They began a push for a form of representative government for the colony and eventually called for Kieft's replacement.

Kieft's War—from 1643 to 1645—nearly destroyed the colony. But in time ships laden with goods appeared again on the horizon. People began buying and selling houses, leasing land from one another, entering partnerships to invest in ships with which to go on trading expeditions. As they rebuilt, they undertook improvements, making the place better, more livable than before. Adam Roelantsen outfitted his house with wainscoting and window frames. Arnold van Hardenberg wanted tongue-and-groove flooring in his home. New tradesmen arrived and set up shop.

Like everyone else, Catalina Trico suffered mightily during the war years. One of her sons was killed. She, Joris, and their children had to start over, rebuilding, planting new crops, grieving. Tempers often flared. At one point she appeared in court within the fort charging that a colonist named Paulus van der Beeck had slandered and abused her. Apparently, he had attacked one of her daughters, and Catalina had gone to him demanding to know why, whereupon he hit her and called her "a whore and a wampum thief."

But Catalina and Joris too recommitted themselves to the colony. They bought land across the river, in Breuckelen, and started a farm. Six months after the peace treaty was signed, Catalina gave birth to her ninth child, a girl they named Anna.

A little over a year after that, the complaint filed by the colonists against Willem Kieft bore fruit. Kieft was recalled, and in May 1647 the new man, Peter Stuyvesant, stepped ashore, signaling the start of a new era.

Chapter 7

THE EXILE

In 1648, as Peter Stuyvesant, the newly installed director general of New Netherland, was immersing himself in local politics on Manhattan, Richard Nicolls left the battlefields of civil war in his home country and traveled across the English Channel to join the young Duke of York in exile in The Hague. It was a perilous time to make that particular voyage. Some of the English vessels prowling the North Sea roadstead known as the Downs were still loyal to the king, while others were under the command of Parliamentary forces. Lethal confusion reigned. At one point, while Royalist officers went ashore, the sailors they left onboard mutinied, took over the squadron in the name of Parliament, and began raising havoc.

Nicolls made it safely to the Continent—and may have felt as if, in leaving his homeland, he had escaped a madhouse. His lifetime, culminating with six years of civil war, was a period of increasingly shrill religious fanaticism in England. Each Protestant sect considered itself outraged by the tenets of the last. The Levellers were committed to extending the vote and to religious toleration, and they were ready to kill to bring about the equality they believed Jesus Christ had espoused. The Diggers took the Leveller manifesto to its extreme by demanding the end of private property, which enraged anybody who owned some. Fifth Monarchists believed the Second Coming (or Fifth Monarchy, following those of Babylon, Persia, Greece, and Rome) was at hand and that they needed to pave the way, with blood if necessary. Ranters—a catch-all term—were the hippies of the seventeenth century, who held that God dwells fully within each individual, so much so that any activity—including public nudity and sex outside of marriage—should be permitted if it was done in the name of the Holy Spirit. Not surprisingly, the Ranters sent ordinary Puritans, with their dour and far less titillating extremism, into apoplexy. It was out of fear of the Ranters that Parliament, in 1650, passed an Adultery Act, which made it a crime punishable by death to have sex with your neighbor's wife—or rather, your neighbor's husband, since the only people actually executed under the law were women.

For many English people the proliferation of increasingly strident sects and the turmoil they caused engendered a longing for order. Richard Nicolls never showed any indications of religious fervor; on the contrary he referred to himself as "a true and faithfull Member of the Church of England without seaming to Poperie or the other, numerous Sects." The implosion of his country—the wholesale destruction of cities and towns, the bloodshed, the tearing-apart of families—seems to have made him an impassioned moderate, if such a thing is possible.

Nicolls must have crossed the Channel shortly after his patron. He likely traveled in a party of other Royalists that included his two brothers: Edward, who was nine years older, and Francis, who at twenty-eight was five years his senior. They were three of a kind. Both of the elder Nicolls brothers had served as infantry captains in the Civil War; like Richard, both, according to the latter's tomb, "preferred Exile, if Exile, it Can be Called, to follow after a banished King."

The three Nicolls brothers split up once they reached the

Continent, following different military assignments. Richard stayed close to James Stuart, whose destination was The Hague. The residence James's sister, Mary, shared with her husband, Willem II, the Prince of Orange, was a grand mansion called the Huis Honselaarsdijk, surrounded by geometrically arranged French gardens. For the time being, the boy-prince would live here. He was not alone. In short order a host of distinguished guests arrived—lords, colonels, captains, a retinue of men loyal to the Stuarts and the monarchy. Richard Nicolls knew many of those who showed up at the Dutch palace. Some of these men he had fought alongside in England, forming what would be lifelong bonds.

If their past and future relationships are any guide, Nicolls functioned as a kind of protector or chaperone to the duke during their time in The Hague. And there was much to do. Within days of his arrival, young James Stuart, serious-minded teenager that he was, received emissaries from the governments of France, Portugal, and the Dutch Republic, and he met with the Queen of Bohemia, who happened also to be his aunt.

Later, Nicolls would give indications that he knew the Dutch language; he must have picked it up during these months in The Hague. Here, too, he began a friendship with a fellow by the name of Robert Moray. Moray was an ardent Royalist, a Scot, a soldier, and most of all an exuberant student of the natural world. He showed up at Huis Honselaarsdijk in June 1648, just after the Duke of York arrived, eager to offer his support for the cause of the royal family. He and Nicolls would become lifelong friends, corresponding on flora and fauna, discussing recent scientific works by the likes of Robert Boyle, Thomas Hobbes, and René Descartes.

James's older brother, Charles, the Prince of Wales, arrived in The Hague in July. It was a hectic time. There was a sea skirmish offshore just then, with Parliamentary forces threatening to take or burn Royalist vessels; the two brothers jumped aboard ships and into the action, but a Dutch squadron swooped in and saved the day. News streamed in from England: of battles, retreats, brave men betrayed. Noblemen showed up, reporting that their estates had been taken by Oliver Cromwell's forces and appealing for financial aid from the royal brothers.

The Stuarts were in no position to help, and things only got worse with time. The court in exile maintained some of the trappings of royalty, but they were dirt poor. Everyone suffered, from Charles himself to nontitled followers like Richard Nicolls and his brothers. As the years of exile rolled on, they had to scrounge for food; their clothes frayed. Charles himself was in "a sad, poor condition for clothes," according to one Englishman who saw him near the end of his exile. Edward Hyde, Charles's chief aide, a man of great opulence before the war who was much devoted to fine living, paused in composing a letter in the winter of 1652 to admit, "At this time I have neither clothes nor fire to preserve me from the sharpness of the season." Another time he broke his train of thought to blurt out to his correspondent, "I am so cold that I am scarce able to hold my pen."

In January of the next year James's mother, the queen, wrote asking him to join her at Château-Neuf de Saint-Germain-en-Laye, the French royal palace outside Paris, where she was the guest of the twelve-year-old king, Louis XIV. James went, as did Richard Nicolls.

Shortly after arriving, James learned that in London the national crisis that had consumed his entire identity had inflicted its most soul-shaking toll. The images conveyed in the reports were appalling in their jarring juxtaposition of details: the calm, dignified bearing of his father, the king, as he stood in the icy cold of a January day on the platform before a vast crowd of his own populace, like an actor before his audience determined to do well in his final performance; the king solemnly bending to rest his head on the block in an ultimate act of submission to reality; the masked figure of the executioner; the outrageous, swift arc of the axe; the collective gasp of the crowd as the neatly severed head rolled into the waiting basket.

The public execution of the King of England was an event toward which all the forces of the previous decade had been tending, but once the act was done, it dramatically altered the trajectory of things. The effects were complex, but they can be distilled. Historian Mark Kishlansky summarized them this way: "Parliament was victorious, yet it did not prosper. Its cause was unified only in opposition to the King, and once this gravitational force was removed the components broke apart in every direction."

From Europe, James and his retinue, Nicolls included, devoured every report of what was transpiring in England. Chaos paved the way for a strongman, and Oliver Cromwell emerged from the civil war battlefields to claim the role. With the title of Lord Protector (he refused "king" but allowed people to address him as "highness"), Cromwell functioned as a theocratic military dictator. He abolished the monarchy and the bishops of the Church of England, believing—correctly—that they were part of the same power structure. He was a complex figure; he had a towering self-confidence that bent others to his will, but he was also wracked by episodes of blackness and self-doubt. He had become a Puritan rather late in life, and his letters and speeches burned with the fervor of a recent convert. A doctor who treated him later wrote that he was "a most splenetick man and had phansyes about the cross." In the heat of battle, it was said that he "did Laugh so excessively as if he had been drunk; his Eyes sparkled with Spirits."

This was the man who wrested power once the king had been removed, and for most of the 1650s he was able to keep the multifarious competing forces and interests in check. But if Cromwell's reign could be called a period of stability, it was a wild and wobbly stability, with English society composed of a frothing plethora of sects and subsects barely restrained from tearing out each other's throats.

The killing of the king stiffened the resolve of his sons, the royal brothers, and of many of their followers, but there was no immediate acting on that resolve. In the interim other problems occupied young James. His relationship with his mother became twisted and nasty. She was a devout Catholic who constantly attacked his Protestantism—which was hardly fair, considering that Catholicism was outlawed at home in England; but then again she had been born and raised in the Catholic faith, and it was a time when religious warfare was as rife within families as it was on the national level. The young duke was also broke: both in The Hague and at the court of Louis XIV, he was expected to maintain a large staff, despite no longer having an income. Maybe the strongest forces operating on him were natural: he was now eighteen and roiling with pent-up energy.

So, in 1652, he took the bold—and, from our vantage, rather strange—step of heading off to war. It was strange because he would not be fighting against Parliamentary forces in England but rather for the French in their own civil war. The Fronde, as this series of encounters is known, pitted the young king of France against his own nobility and magistrates. James offered himself as a warrior for hire to Henri de La Tour d'Auvergne, vicomte de Turenne, the greatest general of the age, who was in command of Louis XIV's army.

When James left the palace, it was a fairly forlorn departure for a prince of the realm; he had no more than eight men at his side.

For the next three years the young duke and his small entourage, including Richard Nicolls, fought their way across north-central France. They gained experience, self-confidence, and an understanding of realpolitik—all of which both James and Nicolls would make use of in later life. The battles were bloody and tortuous, with wagon wheels stuck in mud, horses throwing their riders in fright, night marches through pitch-black forests. There were fusillades of muskets and downhill cavalry charges that resulted in great pileups of horses and riders. They fought door to door in the streets of Paris. Coming into Champagne, the army seized a storehouse of wine, and in the ensuing action

SERENISSIMVS PRINCEPS
IACOBVS DEI GRATIA DVX EBORACENSis
SVMMVS ANGLIÆ de HIBERNIÆ THALASSIARCHIA. SE:
CVNDO-GENITVS SER: & POTENTISS: CAROLI I. NVPER MA:
CNÆ BRITANNIÆ FRANCIÆ, & HIBERNIÆ, REGIS, &c

James, Duke of York, at age eighteen. He was in exile in the Dutch Republic
at the time, accompanied by Richard Nicolls.

the vicomte de Turenne and the Duke of York were exposed
to the enemy because their men were too drunk to join the
battle. There were brilliant tactics to observe and learn from.
At Bléneau, the veteran Turenne arrayed his army against a
far superior enemy in such a way as to give the impression of
greater strength than he had, turning what would have been a
rout into a stalemate.

James had always been serious; combat intensified that quality in him. He learned, grew as a prince and soldier, and was
promoted by Turenne, whom he ardently admired. He would continue fighting in France for the next year.

In 1655, however, Nicolls left his side. For all his loyalty to the
Stuarts, Nicolls might have been excused for feeling the absurdity

Painting of the Battle of the Faubourg Saint-Antoine, during the Fronde, a series of French civil wars in which the Duke of York fought, with Richard Nicolls at his side.

of his situation—risking his life in the service of another nation while his own was in the hands of what he firmly believed to be an occupying power. That year he got his chance to reenter the fray—to return home on a secret mission.

It could have been in October that he made his return, to accompany a man named George Mourton, who was tasked with "communicating with the King's friends and transmitting their advice." Or he might have slipped surreptitiously back across the Channel in the following month, assisting James's emissary Sir Charles Gerard. Most likely, however, Nicolls went to England months earlier, as part of an elaborate but ill-fated Royalist plan to retake the country. Nicolls was particularly close with one of the men involved: Sir Richard Willis. Willis was a leader of a group of Charles's closest comrades who, calling themselves the Sealed Knot, had been plotting ways to restore the monarchy. According to their plan, on a day in March at cities around England, Royalist sympathizers were to rise up simultaneously. The leaders crossed to England in mid-February and began checking into inns under assumed names. But only a few of the planned uprisings ever got started, and those that did petered out. In Yorkshire an army that was supposed to number four thousand ended up being no more than one hundred men, who, when they realized the folly of continuing, vanished into the night. Similar stories played out in Nottinghamshire and Northumberland.

In fact, the plot unraveled even before it began. One of Oliver Cromwell's crucial advantages during his Protectorate was the man who served simultaneously as his secretary of state and spymaster. John Thurloe did for the field of intelligence in the seventeenth century what men like Francis Bacon and Galileo did for science: he began to make it modern. He employed code-breakers who learned how to decipher the secret communications of the Royalists, and he fielded spies all over England and on the Continent. As a result, Cromwell's agents were aware of the Sealed Knot and its plot even before its leaders left the Continent. Thurloe actually had a double agent within Charles's government in exile, virtually peering over the shoulder of Edward Hyde, Charles's chief adviser and head of his council, as he composed his letters. "The writer saw, on looking at the Council notebook yesterday . . ." began one of the spy's dispatches to Thurloe.

Nicolls was one of those who got caught in Thurloe's dragnet. He was thrown in prison. He may have been confined in the infamous Gatehouse Prison at Westminster in London, where some of his compatriots were held. We know that he was held without being charged of a crime, which means the Cromwell government could not directly implicate him in a treasonous plot. We know too that he had some illustrious company in confinement—including at least three of the men who were part of the failed uprising.

And we know that Nicolls's Royalist comrades on the Continent were aware of his situation. Sir John Denham, who had himself been imprisoned by Parliamentarians for a time, wrote a poem in December 1655 to rally the Royalist forces, trumpeting the heroism of their jailed comrades and making light of their imprisonment. The lines "Though the governing part cannot find in their heart / To free the imprisoned throng" suggest that these men had spent some time behind bars while the Puritans tried to find evidence against them. Stanzas of the poem are devoted to the plights of Lord Maynard, Lord Coventry, Lord Byron, Lord Lucas, and others, each with its accompanying rhyme ("Lord Peter wee wonder, what crime he falls under"; "Sir Frederick Cornwallis, without any malice"). Then we get this:

> Dick Nicols (they say) and Littleton stay
> For the Governours owne delight
> One serves hym with Play, att tennis by day
> And the other with smoaking at night.

From this we can infer that Charles Littleton, an attendant to Charles Stuart, had a fondness for tobacco that the governor of the prison shared and that Richard Nicolls was known for his skill with a tennis racket. Making light of their comrades' plight was a show of bravado in the face of danger.

It's not clear when Nicolls was released. He doesn't appear in the records again until the summer of 1659, when he is back among the Royalists in exile, with a vital role in preparations to launch yet another takeover of the Puritan government.

Much had transpired in those four years. The main overseas object of Oliver Cromwell's ire was the Spanish Empire, which in the Puritan mind was Satan's agent on earth. Cromwell hankered to break Spain's control over the West Indies (the Caribbean islands) and the Spanish Main (the coastline of Central and South America that bordered the Caribbean). In 1655 he launched his

Western Design, a military assault on the Caribbean that would loosen Spain's grip on the region. From his perspective, and that of much of the English public, the plan was both economically and spiritually compelling: capturing some of Spain's Caribbean trade would do God's will and fill English coffers. In April of that year thirty-eight ships bore down on the island of Hispaniola. But the army that stormed the beaches wasn't ready for the tropics and quickly succumbed to heat, disease, and Spanish defenses. The fleet regrouped and as a consolation decided to have a go at nearby Jamaica, which they took, then slowly began converting into the base of English operations in the Caribbean.

The Western Design didn't happen, but the plan set certain English minds humming with ideas—of building an empire.

———

Cromwell himself would not long outlive his failed plan for empire. The London *Gazette* for September 2–9, 1658, ran a thunderbolt of a story under the simple headline "Whitehall":

> His most serene and renowned Highness Oliver Lord Protector, being after a sickness of about fourteen days (which appeared an ague in the beginning) reduced to a very low condition of body, began early this morning to draw near the gates of death, and it pleased God about three a'clock afternoon to put a period to his life.

The nation—Puritans and Royalists, Levellers and Ranters, Agitators, Anabaptists, Diggers, and Quakers—was stunned. For a moment the haters stopped hating, and the religious bickering that had engulfed English society and turned it against itself gave way to silence. Cromwell was fifty-nine years old and hadn't been known to be gravely ill, but the shock was due to more than surprise. If there was anything that all parties agreed on, it was that he was the only thing holding the government together—seemingly the only force holding England together.

Though he had eschewed the title of king and gave lip service to the idea of government by the people, Cromwell had, before his passing, done the ultimate kingly thing and named his oldest son, Richard, as his successor. The torch passed to a new generation.

But Richard Cromwell wasn't ready to take it. He was a mild, languid fellow, possessing none of his father's zeal or magnetism. Oliver had assumed power from his role as general in the New Model Army, an army he himself had largely created; his son, as Lord Protector, thus automatically became a military leader. But the army scoffed at a milquetoast general with little military experience. Meanwhile, in the power vacuum left by Oliver's death, Royalists edged their way into Parliament, enraging the Puritans who had fought a civil war to keep them out.

In May 1659, less than nine months after he took office, Queen Dick, as Richard Cromwell was scathingly known in the streets, resigned. He lived a long, strange, postgovernment life: separating from his wife, wandering Europe for decades, returning quietly to England and living under an assumed name—"Mr. Clarke"—for decades more.

Despite the chaos in England, there was no sense that a return to monarchy was inevitable: Puritan will remained dead set against the Stuarts. And yet Royalist sympathizers in England were now readier than ever to show themselves and to act. When news of the departure of the second (and last) Lord Protector reached the king in exile, who was now residing in The Hague, his retinue urged him to authorize a new uprising. Charles agreed, but to the dismay of many of his friends he chose John Mordaunt to lead it. Mordaunt was a relative newcomer among them, pushy and argumentative, and pressed Charles to strike an alliance with Presbyterians, who had allied with Puritans against Charles I.

As the Sealed Knot had done earlier, Mordaunt planned a series of military actions around the country. Richard Nicolls played an instrumental role. Once again central to the operation was his friend Richard Willis. The royal brothers did not lead the effort, but they kept in contact with everyone as the players, preparing to strike, moved around Europe like pieces on a chessboard: The Hague to Paris, Paris to Brussels, Brussels to Calais, Calais to Boulogne, Boulogne back to Calais. Nicolls's role again involved clandestine crossings of the Channel: a false name, messages written in cipher, secret meetings, whispered updates. August 1 was the date selected for the uprisings. In the second week of July many of the central players came together in London and exchanged last-minute information. All was in readiness.

But shortly after the London meetings, soldiers of the New Model Army staged a series of raids across the country, showing up at the inns and houses where the conspirators were staying, bristling with muskets and swords, hammering on doors, hollering for the men to give themselves up. Nicolls escaped being taken prisoner: soon he was back at sea, the cliffs of Dover behind him, making for the coast of France. John Thurloe's intelligence service had continued to function crisply. Once again the Royalist plan to take the government back by force was foiled.

Or was it? "The whole design is not upset," John Mordaunt insisted in a dispatch he sent to Charles from his secret base in England, "for Norfolk, the West, and most of the North are still able to make another effort."

If they were to act, the Royalists needed to be given the go-ahead, and time was of the essence, so in case Charles wasn't there to receive his communication, Mordaunt sent the same dispatch to the Duke of York, in cipher, asking for his authorization of a new effort. For James, Mordaunt added an additional piece of information, concerning a man he knew the duke held affection for: "49. 906. 7. 99. 953. 30. 411. 781." Decoded, the addendum said, "Nicolls arrived safe."

As of September 10, Richard Nicolls was back in England yet again, making preparations for the next uprising. The Duke of

York had been in Brussels and received this dispatch a few days later when he returned to the French coast, looking himself to soon board a barge for England. He had exchanged letters with Charles and expected to find him here. But there was no sign of his brother, and meanwhile another urgent message came—from his mother—telling him to go to Amiens, where the vicomte de Turenne wanted to meet with him.

James decided he would divert to Amiens and see what his mentor wanted. Nicolls had made it back to the Continent by this time and went with him. They saddled up and made the hundred-mile journey to the man in whose service both men had grown to become military leaders.

On arriving, James was immediately aware of a change in the level of pomp that greeted him. Turenne, who was getting his own updates about events unfolding in England, received the Duke of York not as a soldier for hire but as a representative of the English monarchy. Turenne believed the Roundhead government was on

Message in cipher written to King Charles in exile during the English Civil War, one part of which, deciphered, reads "Nicolls arrived safe."

the verge of collapse, and he was making a statement. He offered to put a portion of his army—1,200 infantrymen—at York's disposal for an invasion.

The duke scribbled out instructions, which he handed to Nicolls, who mounted up again and thundered back to the coast. At Calais, breathless, he delivered the message to John Mordaunt, who read it and dashed off a series of coded dispatches. When the messengers returned, Mordaunt composed a letter to Edward Hyde, Charles's chief adviser: "Receiving the dukes commands by Mr. Nichols, I immediately sent expresses to those severall gentlemen [who] had yet preserved their small bodys [of horse] to be ready upon a days warning to march. . . . I was fully assured of 320 horse."

James was now planning an operation involving French troops that would sail from Dunkirk, and Mordaunt was following his lead in organizing a homegrown rebellion. "I have communicated the intent of the Dukes landing," Mordaunt informed Hyde, adding, "My Lord, this affair of Dunkerke is of soe great importance that if it succeeds it may put all England into a flame."

In the same message, however, Mordaunt added important news—that "the arch traytor is discovered." The Royalists believed they had found the reason for the failure of the August uprising. Thurloe had a very highly placed double agent—someone in their inner circle who had been alerting the Roundhead government of their every move. Mordaunt believed it was Richard Willis.

Evidence wasn't conclusive, however, and some refused to believe it. Richard Nicolls in particular was sure that Mordaunt had fingered the wrong man. Another Royalist, named William Rumbold, wrote to Mordaunt in the middle of October that Nicolls had recently met with Willis in England and that others who doubted that Willis was the traitor had been influencing Nicolls: "I promised to inform you of my discours with Nicols," he wrote, adding that "I conceaved [others] . . . might make wrong impressions upon him (& indeed I found he began to warp to that side) so that I thought it fit to acquaint him with the truth of things."

Still, Nicolls was hesitant to believe that his close friend Willis was the traitor in their midst. In November, Charles Littleton, who had been imprisoned with Nicolls four years earlier, wrote to Hyde that Nicolls was still "very earnest" in trying to vindicate Willis.

Nicolls's importance to the operation is evident in the level of concern of its leaders that he be brought around to seeing Willis as a danger. And they seem in the end to have convinced him. In late November, Hyde himself wrote to Mordaunt: "Mr. Nicholls is to be removed from ye good opinion he has had of Sr R. Willis. I have sayd as much to him, as I am sure should satisfy him."

At any rate the plan—an invasion using French forces supplemented by internal uprisings—never materialized. Another far bolder strategy superseded it. George Monck, who had been a relentless general under Cromwell and had become one of the powerbrokers in the post-Cromwellian era, had been assessing the chaos in England and was moving to the conclusion that the only way to stabilize the country and avoid another civil war was to bring back the monarchy. Monck had in fact been on the verge of joining the August uprising before it collapsed. Charles Stuart authorized his agents to open a dialogue with the general through his brother, Nicholas Monck, a clergyman who was known to have Royalist sympathies. Charles sweetened the deal for George Monck by offering him money and the title of Duke of Albemarle.

Edward Hyde, the Stuart brothers, and their comrades and advisers, including Richard Nicolls, moved their operations to the Dutch city of Breda, which was considered neutral territory, and entered formal negotiations with Monck and other representatives of the fraying power structure in England. Monck urged Charles to lay out formal terms under which he would assume the crown. By this time word of the negotiations had gotten out, and people in England, exhausted from years of turmoil, seemed overwhelmingly to support the return of the king.

In April, Charles issued the Declaration of Breda. He promised a "free and general pardon" for those who had acted against him. An exception was made for the men who had signed the death warrant of Charles's and James's father. They were to be hunted down, tried, convicted, and "hanged, drawn, and quartered." What this meant exactly was helpfully elucidated in the case of one of those found guilty of treason: "Your sentence is, that you be led back to prison; laid on a hurdle, and so drawn to the place of execution; there to be hanged, cut down alive, your members to be cut off and cast into the fire, your bowels burnt before your eyes, your head smitten off, your body quartered and divided at the King's will." In the aftermath of the king's return and coronation, the inhabitants of London were treated to a season of spectacles of this kind—which were public events, with children watching from their fathers' shoulders—and months in which the city's outskirts were adorned with rotting pieces of the bodies of regicides. With this vibrant exception the millions of English people who had opposed the Stuarts and driven them to exile were to be forgiven for their lapse in judgment.

Even more significantly, given that this was an era awash in religious hatred, Charles vowed, "We do declare a liberty to tender consciences, and that no man shall be disquieted or called into question for differences of opinion in matter of religion, which do not disturb the peace of the kingdom." The Stuart brothers had both long found religious extremism distasteful. Charles hoped that with his reign he might usher in a new era of tolerance.

Of the three Nicolls brothers who had gone into exile with the Stuarts, only one made the return trip to England. Francis was killed in Paris, possibly in the battle of Faubourg Saint-Antoine in 1652, and Edward died in the Dutch Republic, perhaps of the plague, which was then ravaging the country. There is some evidence that their mother also died in 1652, in London, which meant that from then on Richard was in a sense alone in the world.

He was almost certainly among the groups of English people who could be seen in and around The Hague in the middle of May 1660, as preparations were being made for the royal party's official return to England. They had streamed across the Channel, eager to show their allegiance whether or not they had been in the Stuart camp up to now. The Dutch city had been Charles's base of operations in exile, and Nicolls had spent a great deal of time here with James—so much so that it had come to feel like a second home. It must have been amusing for him to watch as these English arrived for the first time to experience this country that, while only a short boat ride away, was an alien landscape to them, the home of a people who were bitter rivals and at times enemies.

Yet here they were, the cream of English society, acting like tourists, finding it exotic to hear not only the throaty Dutch language but French and Latin on the streets of this most cosmopolitan city. They strolled along the seaside and rode carriages on the Voorhout, the principal tree-lined avenue of The Hague. They took side trips to Delft to see the tomb of William the Silent, the founder of the modern Dutch Republic. They sat in taverns playing cribbage and crambo (a rhyming game), turning up their noses at the Dutch fare on offer, while the English fleet assembled along the wide beach at the nearby seaside town of Scheveningen.

The soon-to-be-christened king and his future bride made appearances at stately homes around town, kissing babies and proffering their hand for ladies and gentlemen. Samuel Pepys, the diarist and admiralty official, opined on first encountering the royal couple at one of these parties that the king "seems to be a very sober man," while the queen "seems a very debonaire, but plain lady." The Duke of York joined the king in making the rounds, as did all of the Royalists in exile, with the exception of Edward Hyde—now the Lord Chancellor of England, soon to be arguably the most powerful man in the country—who was in bed with gout. We can visualize Nicolls at these gatherings, the tattered clothes and desperate, determined demeanor of his time as a soldier in exile replaced by silk and ruffles and relaxed chatter.

Word came during this period of festivities that James had been restored to his title of Lord High Admiral of England. It was probably around this time that Richard Nicolls learned that he was to be given a new position as well, Groom of the Bedchamber to James. It sounds to our ears like someone who went around picking up socks, but the position was high ranking; it spoke to Nicolls being among James's most trusted subordinates, tasked with carrying out important missions. He had been at James's side from boyhood, had stayed steadfast through years of blood and hell. Now a new future was opening up that would forever tie him to the Duke of York.

On the day of the crossing hundreds of people lined the beach to watch. Among those taking part, women dressed as for a ball; men adorned themselves in scarlet waistcoats. "In the morning came infinity of people on board," Samuel Pepys reported. "All day nothing but Lords and persons of honour." Dozens of bottles of wine were consumed; there were toasts, kisses, songs, bows, congratulations. Then, said Pepys, "we weighed anchor, and with a fresh gale and most happy weather we set sail for England."

Chapter 8

DOROTHEA ANGOLA

———

*W*hen Peter Stuyvesant stepped ashore on Manhattan in May 1647, he already had a good working knowledge of the colony he was taking over. During his two-year convalescence from the loss of his leg, he was involved in the West India Company's discussions about the power struggle between Willem Kieft and his colonists. At some point Stuyvesant became convinced that he was the answer to the problem of New Netherland's power vacuum. While serving as a company administrator in Brazil, he had shown that he could handle both the intricacies of a corporate bureaucracy and the harsh conditions of a distant outpost. His zeal was enough to dispel whatever reservations the directors had about sending a one-legged man on a difficult assignment.

He arrived full of plans, but before he could take steps to move the colony in a new direction, he felt compelled to deal with the internal issue: the very people who were on the dock to greet his ship, his colonists. They had engineered Kieft's ouster. Stuyvesant's experience in battle and in the ranks of the West India Company reinforced the biblical injunctions that his father had issued from his minister's pulpit. There was a natural order to things, and "subjects," as Stuyvesant referred to his population, had no business second-guessing their superiors. He signaled as much in his welcome ceremony, for which the whole town turned out, declaring that he intended to function "like a father over his children." Foreshadowing a coming clash, Adriaen van der Donck sneeringly described Stuyvesant's initial performance as "Peacock like, with great state and pomposity."

Stuyvesant called a meeting to chastise the men who had led the popular movement against Kieft. To his bewilderment they came prepared to counterattack. The leaders were Cornelis Melyn, whose property on Staten Island had been destroyed during the war with the Lenape, and Jochem Pietersen Kuyter, a Dane who had served with Melyn on the board of eight men Kieft had convened. They brandished a long list of "interrogatories" they wanted to pose to Cornelis van Tienhoven, Kieft's right-hand man, whom Stuyvesant had decided to keep on. Van Tienhoven had led the attacks on Lenape villages. The questions they proposed to put to him started by establishing that Van Tienhoven spoke "the Manhatans language," thus ruling out the likelihood of miscommunication. They went on in perfect legalese, weaving a web around Van Tienhoven and, by extension, Kieft: "In what year was he, deponent, sent by Mr. Kieft to the Raritanus; and did he not go there with a party of armed soldiers and sailors?" "What order did the Director give him . . . and how did he execute it?" "Did not the Raritans revenge themselves the next year?" The questions had less to do with Kieft and Van Tienhoven than with the men who were posing them. They wanted to use the travesty of the war as a vehicle to gain some degree of self-government. The West India Company, their argument ran in essence, was incompetent and needed to be supplanted.

Stuyvesant was having none of it. He had called them together in order to make exactly the opposite point: that they were to submit to his rule. Instead, he got baited into a spiraling argument. He became apoplectic, asking, "Was it ever heard or seen in any republic that vassals and subjects did without authority from their superiors, conceive, draft and submit to their magistrates self-devised interrogatives to have them examined thereon?" No, he didn't think it was.

Adriaen van der Donck—excitable, ambitious, not yet thirty— was the main legal force behind this popular uprising and the probable author of most of its writings. He went further in the next document, informing Stuyvesant that the Natives had been "slaughtered . . . like sheep" by Kieft's soldiers in the massacre at Pavonia and that in the Natives' counterattacks the homes of colonists were turned to "piles of ashes," all of which devastation was due to inept government. Back and forth they went then, in dueling memoranda, Van der Donck drawing on ancient Greek and Latin authorities on the natural limitations on rulers, Stuyvesant invoking biblical passages ("Curse not the king, no not even in thy thought").

Stuyvesant's tenure thus started on the worst possible footing. And because this matter takes up such a sizable portion of the Dutch records for this period, it has colored the way history has viewed Stuyvesant: as impetuous, narrow, tyrannical, dogmatic. Jaap Jacobs, the Stuyvesant biographer, attempting to balance this portrait, pointed out to me that the Stuyvesant family papers do not survive. "I think it's likely they were burned during the American Revolution," he said. "If we had them, we might have quite a different impression of him." We might see a family man, a wide-ranging correspondent, a man concerned with the well-being of others.

Perhaps so, yet Stuyvesant was still undeniably a hothead, especially in these early years. Even later, when New Netherland was successfully attracting new colonists, the directors of the West India Company in Amsterdam cautioned him not to return to his former ways: "It looks as if many people will come over by every ship and . . . we desire that you shall accommodate all newcomers as well as possible and above all govern the people with the utmost caution and leniency, for you have now learned by experience, how too much vehemence may draw upon you the hatred of the people."

No one benefited from the escalating feud between the new director and his people over the leadership and direction of the colony. Stuyvesant eventually imprisoned Van der Donck, threatened him with capital punishment, then released him, whereupon Van der Donck led a delegation that sailed to the home country to plead the cause directly with the Dutch government. They actually won their case, and the leaders in The Hague issued an order for Stuyvesant to return home to account for himself. But at virtually the same moment Oliver Cromwell declared war on the Dutch Republic, and the States General rescinded its order recalling Stuyvesant; Van der Donck was kept from returning to New Netherland during the period of unrest. He was finally allowed to return to his home just north of Manhattan on the promise that he would stay out of politics.* He died in 1655, probably in the so-called Peach Tree War of that year. Melyn also returned for a time to New Netherland but continued to fight with Stuyvesant and eventually moved his family to the New Haven colony.

Stuyvesant, too, suffered from the ongoing internal strife. Faced with daunting obstacles—dealing with an ornate complexity of Indigenous tribes, with the English to the north, with a recent incursion by the Swedes in the southern part of his colony, and with his temperamental bosses back in Amsterdam—he needed to have the people supporting him; instead, he gave them excellent reasons for mistrusting him. He comes across, in this period of the colony's history, as petulant, almost childlike, suffering from an obstinance that prevented the very success he was so determined to achieve.

---

* Van der Donck's farm was located at present-day Van Cortlandt Park in the Bronx and extended northward into what is now the city of Yonkers, which takes its name from his informal title of "de Jonkheer," or "young gentleman."

But despite the negative effects this clash had on all concerned, it speaks to the vitality of the colony. It was a place unlike any other, and it was experiencing growing pains. New Amsterdam had been established with certain expectations: it was a "staple port," whose mission was to serve as the gateway for trade between the North American colony and the wider Atlantic world. Its mixed population—speaking a variety of languages and with contacts on both sides of the Atlantic—suited this task perfectly. The cause of the colonists—agitating for a form of self-rule—seems of a piece with a multiethnic port that was the brainchild of one of Europe's few republics. These local business leaders wanted what all businesspeople want: an efficient system, freedom from constraints, and taxes as low as possible.

Over the next few years they began to make progress toward these goals. Stuyvesant, as he found his footing, realized he needed to develop ways to work with rather than against the city's independent traders. He started to see himself if not as one of them then certainly as a middleman, reconciling their interests with the West India Company's. We can see the change taking place while Van der Donck and his colleagues were still in The Hague attempting to undercut his leadership. Stuyvesant sent a letter across the ocean to the States General suggesting a radical solution: that the Dutch government grant New Amsterdam a municipal charter.

Making the little outpost on Manhattan an official Dutch city would mean creating a city council, which would function as another power center besides Stuyvesant's colonial council. Even a year or two earlier Stuyvesant would probably have bristled at such an idea if it had come from someone else, considering it a threat to his power. But now he proposed it himself. Maybe he felt stronger, or maybe he realized that he needed to assert his power differently. It was also a simple fact that with all the growth the city had experienced, both in inhabitants and in trade, he needed help in administering things. There were taxes to be levied. There were laws to be passed for the public welfare. For one terribly practical example, the city needed to ban the use of wooden chimneys. Someone also had to stop residents from the inelegant practice of erecting their privies next to public roads. Trade with Native villages had to be regulated. A fixed duty had to be set for all "merchantable beaver skins." The list was endless. A city council could take up some of the burden.

In requesting a city council, Stuyvesant was also trying to outmaneuver his antagonists by giving "the people" their own voice. At the same time, by packing the new council with his own handpicked men, he hoped to ensure he would keep it from getting too independent.

But above all he now saw genuine value in the stability that would come with the city's having an official governing body. Once the request was granted and he was authorized to establish "a bench of justice formed as much as possible after the laws of this city," meaning Amsterdam, the new local government became operational on February 2, 1653.

The next phase in the colony's history, then, was one of growth and increasing stability and of the arrival of a breed of private merchants who would work with one another, and with Stuyvesant as the point man, to create a new kind of business environment: to professionalize New Amsterdam as a city of commerce. Historian Dennis Maika of the New Netherland Institute has recently elucidated a complex network of shippers, skippers, insurers, and financiers, as well as ordinary sailors who bought in on the developing action. What Maika has identified—relying on the work of the New Netherland Research Center and through mining notarial documents in the Amsterdam City Archives—is an "integration process" in which a new generation of savvy Europeans emigrated to New Amsterdam and from there established business networks linking Manhattan to the English colonies to the north and south as well as to the Caribbean and Europe. It was the beginning of Manhattan as a global center.

Maika highlights, for example, Caspar Varlet, part of a wealthy family of merchants from Cologne who had begun backing trading voyages to New Netherland in 1636. Now, sensing a future, Caspar decided to emigrate to the colony with his wife, Judith Tentenier, and seven of their children. Their daughter Anna married a Virginia tobacco farmer, and another daughter, Jannetje, married Augustine Herrman, one of New Amsterdam's most prominent businessmen.

Adriaen Bloemaert, who had previously skippered voyages to the colony, chose this period to emigrate as well. Allard Antonides, meanwhile, sailed into the East River for the first time in 1650 aboard a ship called *Fortuyn*, with the job of overseeing the sale of its cargo, and decided to stay. Within two years he was a member of the new city council. Under the English he would anglicize his name to Anthony, and Nicolls would appoint him sheriff of New York.

Margaret Hardenbroeck, a twenty-two-year-old woman of German background who had grown up in Amsterdam, arrived on Manhattan in 1659 with the plan of working as an accountant for a cousin's trading firm. She came already trained for the job: in contrast to most of Europe, in the Dutch Republic girls were regularly schooled in mathematics and accounting, and it was common for women to read, write, and keep track of family finances.

Hardenbroeck had barely learned her way around the city's sixteen streets when she married a merchant named Pieter Rodolphus De Vries, who was approximately thirty-four years older. If the young woman found it unpleasant sharing a bed with a grizzled man in his fifties, she didn't have to put up with it for long. He died two years later, leaving her with a baby girl and a fortune. Soon after, Hardenbroeck met and married a man in his thirties named Frederick Philipse. In time, Philipse would become one of the richest men in America and be known as the progenitor of the famed Philipse dynasty, exemplified in Philipsburg Manor, which comprised much of the Bronx and Westchester County.

Frans van Mieris, *Young Woman Writing a Letter*, circa 1670. Unlike in other parts of Europe, most Dutch women could read and write, and they often kept accounts.

Though history hasn't given her credit for it, Margaret was the likely force behind the dynasty. She had come into the marriage with a fortune of her own. When she married Philipse, she took care to file a prenuptial agreement—common in the Dutch Republic—that allowed her to retain her own property. She carefully invested her wealth in vessels, real estate, and shipments of goods, including, eventually, enslaved Africans. She also, remarkable for the time, sailed as supercargo on her own vessels; the diarist Jasper Danckaerts traveled as a passenger on one of her ships and recorded lively impressions of her as a no-nonsense, imperious boss of the ship and a woman of "excessive covetousness."

Hardenbroek and Philipse continued to build their empire in the English era, but her role eventually became obscured because under the English doctrine of coverture a woman's property and rights fell under the control of her husband.

Through Maika's work we can see the churning port of New Amsterdam in something like the way Richard Nicolls must have seen it as his ship lay at anchor in Gravesend in the summer of 1664: as innovative and desirable. As Maika says, "These new resident merchants of New Amsterdam, accompanied on these ships by a slew of itinerant traders, farm workers, servants, and craftsmen, energized Manhattan's commercial prospects, encouraging established inhabitants to participate in the emerging commercial opportunities. The short term impact was transformative— when Nicasius de Sille came to New Amsterdam in 1654 to serve as the Company's new fiscal, he immediately remarked, 'All the people here are traders.'"

In addition to paving the way for this activity by redefining his position vis-à-vis the West India Company, Peter Stuyvesant also staked his own claim to the colony at this time. Up to now he had been renting "Bowery Number One," a farm two miles to the north of New Amsterdam, from the company. Use of the farm had come with the job for each director of the colony. Stuyvesant now bought it, signaling his intention to live with his family permanently on Manhattan. He also began personally investing in the colony. Here too Jaap Jacobs noted to me that we would have a fuller sense of this activity if Stuyvesant's family archive had survived. "We know he had one farm on Long Island and another at Wiltwijck,"* he told me. "And he may have been financing some trade. All of this activity would have shown others the depth of his involvement with the community. While he may not have been the most loved person in the colony, in time he came to be respected, especially by the merchants."

---

* The future Kingston, New York.

In May 1660, thirteen years into his tenure, Stuyvesant received a long letter from two of his bosses, Cornelis Jansz Witsen and David van Baerle, directors of the Amsterdam Chamber of the West India Company. The subject was commerce. After several pages of complaints (fees not paid, letters not delivered) and an order that he punish Dutch settlers who were to blame for instigating recent hostilities with the Esopus, they addressed ways to improve trade between Manhattan and the Dutch-held island of Curaçao in the Caribbean. Salt was the first commodity discussed, then horses. After that they brought up tobacco. It had been introduced into Europe nearly a century before, and by this time people were mad for it. There had been many small-scale tobacco farms in New Netherland, including on Manhattan, hoping to fill the demand, but the quality of the product didn't rival that grown farther south in Maryland and Virginia.

There were still hopes of succeeding at producing good-quality leaf, but it was a very labor-intensive crop. Especially for this reason, people on both sides of the Atlantic began to think about developing slavery into a proper industry in New Netherland. This was far from the first foray by the Dutch into the slavery business. The company had been involved for decades, bargaining with West African rulers and middlemen to buy people who had been captured in the interior of the continent, then shipping them to live out lives of hard labor in Brazil and the Caribbean. But there had been no shipments to New Netherland as yet. Six years earlier, however, the Dutch colony on the coast of Brazil, which had used slave labor to produce sugar, had been taken by the Portuguese, leaving the West India Company with a large deficit. Maybe, the directors began to think, it could be profitable to divert northward the human cargo in which the company had established a supply network. Despite the success that its independent traders had had, New Netherland had yet to turn a profit for the West India Company itself. Applying a forced labor pool to the cultivation of tobacco might turn around its fortunes in North America.

The idea then was to begin sending Africans from Curaçao to Manhattan and to allow independent traders there to buy and resell them to farmers. Witsen and Van Baerle spelled it out to Stuyvesant:

> As the cultivation of the soil there could to a great extent be carried out by Negroes, and as its continuation is very important, and as the welfare of that country mostly depends on it, we have agreed and resolved to experiment with a consignment of Negroes, whom we shall have sent to your honors by the first ship or ships from Curacao. They must be sold at public auction to the highest bidder, on the express conditions that they are not to be transported away from there, but that they must be employed in the cultivation of the soil.

In fact, the vagaries of transatlantic communication being what they were, the initial "consignment" had already arrived, in 1659, months before the directors' letter reached Manhattan. It consisted of five children—"four head of Negro boys and one little Negro girl," as Stuyvesant put it—who had been shipped from the Caribbean and up the coast of North America together with a cargo of salt.

It was not an auspicious beginning to a business venture. In fact, it was appalling in every detail, which perhaps makes it an appropriate event to single out as the commencement of New York's life as a slaving port. (I say "New York" because this was late in the history of the Dutch colony, and the experiment took several more years to get off the ground so that it would eventually fall to Richard Nicolls to develop it.)

Stuyvesant did his determined best over the few years left to him to run the place to ensure that the new industry would succeed. He worked with his lieutenant on Curaçao, Matthais Beck, to set prices. He declared that he would only accept "very stout and strong" Africans. A twenty-first-century researcher scours the records in vain for indications of moral unease on the part of those involved in developing this trade. In defending himself against blame in the death of the child in the initial shipment, Beck insisted that the five youths had left his port "in dry and good condition," as if he were talking about kegs of flour. And, as above, Stuyvesant, Beck, and the traders and shippers with whom they corresponded routinely used the term *stuck* in referring to these human beings. The Dutch word means "piece" or, in reference to animals, "head," as of cattle. A passage from Beck to the directors in Amsterdam gives the flavor:

> Thus it was with the Cabo Veersche [Cape Verde Islands] Negroes whom I gathered together with great difficulty from the Company as well as private parties, and obtained in all 62 head among whom there were some young and old, for which reason two head less have been calculated, as appears on the original receipt accompanying this, of which they then paid me here for 46 head, according to the contract, at 120 pieces of eight, amounting to 5520 pieces of eight, so that the remaining 14 head of Negroes are to be paid to your honors in Holland by the aforesaid Messrs. Hector Pietersen and Guilliamme Momma.

A few months after the first group of enslaved children arrived on Manhattan, Beck sent the second "consignment," which consisted of twenty healthy men along with some horses. This presumably made Stuyvesant feel they were on the right track. The Africans were sold at auction. And within a short time, as Dennis Maika incisively puts it, the merchants of New Amsterdam began "devising speculative strategies to incorporate enslaved people into their commercial portfolios."

If Dorothea Angola heard it asserted that the year 1659 marked the beginnings of slavery on Manhattan, she might well have registered surprise. Thirty-two years earlier, on a late summer day in 1627—three years after Catalina Trico and a handful of other Walloons began to carve out a life in the colony of New Netherland and at a time when New Amsterdam was nothing more than a few dirt roads and a muddle of rough dwellings—the first ship carrying Africans dropped anchor off the tip of Manhattan. Twenty-two individuals stumbled ashore, dazed from an epic sojourn, and learned that they had become the property of the Dutch West India Company. We don't know for sure that Dorothea Angola was among this group—there wasn't a ship's manifest listing the names of those offloaded—but there is no record of another early voyage that brought Africans.

The difference between this early arrival and the slave trade that Stuyvesant oversaw beginning in 1659 was in scope and intent. The first Africans to appear on Manhattan were to some extent a result of happenstance. They had had a brutal time getting to a destination that none of them had ever intended to reach. Earlier that year a flotilla of Dutch privateers on the hunt for enemy ships in the war against Spain and Portugal had captured a Portuguese vessel near Venezuela. The Portuguese were en route from São Tomé, off the coast of West Africa, and carried 225 Africans. (Portuguese middlemen more or less invented the slave trade in the fifteenth century and were far ahead of everyone else in the early seventeenth century.) The vanquished ship was in bad shape after the fight; we can imagine screams and moans of horror as the awareness spread among the chained prisoners that it was slowly sinking. The Dutch victors clambered aboard, surveyed the situation, and decided to take 22 of the Africans—the healthiest of the lot—as prizes, which was all they could carry, and leave the rest. They couldn't haul their captives all the way back to the home country: it was too far, and anyway slavery was illegal there. But word had gotten round of the recently founded colony in North America.

Slavery for most of the life of New Netherland was likewise a disorganized affair. There were no West India Company shipments from Africa. There were no regulations governing the practice of slavery. Dorothea Angola's life gives us a sense of what it was like and of how unlike our mental image of American slavery it was.

We can begin recovering her identity by considering her name. It became a common practice among European slavers to append place names onto the given names of Africans to indicate their point of origin. In addition to Dorothea, the records of New Netherland include Susanna van Angola, Domingo Angola, Mayken van Angola, Isabel d'Angola, Emanuel de Angola, Catalina van Angola, Susanna Simons van Angola, Anna van Angola, Jan Francisco van Angola, and several others—making them seem to a disinterested reader like one large extended family. People from other regions who were forced to make a life on Manhattan Island in the Dutch period include Simon Congo, Louis Guinea, Anna van Capoverde, Manuel de Spanje, Francisco Cartagena, and Pieter Santome.

Then there was her first name. It can be a challenge identifying Dorothea as she makes her way through the decades leading up to Richard Nicolls's appearance in the harbor. At times she is called Etoria, or Elaria, or Reijtorij. Jeroen Dewulf, a professor of history at the University of California at Berkeley, who has done research into the ancestry of the enslaved in seventeenth-century America, gave me some assistance. "As for the names," he wrote in an email, "those typically refer to saints, in this case, most likely St. Dorothea, and the equivalent Portuguese name is Doroteia. Judging from the way this name is pronounced in Portuguese, Etoria and Reijtorij could be attempts by native speakers of Dutch to write the name the way they (mis)understood it."

That many of the Angolans who wound up in Manhattan were named after Catholic saints adds to our understanding of their identities. A standard trope of the history of American slavery holds that Christian faith among enslaved Africans was a result of their captivity—that, often, owners encouraged them to adopt the faith as a way to keep them docile. But many Africans who were shipped to the Americas during the seventeenth century were already Christian thanks to the extent of Portuguese colonization on the African continent A European traveler in the Congo in the 1640s found that "there are many churches, where Portuguese papists conduct daily services and other ceremonies." The Portuguese presence in Angola was profound enough by Dorothea Angola's time that she may well have been born and baptized a Catholic and thus would have carried her faith with her to the New World.

It also means that once in New Amsterdam these first enslaved Africans on Manhattan had strong natural bonds with one another. They may have come from villages that were hundreds of miles apart, but they probably shared a common language—Kimbundu, which today is spoken by more than two million people in Angola (where Portuguese is still the official language)—and customs. Many of them would go on to live through the decades of the Dutch colony's history together, becoming a tightly knit community. Together they experienced deaths, marriages, births. Probably shortly after arrival, Dorothea married Paolo Angola. And she must have been particularly close with one other early arrival, a woman named Mayken van Angola. They were likely about the same age, spoke the same language, shared customs and a region of origin. Year after year they saw one another around town, attended many of the same functions, commiserated, raised children, ultimately grew old together. Their fates were intertwined.

Dorothea gave birth to three children that we know of— Dominicus, baptized in 1646; Janneken, in 1649; and Jacob, in 1653. Historian Susanah Shaw Romney has tracked Dorothea's life as a mother and concludes that she and Paolo "were spacing their children every three to four years, in keeping with West African customs of allowing time between births." She speculates that Dorothea may have had as many as four earlier children as well, in a period for which the baptismal records are lost.

This growing family probably lived, during these early years, in one house with all the other enslaved people owned by the West India Company. It was located on present-day South William Street. There was a garden in back, where they would have grown much of their food. There may have been, buried somewhere just outside the house, a basket filled with a collection of what looked like odds and ends: pipestems, marbles, buttons, coins, animal bones. An *mpungu* like this, used in ritual healing in certain parts of Africa, was found in an archaeological dig in 1984 near the site of a former New Amsterdam home. The objects would have been chosen by someone with training in *bilongo*, faith-based medicine.[*] A ritual healer would gather them and visit them regularly to ward off bad luck or cure disease. Though Dorothea was a devout Christian, it was common for Africans in New Amsterdam to hold on to traditional beliefs as well.

The house was a very small building, so that many families would have been crammed together. For that matter New Amsterdam was a tiny settlement, and everyone lived cheek by jowl. In her book *Spaces of Enslavement*, Andrea Mosterman has charted the way Blacks moved through this polyglot village. They apparently were free to go out in the evenings, and they had establishments they frequented. The City Tavern, the boisterous center of New Amsterdam life, conveniently located adjacent to the dock where rowboats from anchored ships tied up, was a short

---

[*] Archaeologists Anne-Marie Cantwell and Diana Dizerega Wall suggested in 2015 that the collection might be an *nkisi*. However, art historian Barbaro Martinez-Ruiz told me in 2023 that it was more likely an *mpungu*: "An *nkisi* is a type of object that is more anthropomorphic. For a container, the term is *mpungu*." Martinez-Ruiz also explained its use within the context of *bilongo*.

During a 1984 excavation in Lower Manhattan, these objects were found in a basket buried outside the New Amsterdam house of West India Company official Cornelis van Tienhoven. They are believed to constitute an *mpungu*, a collection used for ritual healing in central African culture.

walk away, but Black people tended to favor Madaleen Vincent's tavern near their dwelling or Jan Rutgersen's bar on the Herenweg (i.e., Broadway). You can see them there, in your mind's eye, gathered around a cheer-giving fireplace of a winter's evening, letting go of some stress, drinking, laughing, tearing up over stories of suffering and loss.

Dorothea Angola would have shared many experiences as well with Catalina Trico. For years the town's population numbered only in the dozens or low hundreds: white or Black, everyone knew everyone else, and both women were at the bottom of the socioeconomic spectrum. We can only guess at how the division between free and enslaved played out in the streets and markets of New Amsterdam—whether the two women would have stopped to chat, coddled one another's children, or kept some social distance.

There was at least some social fluidity. Everyone worshipped in the same church. And mixed-race marriages weren't forbidden: we have records of both a white man marrying a Black woman and the reverse. The Dutch had two historical models to look to with regard to slavery: the Bible and ancient Rome. Slavery existed in both of those past worlds, and in neither was it race based; that is, the color of your skin was not a tipoff to your status. In Rome people of different races and backgrounds might be enslaved for a portion of their lives and then freed. Likewise, in New Amsterdam race wasn't an automatic indicator of being enslaved, and slavery wasn't necessarily permanent. In Amsterdam itself a population of free Blacks had grown up over the course of the century, most of whom lived in the Jewish quarter, the same neighborhood where Rembrandt had his house and studio.

Rembrandt van Rijn, *Two African Men*, 1661.

Probably the most surprising aspect of Dorothea Angola's condition for us is that the enslaved could petition for their freedom. Her two earliest appearances in the records both involve expressions of agency—of her asserting her will, laying claim to something. In the first, in 1643, she took her place in the Dutch Reformed Church as the godmother of a little boy named Anthony; after his mother died a few weeks later, Dorothea effectively adopted him, never mind having children of her own. We might reasonably conclude that she was strong, devout, loving, and committed to her community.

The second instance in which she peeks out from the records occurs a few months later. In February 1644, eleven enslaved men, including Paolo Angola, petitioned the company for their freedom and that of their wives. Willem Kieft and his council granted their request, "setting them free and at liberty on the same footing as other free people here in New Netherland," and noted that this was warranted "especially as they have been many years in the service of the honorable Company here and long since have been promised their freedom."

It wasn't entirely true that they were as free as others. The company demanded that the eleven couples make annual payments in the form of crops. They weren't being singled out in this regard: white settlers who were given land also had to make crop payments to the company. But Kieft also inserted a clause that the children of the freed couples "at present born or yet to be born" would remain enslaved. This unbelievably cruel caveat would certainly have ensured that the parents would continue to do whatever the company asked of them. There is no evidence that the government of the colony followed through on this onerous demand, but the mere assertion of it kept the couples on the alert.

So freedom came with conditions. In this way the Dutch were perhaps following the model of ancient Rome, where freed slaves remained obligated in certain ways to their former owners.

Later that same year, Paolo and Dorothea were granted their

own land, a six-acre tract two miles north of the city, encompassing much of present-day MacDougal, Sullivan, and Thompson
Streets—the part of Greenwich Village that three centuries later
would be made famous by the likes of Bob Dylan, Joan Baez, and
Lenny Bruce. Dorothea and her husband formed a community
with other freed couples who were given land nearby, which in
time became known as the Land of the Blacks.

For several years the couple seem to have had what you
would call a full life: land, a home, and a family. Then, sometime
in late 1652, Paolo Angola died. Within months Dorothea got
married again, to a man named Emmanuel Pietersz. This was at
the time when Stuyvesant was altering his approach to running
the colony so that Dorothea presumably benefited somewhat
from the increasing wealth and stability of the place over the
ensuing years. She surely would never have considered herself
on equal footing with Europeans, and she and her second husband had the onerous burden of paying a substantial portion of
their crops to the company, but Dorothea was a landowner, a
mother, a member of the church in good standing. She had lived
most of her life on Manhattan, had grown to middle age, had
skillfully worked the angles to move herself up from the bottom
of a system that was rigged against her. She probably spent her
days working alongside her husband and children in growing
maize, wheat, peas, and beans, those being the crops specified
in the grant of freedom that were to be paid to the company. Life
was surely not easy. But she had come far, largely through her
own will and intellect.

If there are things that we can admire and appreciate in New
Netherland as a foundation to our history, its role in the development of slavery is not one of them. The best that can be said
of it is that compared to other regions under the control of the
West India Company, the New Netherland slave trade was minus-
cule. Out of an estimated half-million people the company trans-
ported across the Atlantic into lives of bondage, the total in New

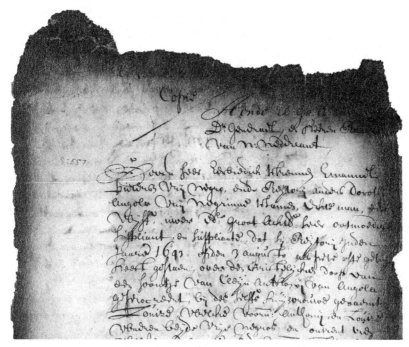

Dorothea Angola appears several times in the Dutch records. Here, she and her second husband petition the West India Company to ensure the freedom of their adopted son, Anthony. Dorothea stresses that she raised the boy "with maternal attention and care without having to ask for public assistance."

Netherland was in the hundreds. But that was due to circumstances, not any pangs of morality.

In 1661, three years before Richard Nicolls showed up in the harbor, Dorothea Angola and Emmanuel appeared before Stuyvesant with a request that for all their achievements spoke to the precariousness of their positions. They asked Stuyvesant and his council to formally declare their adopted son, Anthony, who was now eighteen, to be a free person "in order thus to be qualified to inherit his or your petitioner's temporal goods by last will and testament." The boy's birth parents had been free and so had his adoptive parents, but Kieft's order about children remaining the property of the company hung over all their heads. The lack of formal regulations regarding slavery cut both ways: there was latitude that the Africans could exploit, but then too there was no telling whether on the adopted parents' deaths the colony's director might pull the boy, whom Dorothea had loved as a son and reared as her own, back into servitude. Having something in writing would give them some peace of mind.

Stuyvesant pondered briefly—his secretary Cornelis van Ruyven pausing, pen ready; Dorothea holding her breath as yet again her family's fate was about to be decided by the whims of others—then ruled: "The matter being so as the petitioners have herein stated, their request has been approved."

Chapter 9

RESTORATION LONDON

———

"The Palace of Whitehall" is a phrase that suggests stately grandeur. In fact, the home of the kings of England through most of the sixteenth and seventeenth centuries, until it burned down in 1698, was more like a medieval village. Estimates of its size ran from 1,500 to in excess of 2,000 rooms. That it wasn't easy to come up with a precise number hints at higgledy-piggledy development, and indeed, it was actually a vast rabbit warren of structures—"a heap of Houses," one visitor called it—cobbled together decade upon decade along the banks of the Thames. To get from one office to another, as Richard Nicolls would have done as part of the regular course of his work in the early 1660s, might mean trundling along narrow corridors, following odd bends and twists, marching through meetings in progress, crossing one or more of the dozens of open-air courtyards (most famously Scotland Yard, less famously the Wood Yard and the Small Beer Battery), past chapels, guardhouses, bowling greens, and tennis courts.

From the time of his return in 1660, through his formal restoration in April 1661, and until his death in 1685, King Charles II lived here (with regular stints at Windsor Palace and Hampton Court). So, after their wedding in 1662, did his queen, Catherine of Braganza, in an adjoining suite. (The king's principal mistress, Barbara Palmer, was domiciled in a house adjacent to the palace.) The Duke of York had his quarters down a nearby passage. The palace also housed dozens of other nobles and assorted government officials. As Groom of the Bedchamber to James, Nicolls would likely have lived in one of the smaller apartments near the duke's suite.

The royal return, after nine years in exile, and the formal restoration of the monarchy, set off a season of festivals and parties. It's commonplace in historical literature to characterize Restoration London as a Gomorrah, where immoral primal urges were vented day and night. There is surely something to that, but my inclination is to turn the matter on its head. It was in the preceding era of Puritan rule that true immorality reigned, an eighteen-year period when a fundamentalist cult bent all of soci-

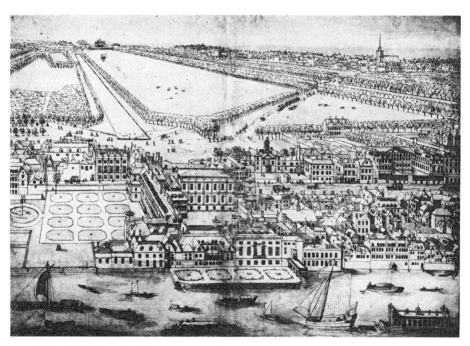

Whitehall Palace in the seventeenth century.

ety to its harsh and narrow will, when people were arrested and imprisoned for holding religious services to celebrate Christmas, when families were fined for letting their children play on the Sabbath. The Stuarts didn't so much promote wantonness as reopen the playhouses and other entertainment centers and allow people (within limits) to practice the faith of their choosing.

The result, after years in which ordinary impulses and desires were stifled, was an emotional unleashing. People learned to dance again. They rediscovered Shakespeare and packed houses for newly written plays, especially newfangled comedies that reveled in sexuality. Theater audiences were ready for a bold new innovation: the introduction of actual women playing female roles.

Saying that the Stuarts weren't outright promoters of public wantonness doesn't mean that they were prudes. Both Charles and James were inexorable rakes who sired dozens of illegitimate children and fostered a court composed of, as one poet put it, "Pimp statesmen, bug'ring priests, court bawds, and whores." As adulterers, both brothers were particularly drawn to the wives of noblemen. (One of Charles's high-born conquests was instructed by her clergyman that she "should have no more commerce with that known enemy to virginity and chastity the monarke of Great Britain.") Of the two brothers, James was apparently the more rampant. While trading stories of conquest with the French ambassador one day, the king remarked, "I do not believe there are two men who love women more than you and I do, but my brother, devout as he is, loves them still more."

And yet you have to square your mental image of the hedonism of Charles's court with the fact that the same people who were so devoted to sexual high jinks also oversaw the recasting and redirection of the government of England, setting it on a course toward empire. Working hard and playing hard is perhaps a way to think of the Stuart regime. But the push to empire, too, had a measure of self-interest in it. Charles and James were acutely aware of how unstable their position was, of how many of their subjects, including some very powerful ones, had fought against them, still hated their guts, and longed to give them the same treatment that had been afforded their father. In the face of simmering opposition, the way forward, they and their advisers concluded, was through vibrant manifestations of power. Case in point: Oliver Cromwell's body was ordered to be unearthed from its grave in Westminster Abbey, hanged, then decapitated, and the ghoulish head, with desiccated flesh still papered over it, mounted on a pike twenty feet above Westminster Hall. Would-be enemies of the Stuarts didn't have to rush to get a glimpse of it. It stayed there for the twenty-four years that remained of Charles's rule.

Less symbolically but more historically resonant, the Stuart government, along with a group of private merchants, decided to improve on the expansion efforts attempted under Cromwell. Straightaway—within months of taking power—they created three new organizations that shaped the future not only of England but of the entire world. One operated within the government. In its very name the Council for Foreign Plantations made clear that the English state would henceforth look outward, toward empire, with an emphasis on North America and the Caribbean. The Royal African Company expressed a similar objective from the perspective of a private business concern and in time became the main moneymaking engine of the British slave trade. The Royal Society—formally the Royal Society of London for Improving Natural Knowledge—has, ever since its founding in November 1660, been known as one of the world's premier organizations for the advancement of science, but its origins were also tied to dreams of empire—to mastering not only the natural world but foreign lands and populations.

***

While there may be a tendency in our time to think of royals of the seventeenth century as spoiled brats living in a bubble of excess who let men beneath them do the actual work of governing, James was—some of the time anyway—a serious and hardworking administrator. He oversaw the Council for Foreign Plantations and was the principal sponsor of the Company of Royal Adventurers Trading into Africa. He was thus at the center of the handful of people plotting a course of empire, a plot that would include Richard Nicolls's mission to Manhattan. The British Empire, which he would not live to see, owed a good deal to the groundwork he laid. And James's personality, a mix of waywardness and intense focus, became imprinted on the effort. He was now Lord High Admiral of the Navy, the largest organization of any kind in the country, and he had latitude in running it thanks partly to the differences between his nature and his brother's. Charles was a man of ideas who lacked the drive to carry them out. He had fought doggedly to win back the crown, then, as king, seems to have spent as much time behaving royally—dress, courtiers, banquets, storied expenditures on royal portraits—as he did governing, earning him the moniker the Merry Monarch. He adored pageantry, which made him rather popular. He was also deeply cognizant of political infighting at court and adept at getting his way.

James was the more driven of the two brothers—to a fault, as would become clear when he himself became king twenty-five years later and all but willed a revolt by trying to impose both an absolute monarchy and the acceptance of Catholicism on the English people.

James's drive propelled him in many directions. He was a passionate hunter, for instance, who practically invented foxhunting as a pastime of English royalty. Another, quite different example of his willfulness manifested itself before the Restoration. After impregnating a young woman who was beneath his station—Anne Hyde was the daughter of Edward Hyde, the Lord Chancellor, but still a commoner, and at the time was a mere lady-in-waiting to his sister, Mary—he insisted, against all advice, on marrying her. (To skirt scandal, though, he agreed to hold a shotgun wedding in the middle of the night.) James seems to have genuinely loved her, never mind his serial adultery. (Then too, Anne, while fond of her husband, may have had an affair with her riding instructor.)

James was tall, broad, brash, and handsome. With his long curly wigs and pouty lips, he could have passed for the lead singer of a 1970s rock band. He attended meetings regularly and kept a journal of the goings-on. A man who knew both royal brothers well noted that James "has not the King's quickness but that is made up by great application and industry."

As he had been on the Continent, Richard Nicolls was at James's side throughout this period. For the first year of the Restoration he was James's only Groom of the Bedchamber (later

James, Duke of York, after whom Richard Nicolls named New York, at about age forty, dressed as Mars, the Roman god of war.

there were eight), making him an eyewitness to the creation of several world-changing organizations. Nicolls would have managed James's appointments, such as meetings of the Privy Council and the Navy Board, and his other affairs, perhaps including those with young ladies of the court, so that a picture of his life at Whitehall comes into view: hurried mornings, the pulling on of silk stockings, getting the wig in place, maybe greedily taking part in the new fad of gulping down cups of coffee.

Samuel Pepys, the diarist, naval administrator, and most prolific and detail-oriented chronicler of Restoration England, surely interacted with Nicolls. Both worked within Whitehall under James and his secretary, William Coventry. From Pepys we get gossip about the whole group. For example, he was first with the news that "the Duke of York hath got my Lord Chancellor's daughter with child" and that "he did promise her marriage." Through Pepys's observations, too, we catch glimpses of what a life such as Nicolls had in London was like beyond the gates of Whitehall: meetings in taverns and inns over bottles of sack and claret and meals of stewed carp, pickled oysters, and the odd "jowl of salmon"; murmured conversations during walks in gardens; while in the streets being careful to dodge the emptying of chamber pots from upper windows.

Nicolls's world now was vastly different from what he had experienced growing up in Ampthill or had lived through in battle on the Continent. He was seemingly at the center of everything: art, politics, invention, sex, spectacle. It was a new age, and discovery was in the air. Robert Moray, his friend from The Hague, was among those who formed the Royal Society and in fact became its first president. The two men were close enough that in an age of formality, of Sir This and Lord That, Moray called him Dick.

It may have been through Moray that Nicolls became aware of the burgeoning exploration of the natural world that people all over Europe were suddenly engaged in. Moray had spent years roaming the continent as a soldier, but in between battles he had studied rocks, plants, tides, and winds and built up a network of kindred spirits: amateur scientists, we might say, but then again all scientists in the seventeenth century were amateurs. Universities, where professors were more likely to propound medieval theories based on the work of Aristotle than to engage in real-world experimentation, were most often behind the times.

The Royal Society was not to be a mere forum for lectures: its members wanted to promote observation and experimentation. And many of the early investigations it promoted were conducted at Whitehall itself. Nicolls could have been among the group of enthusiasts who accompanied his friend Moray in June 1662 as he studied "the variation of the needle," presumably a magnetic compass; or when he observed the eclipse of the moon from the palace grounds; or in March 1663 when he was involved in an experiment "producing maggots by cheese and sack." We don't know that Nicolls took part in these explorations, but he was deeply interested in what science was discovering and later, from Manhattan, would correspond with Moray about America's natural world.

The most vital member of the inner circle of men who dreamed up the idea of empire was Edward Hyde, the Lord Chancellor and Anne Hyde's father. He had been a trusted adviser to Charles I and joined his son Charles in exile. He was large, wheezy, arrogant, and had a brilliant political mind. James held him in such esteem that for the first years after the return from exile, he would sit beside him in the House of Lords so that he could get "advice on how best to behave himself," Hyde later wrote.

An indication of Hyde's political savvy was his initial opposition to his daughter marrying the prince. It would surely elevate his own status, but that was just the problem. He was devoted to the kingdom and saw it as his life's work to turn England from an inward-focused island to a global power. He knew that the match would make him the object of envy at court and thus threaten his effectiveness. When he was elevated to the peerage afterward, becoming the Earl of Clarendon, it confirmed his enemies' fears.

Nevertheless, he used his increased power ably, steering the ambitious circle of James's advisers toward their objectives.

If there is one person in English history who might be thought of as the mastermind of the idea of a British empire, it must be George Downing, and he wasn't even in the country for much of the period of the Restoration. Some historians consider him nothing less than the architect of the modern British state. And yet one English historian has also called him (in a handsome turn of phrase) "the most unscrupulous person of whom record survives." He was universally hated, even—especially—among those, like Edward Hyde, who worked closely with him. Pepys, who served directly under Downing, called him "a perfidious rogue" and "so stingy a fellow I care not to see him." Downing's own mother complained that even after he had made himself one of the richest men in England, he kept her in near poverty.

Two constants animated Downing's career: he was utterly devoted to himself, to his own wealth and power, and equally devoted to seeing England rise to global greatness. The naming of Downing Street in London is one testament to how well he succeeded. His devotion to England's rise coupled with his profound intellect made Downing indispensable to Charles and James. He was one of those figures—they exist in every era—who could adjust himself shamelessly to suit every shift of the political winds. As ambassador to the Dutch Republic under Oliver Cromwell, he had been a vigorous mouthpiece for Puritan, anti-royal ideals and a great promoter of the Western Design. Once the Stuarts were back on the throne, he changed his stripes instantly, was reappointed as ambassador (and knighted to boot), and proved his worth to the new King Charles by hunting down several of the men who had taken part in the execution of his father. This group of regicides had fled to the Continent. Using skills he had obtained as head of England's spy service, Downing located them in the Dutch city of Delft, personally captured them (while they were having dinner), dragged them back to England, and oversaw every step of their punishment: the hanging, the cutting off of the "privy members," the decapitation, and finally the quartering of the body. One of those who received this treatment had been Downing's superior officer under the old regime, a man who had considered him a close friend.

Downing was uniquely experienced for contributing to the plan that was about to unfold. He had grown up in New England—he was part of Harvard's first graduating class—and had spent years in the Dutch Republic, which growing numbers of the English ruling class were now coming to think of as their primary impediment to economic and military greatness. Downing's powerful intellect imaginatively connected these pieces of his past life. He had a unique insight into how the American colonies could be made profitable, and he had learned where Dutch weaknesses were and studied the new methods of finance that the Dutch had developed, with the intention of copying them in England.

As soon as he had seen his onetime friend and the other two regicides punished for their crime, demonstrating himself eminently worthy of the king's confidence, he turned his attention to the next matter: empire.

———

In the summer of 1660, just weeks after King Charles, the Duke of York, Richard Nicolls, and the rest of the royal party in exile returned to English shores, a ship slipped into London from Boston. A man—grizzled, pushing sixty, tough as nails—disembarked with a purpose; he knew his way around the city. Not long after settling himself in quarters, he appeared at the gates of Whitehall Palace. He managed to make his way inside, strolled down the long, elegant central courtyard, turned right past the Banqueting House, and was admitted into the Privy Council chamber.

Samuel Maverick—that maverick of a fellow we met earlier—explained to the gentlemen of the esteemed body that he was an Englishman who had helped to found the city of Boston in the 1620s, that it was his belief that America was an impossibly rich and fertile place ideally suited to fostering the growth of English civilization, but that shortly after his arrival the Puritans had started coming. They had turned the place into an independent state ruled by dogmatism; they hated the Stuarts; and despite the fact that the man was dead and gone, they remained essentially Cromwell's men. If the monarchy were to take advantage of the unparalleled opportunity that North America represented, he argued, it had to meet this threat.

Maverick knew a great deal, which attracted the attention of no less a person than the Lord Chancellor. Edward Hyde encouraged him to make his case in writing, and Maverick produced a small book packed with information about both the opportunity of America and the transgressions of the Puritan settlers of New England. Feeling that he hadn't fully expressed himself in it, he followed up in a stream of subsequent letters to the Lord Chancellor in which he hoped "in all humilitie [to] lay open my pticular thoughtes." The Restoration of the Stuart monarchy, he said, had come not a moment too soon, for the rulers of Boston, not content with their own colony, had "swallowed up" other pieces of New England and in other ways asserted themselves as if they were a sovereign state.

Hyde admitted Maverick into his office time and again, asked for further information and for updates as these arrived in the form of letters from correspondents in America.

In December the king empowered the Council for Foreign Plantations, giving the members a meeting room within the palace, authorizing them to raise a staff and pay salaries, and commanding them to bring "the severall Colonies and Plantacôns, within themselves, into a more certaine civill and uniforme of government."

Maverick appeared repeatedly before this new council and got to know many of its members. They were eager for information. Several of them—earls and viscounts, knights and wealthy merchants, men who had a vested interest in seeing England expand—had long been curious about America, which had been claimed by England decades earlier but had been allowed to go its own way while the nation was preoccupied by its civil war. They hoped to turn America at last into a profitable satellite of the home country.

And Maverick was not the only New Englander in London. More than a dozen disgruntled colonials trooped in and out of the council chamber over the next couple of years, petitioning, pleading, offering information, hoping that the return of the monarchy meant that the English government realized it had let the American colonies grow like mad weeds and would, like a suddenly attentive gardener, finally address the problem.

While the American colonies were indeed on the minds of England's ruling set, they were also interested in other properties. It was a giddy time for would-be colonizers, slavers, and exploiters. In these months following the return of a king to England's throne, dozens upon dozens of meetings were held, petitions read out in echoey stone halls. Faraway place names were summoned, and with them echoed the promise of fantastic wealth. Within a remarkably short time England began the process of putting its stamp on the world. At Whitehall minutes were recorded, licenses were granted, petitions were received, proclamations went forth:

The King to all Captains and Commanders of ships, and all his subjects in Newfoundland . . .

An Act for encouraging and increasing Shipping and Navigation, to the Governors of Virginia, Maryland, Barbadoes, St.

Christopher's, Nevis, Montserrat, Antigua, Surinam, Jamaica, and New England . . .

Grant of a Charter to Rhode Island . . .

Minutes of a meeting of the Lords Proprietor of Carolina . . .

Petition of the Company of Royal Adventurers of England trading in to Africa to the King. That petitioners in order to induce the Spaniards to trade with the West Indies, had sent a ship with 160 negroes to the Spanish main . . .

License for Mr. Willoughby to transport 100 horses to Surinam or any of the Leeward Islands . . .

Petition of officers and mariners late of H.M.S. Diamond. On February 21st, petitioners seized a Flemish ship in Jamaica harbour, which with her apparel and furniture, negroes, and other goods and lading amounted to a good value, and was condemned as prize by General D'Oyley; pray that they may receive a proportion thereof. Indorsed with an order recommending the Duke of York to grant the petition. . . .

[A] Dutch merchant ship came into Cagway Road, freighted with negroes, which Col. D'Oyley, then Governor, bought contrary to the Act of Prohibition of Trade with Foreigners. . . .

Warrant for Privy Seal of 3,000*l.* to be paid to Edw. Morgan . . . for his Majesty's service for Jamaica.

The King's warrant to the Governors of Barbadoes and Jamaica, and all officers by sea and land, of safe conduct for the St. Jean Baptist to carry negroes to the Spanish Indies and bring back money and merchandise from thence to pay for same. . . .

The Trade of Africa . . . the supply of negro servants . . . above
160,000*l*. in cargoes . . . 40 ships . . . very considerable quantities of gold and silver.

Three months after Samuel Maverick showed up at Whitehall,
another Royalist from Boston, a merchant by the name of Thomas
Breedon, arrived in London and made a similar petition before
the council. He echoed the outrages of the Massachusetts Bay
Colony, declaring that its leaders "looke on themselves as a Free
State" and were against "having any dependance on England,"
and that they demanded an oath of allegiance not "to his Majestie
but in stead thereof force an oath of fidelitie to themselves and
their governmt." He stressed too a dark fact: that two of the regicides who had escaped English justice had fled to Boston, that he
himself had personally arrested them and brought them before
the governor of the colony for justice, but that the governor and
his council refused to send them to London and instead offered
them hospitality. For attempting to bring these murderers of the
late king to justice, Breedon said, "I was abused by many."

Breedon also highlighted the polarization in the colony,
explaining that many of its inhabitants had grievances against
the Puritan rulers and would welcome a commission sent by the
king to assert control.

Breedon too remained in London, coming in and out of the
council chamber, ready to give assistance should the government
make a move toward taking control in America.

Richard Nicolls, as the Duke of York's liaison, was around
these men during the early 1660s. He got to know Maverick, read
his book on the situation in America, and found the older man to
be trustworthy and deeply informed if a little excitable.

What's more, Maverick in his petition underscored for the
council not only the situation in New England but that in New
Netherland as well. He drew the lords' attention to the fact that
the whole eastern seaboard of North America was claimed by

the English but that the Dutch had "intruded," creating a barrier between Virginia to the south and New England to the north. And from their base on Manhattan Island they were conducting a vigorous "trade and Comerce," especially with the Native people of the region, "gettinge yearely from the above one hundered Thousand Beavar skines, besides much other good Pelterey." He noted that the land they occupied was "exceedinge good" and there were "two gallant rivers running farr up into the land."

These insights resonated with information that George Downing was feeding to the council. Working in tandem with John Thurloe, the spymaster who had built up Oliver Cromwell's intelligence network, Downing had developed a ring of informers in Amsterdam and The Hague—to whom he paid as much as 1,000 pounds per year, about $200,000 in today's money—from whom he learned details of the Dutch military and the country's great trading operations, the East and West India Companies. Perhaps the main insight he gleaned was how these vast companies, which spanned the globe with their militarily fortified trading outposts, acted in effect as an outsourced Dutch military. The Dutch people saw their tiny nation's tremendous economic success on the world stage as vital to their own wealth and contentment. They were willing to put up with high taxes because the money went to protect the elegant fleets of wooden sailing vessels that gave them trading supremacy. That, Downing observed, was "the mystery of this state."

As a way to attack this system, Downing advocated for Parliament to support a revision of the Navigation Act it had passed years earlier. This protectionist measure, aimed directly at the Dutch, who had become Europe's trans-shippers par excellence and whose traders in New Amsterdam had developed a business that Downing believed should by rights go to New England, stipulated that only English ships could bring goods into England.

Through the early 1660s, Dutch spies also fed Downing information on the West India Company, which administered New

Netherland. Peter Stuyvesant had appealed for arms and soldiers, but the West India Company had ignored these appeals.
Manhattan was ripe for the taking and all but unprotected.

Of course, to attack it would be an outright provocation. But
provocation was part of the plan that Downing pressed his government to adopt and one that many wealthy merchants—members
of the council and shareholders in the Royal African Company—
supported as well. In their estimation a war just now would be
very winnable and would catapult them ahead of the Dutch.

A propaganda campaign cranked up—by means of pamphlets, the blogs of the day—whose purpose was to fan English
resentment of the Dutch. People in the streets of London, Bristol,
and Birmingham read of Dutch ships firing on English vessels
that approached the East Indies (which the Dutch considered
their territory) and were informed that the Dutch were the main
cause of the economic depression that had recently swept the
country. A parliamentary commission reported that "the wrongs
inflicted by the Dutch are the greatest obstacle to foreign trade"
and that "His Majesty should be moved to take a speedy course
for their redress."

The king didn't need persuading. He wrote to his sister,
"I am now sending Sir George Downing into Holland to make
my demands there. . . . I will have full satisfaction, one way or
another."

Downing was ready. He had, after all, been huffing and puff-
ing his way around Dutch cities long enough to see firsthand the
rival nation transform itself into a powerhouse. Formerly dour
burghers were now fantastically wealthy men of the world, swaggering creatures who adopted French fashions and tricked out
their houses with Italianate flourishes. That was precisely how
Downing himself looked and behaved—with his flaccid face and
long, aquiline nose, his penchant for dressing his large frame in
ruffles and silks—but that was beside the point. There was no

other way of looking at it: the Dutch now had an empire. England had to play catchup.

A plan—a two-part plan—was coalescing. By picking one's way through the millions of documents filed at the UK National Archives at Kew, it's possible to see the plan come together in the minds of this coterie of government officials and merchant princes. More than nine months before it was given life in official orders, before its features were fully apparent, Richard Nicolls was already attached to this plan. Edward Godfrey, one of the petitioners from New England who was in London, who had for years been complaining about the Massachusetts Bay Colony swiping land outside its patent, gossiped in April 1663 that "one Mr. Nicolls, belonging to the Duke of York, is to go for New England." Nicolls, then, had a full year in which to contemplate what he would be doing, a year to chat up Maverick, Breedon, and other men recently returned from the colonies.

Three months after Nicolls was tapped to lead an American expedition, it became apparent that it would involve more than New England. The Council for Foreign Plantations heard yet another complaint: that "the Dutch have of late years unjustly intruded" on English properties in America—meaning properties that the English had belatedly decided were theirs—including "Manhatoes and Long Island." In August, Samuel Maverick was back in their chamber, making two more petitions, in the last whining that "for near three years" he had been "a constant solicitor for relief from his Majesty," but as of yet he could not "perceive anything done effectually towards it" and therefore he urged "that some persons may be speedily sent over."

One thing that emerged from the stream of New Englanders with their petitions and complaints was a fuller sense than anyone in England had previously had of what New Netherland was—of what the Dutch had accomplished on the island called Manhattan (or Manahatta, or Manhattes, or Manhattoes), how New Amsterdam had connected itself not just to Amsterdam but to other cities in Europe as well as the Caribbean. Maverick made the strategic placement of Manhattan clear for them. "Hudsons river," he said, made the island "most Commodious for comerce from and with all pts of the West Indies," so that it "may in tyme on that Account prove very advantagious to ye Crowne of England if Regained, and as priudiciall [prejudicial] if not."

Palpable in the complaints the New Englanders vented toward the Dutch was what could only be called jealousy. Nobody in Boston or elsewhere in America seemed to be able to match New Amsterdam's shipping and trade prowess, and nobody could figure out how the place, with its confusing mix of languages and religions, functioned. Outsiders had a hard time fathoming that a multiethnic population could be a strength. New Amsterdam was a trading center whose inhabitants had family and business ties in far-flung places. Those same inhabitants also engaged in what we would call capitalism, personally investing their savings in voyages in hopes of future profits. What seems commonplace to us today was bewildering to the English of the time. It didn't seem to make sense, but it worked, and the English couldn't stand it.

Exactly who on the council perceived that New Amsterdam was doing something novel and valuable is an interesting question. Likely William Coventry, James's secretary, realized it. Certainly Richard Nicolls, as he prepared for his mission, was another of those who was coming to understand the value of Manhattan—strategically, but also in terms of the social and economic system the Dutch had built there.

Finally, in January 1664, a committee of members of the council, which included Coventry, issued a report. Having "discoursed with several persons well acquainted with the affairs of New England," it noted that the Dutch in New Netherland "do not exceed 1,300 men"; that there were about 600 Englishmen within the colony who would presumably be loyal to England in the event of an invasion; and that from the surrounding area they could expect to gather "1,300 or 1,400 men, besides other English which will come freely from other colonies." The committee reasoned that "it seems very probable the Dutch may either be reduced to his Majesty's obedience or dispossessed of their usurped dwellings and forts if the King will send three ships and about 300 soldiers under good officers." It would be up to the king to decide, but the members of the committee advised moving on Manhattan.

His Majesty made his decision. The next month— February—he sent his brother James, in his capacity as Lord High Admiral, instructions to assign ships "for a voyage to New England." James had already, months earlier, tapped his Groom of the Bedchamber, his loyal aide, the friend of his youth who had been at his side through the long hard years of exile, to lead a pos- sible mission to the New World. Now it had become a reality. He would leave in the spring, at the start of the sailing season. That gave two months to prepare.

And so the operation moved through the bureaucracy.

On February 25, Colonel William Legg, Lieutenant of the Ordnance, received a warrant to deliver to Richard Nicolls "500 firelocks, 500 matchlocks, pikes, pistols, 50 carabines, saddles, bridles, 2 mortar pieces, powder, match and ball, pickaxes, spades, and shovels, 2 brass sakers with field carriages, 1,000 bandoleers, holsters, bells, 500 swords, axes, hatchets, saws, wheelbarrows, hand baskets, tents, halberds, 6 drums, 3 colours, 40*l*. worth of nails and ironwork, one barrel of flint stones, and carriages and tackle for the mortars and sakers."

Four days later the Clerk of the Signet was told to prepare a bill for the king to sign to pay the Treasurer of the Navy the sum of 4,000 pounds to cover costs of the expedition. A separate warrant noted that this money was to be paid over to "Richard Nicolls, groom of the bedchamber to the Duke of York."

On March 17, Nicolls received a commission to raise and arm soldiers and officers from the precincts of London and Westminster. A notice went out on the same date stating that "Justices of the peace, mayors, &c. are charged to permit them to march to the place of embarking."

Preparations were proceeding smoothly, but one rather enormous alteration in affairs occurred at this point. There had been so much fussing over ownership of portions of North America—not only the Dutch claim to New Netherland but the squabbling among the various New England colonies—that the king decided on a simple expedient for clearing the way for Nicolls's mission. He claimed that a huge swath of it had been in his possession all along and that he would now hand it over, as a royal gift, to his brother.

A patent was thus executed—swirling handwriting, sealed in a great gob of red wax—and made public:

> CHARLES the second, by the grace of God, king of *England, Scotland, France* and *Ireland*, defender of the faith, &c.
> To all to whom these presents shall come, greeting:
> Know ye, that we, for divers good causes and considerations, have, of our especial grace, certain knowledge and mere motion, given and granted, and by these presents, for us, our heirs and successors, do give and grant unto our dearest brother, *James*, duke of *York*, his heirs and assigns, all that part of the main land of *New-England*, beginning at a certain place, called or known by the name of *St. Croix*, next adjoining to *New-Scotland*, in *America*; and from thence extending along the sea coast, unto a certain Place called *Petuaguine* or *Pemaquid*.

Well, the geography of North America was confusing: the royal cartographers and scribes did their best. The patent—which was aimed at the land-greedy zealots of the Massachusetts Bay Colony as much as at the Dutch—went on to include features that, since 1609, had been under Dutch claim, including "all that

Island or Islands, commonly called by the several name or names
of Matowacks or Long Island, Scituate, lying and being towards
the west of Cape Codd . . . abutting upon the main land between
the two rivers there, called or known by the several names of
Conecticutt or Hudsons river; together also with the said river

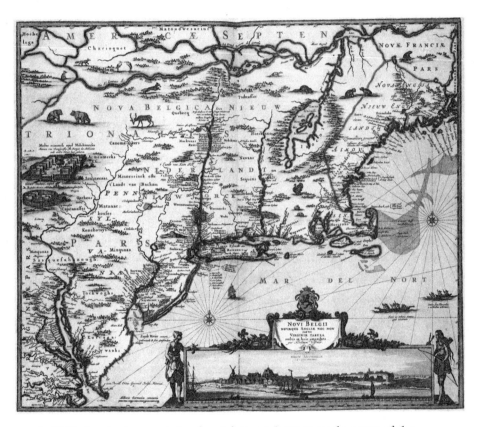

In 1651, Amsterdam cartographer Johannes Jansson made a map of the
portion of the North American continent in which the colony of New
Netherland sat. Boundaries were never agreed on, but Jansson's map, later
engraved by Nicolaes Visscher, shows "Nieuw Nederlandt" occupying a vast,
central stretch of territory and seeming to push "Nieuw Engelandt"—i.e.,
the New England colonies—into the Atlantic Ocean. The map was revised
and reprinted twenty-eight times over the course of the next century. This
edition clearly dates to early in the English period, as it indicates both
"Nieuw Nederlandt" and "Niew Jorck."

called Hudsons river, and all the lands from the west side of Conecticutt, to the east side of Delaware Bay."

That the territory in question—however vaguely the geography of it was understood in London—was the king's to give is a question that goes right to the dark heart of the age of colonial expansion. England's claim of territorial rights rested on notions of European specialness. Put another way, King Charles was playing a kind of real-world game of Risk in which the only authorized players were other European leaders. The "first" in the Doctrine of First Discovery referred to European nations—whoever got there first won that piece of the board. Related to this was the curious notion of "contiguity": not only was the exact spot where a given European nation's explorer made footfall to be considered the property of that nation but so was all land contiguous to it. How far contiguity could be made to extend was in turn dictated (as was the Doctrine of First Discovery) by how much force one was prepared to use. In this case it hearkened back to the Italian explorer Giovanni Caboto, aka John Cabot, who reached Newfoundland in 1497 under English auspices and magically, according to the assertion, extended English domination to the entire continent. Richard Nicolls was about to put contiguity to the test against the Dutch, and at the same time, the king was asking him to reassert sovereignty over the rebellious-minded English colonies.

A royal decree and gift sent a sharp signal both to the Puritans and the Dutch: there would be no fussing about legal niceties. Charles had given this to James; it was James's now to do with as he pleased.

On April 2, James formally named Nicolls "his Deputy Governor there with all the powers granted to the Duke by said Patent." Three weeks later Nicolls's three fellow commissioners were named—and when Samuel Maverick learned that he was to be one of them, and would be heading back to face his longtime nemeses now with a royal commission in his pocket, he surely felt the glow of vindication flooding his veins.

———

At Whitehall, on the 23rd of April, 1664, Nicolls received his instructions. Poring over them, he saw that the essence of his mission was "to visit our Colony of ye Massachusetts" and to let the governor and council there "know ye kindnesse wee have for them and ye extreme desire wee are possessed wth to advance that plantacôn."

But of course a mere "visite" didn't require a flotilla of gun-ships packed with an arsenal of military hardware. In the same session Nicolls was handed a set of secret instructions, which spelled out his real objectives. "Though the maine end and drift of yor employmt is to informe yourselves and us of the true and whole state of those severall Colonies," he was told, and while he was to achieve this "by insinuateing yourselves by all kind and dextrous carriage into the good opinion of ye principall persons there," he was in fact ordered to go further. He was to do whatever was necessary to bring within the laws of England and her king "whatsoever [colony] hath swerved from it." He was to study in particular the laws of Massachusetts that had been published "during the late usurping Government" and identify those "indecent expressions and materiall and important points . . . which are contrary to our dignity." He was to keep uppermost in mind that "it is very notorious that there are not only very great factions and animosityes in one Colony against the other, but in one and ye same Colony betwene persons of different opinions in religion," and for this reason he was to "be very wary in your conversation."

His mission, therefore, had everything to do with bringing the Massachusetts Bay Colony to heel.

Then there was the second task stipulated in the instructions: "the possessing Long Island, and reduceing that people to an entyre submission and obedience to us & our governement . . . that the Dutch may noe longer ingrosse and exercise that trade which they have wrongfully possessed themselves of."

By "Long Island" the king meant, of course, the Dutch colony of New Netherland, which stretched from the borders of Massachusetts south to the Delaware River and had Manhattan Island as its fulcrum. The king and the duke had some idea now of what a swath of territory it covered, what the Dutch had created there in forty-odd years, how strategically situated it was, and what an impediment it was to the development of the English colonies in North America.

The end result, then, of this series of petitions, meetings, and depositions was the realization that what it had all concerned—America—had become important to the Stuarts. And one can't help but see this realization not just in nationalistic and world-historic terms but psychologically as well. There was a determination on the part of the two brothers, now that they had clawed their way to power, not to lose their heads as their father had but rather to go big and bold at the world, attacking their two greatest enemies of recent years: the Puritans, who had wounded their family so deeply, and the Dutch, who had shot past England in this age of colonization, enriching themselves and flaunting their superiority. The Puritans and the Dutch were demons to be exorcized. They were twin obstacles to Stuart greatness—and to England's rise.

The instructions contained a laundry list of other, related issues the king wished Nicolls to take care of in America. He was to hunt down the two men who had been accused of ordering the execution of his father—known to be hiding out somewhere in New England—and haul them back to meet their punishment. He was to visit all the other New England colonies, see what mischief they had gotten up to, and let them know that the King of

England now had his eye on them. Nicolls was to bring these far-flung religionists "to an entyre submission and obedience to our government." And once he had subdued the Dutch, he was to set his mind to studying this most inscrutable colony that they had planted, which was prospering in such unfathomable ways, unlock its secrets, and somehow make it English.

Altogether, this was a mission of staggering scope. Because of the ocean that lay between London and North America, Nicolls was given similarly sweeping latitude in carrying it out. There were no government committees or ministers he could confer with or get orders from. Exactly how it was to be done "wee cannot tell," the king admitted. Rather, he informed Nicolls with a rhetorical wave of the hand, he would "leave it to your skill & dexterity."

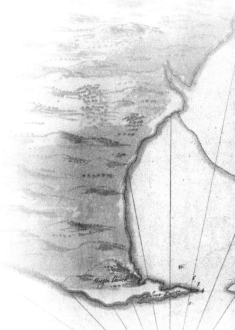

Map of "Manhattan situated upon the North River" made in 1639 for Willem
Kieft, director of New Netherland. It shows the future New York Harbor in its
entirety: the theater in which the standoff between English and Dutch forces
played out in 1664.

Part Three

A GAME OF CHESS

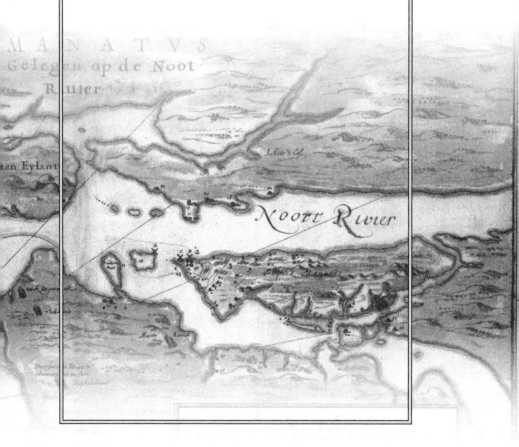

Chapter 10

DOPPELGANGER

———

A particularly ugly type of violence animated Anglo-Dutch relations in the era in which the fate of Manhattan was decided.
It played out in a series of tropes that featured sailing vessels and
coastal forts firing murderous volleys at one another. Elements
included heat, acrid smoke, blasts of fire, wood-shattering colli-
sions, and the screams of men being impaled or torn apart. The
results of each battle were published in luridly detailed pamphlets
and immortalized on great stretches of canvas.

We might take a moment to assemble this activity frame
by frame. A single iron ball that was unleashed from, say, a
culverin—a type of extra-long cannon—by three or four pounds
of gunpowder was accompanied by a thickly clustered shower of
sparks, a high-decibel explosion, a six-foot recoil of the cannon,
and with any luck a ragged hole through the target, followed perhaps by potentially lethal foot-long splinters of wood whirligigging
about the deck of the enemy ship. Now envision five wooden vessels, each with about forty such guns, arrayed against one another
in a vicious dogfight under a blazing sun and beneath the ramparts of a fort whose cannons, manned by Dutch gunners, pump

lethal projectiles into the English enemy flagship. Despite this barrage the English ship manages to set two of the Dutch vessels huddled against the walls of the fort ablaze. As the hours tick by, light begins to fade, and the Englishman retreats, the captain later penning in his journal, "My mast and rigging being much shattered I was forced to hale off out of shott to repaire them." Meanwhile one of the opposing vessels, a great castle of wood, teeters and eventually succumbs to the deep—"by reason of so many shott she had received between wind and water." The battle is over. Blood and death own the seascape. The battered English have command of the fort and the island.

This was the essence of Anglo-Dutch conflict in the seventeenth century. We are not in the harbor at the base of Manhattan Island, however, but off the coast of West Africa. It is January 1664—three months before Richard Nicolls is to set sail for Manhattan. The fort under attack sits elegantly hulked above Gorée, a tiny jewel-like island off the coast of modern-day Senegal.

Let's pause for a moment to orient ourselves. This book is about how New York came into being. There were two European nations involved in its birth—parents, as I have suggested, who would each contribute genetic material to the newborn. In Part One we set the scene in the future New York Harbor as that act of conception was about to take place. In Part Two we stepped back and looked at the forces at work on both sides in the previous decades.

As we return to the events that would unfold in and around Manhattan in the late summer of 1664, a further bit of context regarding the scope of activity and the nature of English animosity toward the Dutch may sharpen the picture. The trading empire that the Dutch Republic had established through its East India Company was the envy of Europe, but especially of England. England had its own East India Company, which also funneled wealth from Asia to the home country, but it couldn't compete with the Dutch in part due to structural differences. The

Dutch company was an arm of the government and empowered
to make treaties, establish forts, and set soldiers against local
populations if that was what it took to gain the trading monopoly
it sought. It stood supreme among all trading companies in the
world. Economist Lodewijk Petram has called the Dutch East
India Company "the Apple of its time."

From their side of the Channel the English were acutely aware
of the wealth that the East India Company brought to Dutch
cities—Amsterdam quintupled in size over the course of the seventeenth century—and their envy was magnified by bitterness
over the brutal tactics Dutch vessels employed in their determination to keep their power. An event that had taken place four
decades before Richard Nicolls set off on his mission remained the
touchstone of English ire. In 1623, amid the struggle for control
of the spice trade in the East Indies, Dutch soldiers on the island
of Ambon in present-day Indonesia—then called Amboyna—
tortured and murdered a number of men in the employ of the
English. The English produced a best-selling pamphlet that was
reprinted throughout the ensuing decades, replete with woodcut
illustrations and elaborate descriptions of how the Dutch devils
had gone about their torture. Each man, generations of horrified
and fascinated English readers learned, was bound, then had a
cloth wrapped tightly around his face and neck:

> That done, they poured the water softly upon his head untill
> the cloath was full up to the mouth and nostrils, and somewhat
> higher; so that he could not draw breath, but he must withall
> suck in the water: which being still continued to be poured in
> softly, forced all his inward parts, came out of his nose, ears,
> and eyes, and often, as it were stifling and choaking him, at
> length took away his breath, & brought him to a swoun or faint-
> ing. Then they took him quickly down, & made him vomit up
> the water. Being a little recovered, they triced him up again,
> & poured in the water as before, eftsoons taking him down

as he seemed to be stifled. In this manner they handled him three or four several times with water, till his body was swoln twice or thrice as big as before, his cheeks like great bladders, and his eyes staring and strutting out beyond his forehead. . . . Afterwards they hoised him up again as before, and then burnt him with lighted candles in the bottom of his feet, untill the fat dropt out the candles; yet then applied they fresh lights unto him. They burnt him also under the elbows, and in the palms of the hands; likewise under the arm-pits, untill his inwards might evidently be seen.

The Dutch disputed such accounts, but even decades after the events the English kept reliving Amboyna. As late as 1673 the celebrated dramatist John Dryden would produce a bluntly propagandistic play, *Amboyna, or the Cruelties of the Dutch to the English Merchants*, to stoke resentment during yet another Anglo-Dutch war. Focusing on Amboyna eased English envy, allowed the English to feel that the phenomenal Dutch success in building a global trade empire was thanks to their employing unsavory tactics that Englishmen would never stoop to.

Now, at last, it was time for the English to vent their frustration, attack the Dutch empire, and begin the work of building their own. The first strike was not Manhattan Island but Gorée, off the African coast.

Gorée is an eerily pleasant place today, with clashing overtones of tragedy and paradise, a UNESCO World Heritage Site that has been visited by the likes of Nelson Mandela, Pope John Paul II, and US presidents Obama, Clinton, and George W. Bush. Fewer than two thousand people inhabit it, their homes scattered among palm trees. Without a single car on the island, its loudest sounds come from children playing and the pounding surf. Visitors to the crumbling architecture of slavery are hushed and solemn, as if walking among temples.

For 312 years—while Europe went from knights and castles

Seventeenth-century Dutch engraving of Gorée Island.

to the age of steam engines—Gorée was a central slave-trading depot. Because of its protected harbor, deep waters (which discouraged prisoners weighted with chains from escaping), and proximity to the mainland, European slavers repeatedly fought one another for control of it. In 1664, at the same time they were plotting Richard Nicolls's mission, Charles II and his advisers, having succeeded in engineering support for a conflict with the Dutch ("all the Court are mad for a Dutch war," Samuel Pepys, the naval administrator, wrote in his diary), hatched the accompanying idea of goading their upstart neighbors across the Channel into war by sending a convoy to harass slaving posts on the African coast that were in Dutch possession.

Thus, though Gorée was an ocean away from Manhattan, their fates were connected. Indeed, the man the English chose for the African assignment, Robert Holmes, was seemingly a mirror image of Richard Nicolls. They were close in age, had similar backgrounds, and were alike in their grit and their loyalty to the Stuart brothers throughout the years of exile on the Continent. And now they were given parallel assignments on opposite sides of the Atlantic. The two men had so much in common, in fact, that some past historians merged them in their accounts of English derring-do in the seventeenth century, asserting that Holmes, after attacking Dutch ports in Africa, sailed west and took Manhattan.

One crucial difference between the two men was in temperament. Where Nicolls kept his cool, Robert Holmes had a swashbuckler's demeanor, and James clearly selected them for their respective missions with this in mind. The American assignment required nuance and the ability to maneuver with care among various Dutch, English, and Native American parties and interests. The objectives were complex, and the strategy behind them involved playing out scenarios into the future. The journals of Holmes's voyages suggest that had he been given the North America assignment, he would likely have inflamed the Puritans in Boston, then gone at Manhattan with murderous intent, setting off a like response and ending up with the destruction of New Amsterdam and unending war with the tribes of the region. American history would have veered in a very different direction.

The Africa job, by contrast, had Holmes's name written all over it. In fact, James's team in London seems more or less to have banked on him exceeding their instructions. It would have been diplomatically inappropriate for them to bluntly order an emissary to attack another country's possessions in a time of peace, so the instructions written by William Coventry, James's secretary, vaguely ordered Holmes to head for Africa and set about "protecting and promoting the Interests of the Royal Company, which is the sole end of your present voyage."

Even before he reached Africa—when he sailed within sight of the Cape Verde islands, some hundreds of miles to the west of the continent—Holmes made clear how he would interpret the order. On sighting a Dutch ship sailing eastward toward the mainland, he ran it down, fired a warning shot, and, when it did not surrender, ordered his men to blast away. The Dutch captain quickly gave up, and Holmes took ship, sailors, passengers, and cargo. This was in a time of peace, and Holmes's actions on reaching the mainland showed that he saw it necessary to drum up justifications for his behavior. In the Gambia he found an official who swore that the local representative of the Dutch West India Company had been attempting to get the King of Barra, a principality in the region, to declare war on English traders, hence the need for the militant action.

Then Holmes—a powerful man with a wide, strong face and surprisingly vulnerable eyes—made for Gorée Island, which controlled much of the coast, opened fire, and took the Dutch-manned slaving fort for England. He knew he was going beyond his written instructions, and at the same time he knew that what he was doing was precisely what his superiors wanted him to do—and he voiced the subtext of the little drama, reminding them that he was following their wishes and that he expected them to have his back. "If I goe beyond my instructions I hope you and the rest of the royall Company will mediate for mee," he wrote to Coventry.

From Gorée, Holmes continued south, toward Sierra Leone, where he captured more Dutch vessels and bullied local rulers into shifting their trading ties from the Dutch to the English. Then, continuing his remarkable one-man mission of havoc—for he had only his one ship, the forty-gun *Jersey*, along with the few enemy vessels he captured along the way and turned into a squadron under his command—he made for present-day Ghana, where he brought hell and destruction onto Dutch-controlled ports, turning them English. Here he touched off an ugly incident—involving the one hundred Dutch prisoners he had taken as well as Dutch and African merchants on the mainland—in which a depot was blown up, killing dozens of men. This led the Africans in charge to retaliate by decapitating all the Europeans that were within reach.

The Stuart government was delighted by Holmes's overreach. When the news reached Whitehall, Samuel Pepys recorded in his diary that "the King do joy mightily at it."

The link between Holmes's mission in West Africa and Nicolls's in North America was, of course, empire, but it may be worth noting that neither of them would have seen it quite that way. No one caught up in the English scheming in the year 1664 was envisioning the expansive and rapacious manner in which history would unfold over the coming decades, though one or two people involved in the planning surely had dreams of something like it. In hindsight we can see how those movements went together with events that would follow in the coming decades, each season's activities—bloody pitched sea battles, state-sanctioned piracy, a growing sophistication in how to do business with slave-trading African potentates, refinements in corporate structure—building on the last and coalescing into a global strategy, culminating in the great and mighty British Empire of the eighteenth century, one component of which was the thirteen American colonies. But the focus in 1664 was on specifics—on making money and maintaining power.

The very name of the Company of Royal Adventurers Trading into Africa points to the source of the future wealth they had in mind. And it suggests too that this early stage in the formation of the British Empire wasn't entirely the work of the Stuart government. Historian Lou Roper has underscored the extent to which the colonizing activity that Charles and James oversaw from the moment they came into power was encouraged by a cluster of English businessmen who had interests in foreign lands. It was obvious to these men that a slave trade would make those overseas properties more valuable. At Whitehall, Richard Nicolls met and interacted with, for example, Thomas Povey, whose family owned chunks of Barbados and Jamaica. Povey had gotten himself appointed as James's personal treasurer and used that post to push the idea of linking continents for his family's gain.

And the link between Gorée and Manhattan also involved slavery. As in other ways, the Dutch were ahead of the English in developing a slave trade. The West India Company may only recently have set itself to establish a slave trade in New Netherland, but the Dutch had had a base at Gorée since 1621, from which they oversaw shipments of human beings to the Caribbean and South America.*

The Dutch had other slaving posts on the African coast besides those that Holmes captured. In fact, a Dutch slaving mission that would bear directly on New Netherland overlapped with Holmes's trip. At about the time that Holmes was meeting in London with government leaders to plan his voyage, a Dutch adventurer named Simon Gilde was sitting down in the elegant Amsterdam mansion that housed the West India Company. Company officials Jacob Pergens and Abraham Wilmerdoncx contracted him to sail to Africa, purchase a shipload of slaves, and transport them to Manhattan in what would be the first significant effort to make good on the "experiment with a consignment of Negroes" that Stuyvesant had begun four years earlier.

Gilde, in his ship *Gideon*, reached Loango, a kingdom that stretched across modern-day Gabon and parts of Congo, at about the same time that Holmes was attacking Gorée, two thousand miles to the northwest. There he bought 421 men, women, and children and began an Atlantic crossing that was even more har-

---

*Dutch colonizers had long since considered this activity vital. In the 1630s, Johan Maurits, the leader of Dutch Brazil, pronounced matter-of-factly, "It is not possible to effect anything in Brazil without slaves . . . and they cannot be dispensed with upon any occasion whatsoever: if anyone feels that this is wrong, it is a futile scruple." The East India Company had likewise been in the slaving business in Asia for decades. In 1623, Jan Pietersz Coen, governor of the Dutch East Indies, argued in favor of not just amassing an enslaved population but "breeding" for long-term benefit.

rowing than most: 73 died en route—a death rate, nearly 18 percent, that was significantly higher than the average for slaving
voyages of the period. After putting into port at Curaçao, Gilde
sailed into the future New York Harbor and anchored off the tip
of Manhattan on August 15, two weeks before Nicolls showed up.

This was precisely the type of mission—bold, richly exploit-
ative, defiantly profit centered—for which the English envied
the Dutch. The Dutch trading companies functioned as arms of
the government, with enormous latitude to exploit distant lands.
Holmes's mission was an opening gambit on the part of the Stuart
government to assert itself in what would be a lengthy and bloody
showdown between two European powers, the results of which
would shape the coming centuries.

After Holmes's five-month voyage of intensively focused may-
hem, he sat down and wrote William Coventry a summing-up letter, informing him that thanks entirely to his actions, "You have
now all the trade in your owne hands from Cape de Verd to the
Gould Coast." He was yet again making clear that though he had
not been overtly instructed in this objective, capturing the Dutch
trade in Africa had been the underlying purpose. And as far as
Holmes was concerned, he had delivered: he declared to Coventry
and the Royal African Company that his spree had resulted in
nothing less than the English possessing "the most considerable
trade in Cristendome," and he concluded cheekily, "I hope you
will take a resolution to keepe it."

Holmes had taken a murderously bold step in advancing
the English cause against the Dutch, one that would also move
England a big step forward toward becoming a slaving power. Now
it was time for Holmes's doppelganger, Richard Nicolls, to fulfill
his own task on the other side of the Atlantic. There was good
reason to expect that it would be equally violent.

Chapter 11

GRAVESEND

———

Midland Beach, on eastern Staten Island, is a skinny strip of sand flanking the brawny expanse of New York Harbor. Behind it lie the communities of New Dorp and Old Town. *Dorp* is the Dutch word for "village." New Dorp is three-and-a-half centuries old; its name reflects the fact that it was founded after Old Dorp, which later became anglicized to Old Town. The present-day neighborhoods hearken back to the earliest European settlements on Staten Island. These communities that existed on the island under Dutch rule were barely that: each amounted to nothing more than a few houses made of "straw and clapboard." The most substantial structure was a blockhouse—a small fort, eighteen by twenty feet, made of wood. Its purpose was to house lookouts who would scan the harbor for threats.

The blockhouse was manned, in August 1664, by "six old soldiers," according to an account Peter Stuyvesant later gave to officials in the Dutch Republic. The tip of the Sandy Hook peninsula lay four miles away across the Lower Bay. For two days the lookouts had had a clear view of the long-feared existential threat to their colony: the *Guinea*, resting there at anchor, menacing but alone. They had sent word of it to Manhattan.

Then, on Thursday, August 28, three more English vessels sailed into the mouth of the harbor to join her. The lookouts noted that the ships didn't linger for long but rather, once together, moved as a convoy—heading their way.

The soldiers sent someone racing toward New Amsterdam with the alarming news. The messenger would likely have gone on horseback north to the Kill van Kull,* the channel separating Staten Island from the mainland; by sloop across to the future Bayonne, New Jersey; then north by horse to the Bergen ferry; and so across to Manhattan, a distance of about eighteen miles, which could be covered in a few hours.

Word spread through the city. Weeks of doubts as to the intent of this fleet—fed by English misdirection at the diplomatic level in Europe and swelled by wishful thinking among the West India Company directors—were swept aside. "Niccles" was coming for them.

The city became a study in contrasts: pandemonium and order, confusion and clarity. Soldiers went about their preparations; the burghers on patrol assumed their stations. Such orderly activity itself led to a certain amount of panic—the populace was "not a little frightened," said a Dutch minister—since everyone knew it meant that bloodshed and horror and destruction were imminent. And yet what were people to do? Where could they run? What of their possessions, their homes?

Through the streets of the city in this moment of controlled confusion strode John Lawrence, making for the fort. He was an Englishman, aged about forty-six years, a merchant who dealt in beavers and other commodities. He had lived in New Netherland for years, had assisted Peter Stuyvesant in the past in attempt-

---

Kill was seventeenth-century Dutch for an estuary. The word is no longer in use in modern Dutch but lives on in place names throughout the New York region.

ing to fix a firm boundary line between New Netherland and Connecticut. He'd been loyal.

But now he was feeling the general panic. We can picture him bursting into the council chamber. Stuyvesant looks up, stares as Lawrence blurts out what he has come to say in English, and Stuyvesant's secretary, Cornelis van Ruyven, grabs a pen, dips it into ink, and gets it down as best he can for the official record, Dutch spellings and all. (Note that the Dutch *-ij* approximates an English *-y*.) The helter-skelter of it gives, I think, a nice flavor of the moment of alarm and anxiety. Lawrence stammers that while he has always been a good resident of the Dutch colony, he now feels that taking up arms would be

> an obstruction to the Contrarij power & Commission from his Kinglij Maiesty of Great Brittayne mij naturall King & Superior souverrainge unto whose Authoritij I dare not nor cannot open mij mouth nor act mij waijes aginst his Commands but must shew mij obedience to the same wherein I humblij desire your Concurrance. . . . So that if any Appearance of hostilitij show it selfe Against this place & your Command therein as present Governour bij A power and Commission from his majestij: that you would please to excuse me if any Command should ishue from your selfe that I should arme as a burgher of the place to make resistance for the Defense thereof.

In other words, please don't make me fight against my countrymen.

John Lawrence's panic, and his conviction that attack was imminent, reflects the general alarm. Many residents guessed their fort was poorly stocked with gunpowder, and all knew the rules of war as practiced in the seventeenth century: if they put up a fight and lost—if they so much as let loose a single cannon volley—they opened themselves up to pillage. As Stuyvesant later told his superiors in Amsterdam, speaking of the city inhabitants in his charge: "By effective resistance everything would be ruined and plundered, and themselves, with wives and children, more than 1,500 in number, reduced to the direst poverty."

But the expectation of an imminent attack was wrong. By the time the messenger from Staten Island reached New Amsterdam, his news was already out of date, or at least in need of revision. Instead of sailing past the soldiers in their blockhouse, through the Narrows, and so on toward Manhattan, the English vessels rounded the end of the Coney Island peninsula and came to anchor in Gravesend Bay, at the tip of Long Island—a good eight miles from New Amsterdam and directly across the channel from the little blockhouse that guarded the harbor. It was as if the half dozen grizzled Dutch soldiers stationed there were to have a private show of whatever was about to transpire.

But no. In the next beat they became part of the show. One of the English vessels crossed the Narrows, bearing down on their position. The Dutch soldiers scrambled out of the blockhouse and ran, as the English troops clambered ashore and marched into the unmanned structure, taking possession of it and of Staten Island. Meanwhile, the other English ships sent boats rowing for the Long Island shore, each crammed with soldiers. The men landed and made a beeline for the village of Gravesend, which sat at the tip of the island, its houses looking out into the bay and across the channel to Staten Island.

In deciding to make Gravesend his base, Richard Nicolls was showing that he intended to go about his task quite differently from the way Robert Holmes had pursued his mission in West Africa. This was going to be a methodical operation.

Gravesend was part of the Dutch colony but had English roots and mostly English inhabitants. It had been settled two decades earlier by Lady Deborah Moody, an English noblewoman who had emigrated to Massachusetts in 1639 in search of religious freedom. Instead, she found just the opposite; the Puritans took to calling her "a dangerous woman" for professing her Anabaptist faith (the belief that baptism should not be given to infants but should wait until a child is old enough to comprehend the act), which made her a champion of religious liberty to future generations. In 1643 the then-director of New Netherland, Willem Kieft, invited her to his colony, informing her that it was both a haven of religious toleration and in need of settlers. She took him up on the offer, brought her followers with her, had a surveyor draw up a plan—a central quadrant around which homes would be erected—and became the first and perhaps only woman to found a town in colonial America.

Over the next twenty-one years Gravesend became an English enclave, and Lady Moody, as she was known, commanded great respect, serving as its spokesperson, communicating with the director and council of the colony on official matters. When Nicolls arrived, the village was still quite small, basically just the tidy square that Moody (who had died a few years earlier) had outlined, protected by palisades and bisected by a north-south and an east-west road: today's McDonald Avenue and Gravesend Neck Road.

At Nicolls's side, guiding him up the path from the beach, passing meadows left and right, over a little bridge crossing a creek, stepping around pastured cows and through a throng of wide-eyed English inhabitants in the center of the village, was a man named George Baxter. Baxter had been among those who showed up at Whitehall and appeared before the Council for Foreign Plantations. He'd been on the *Guinea* with Nicolls when it left England. The two men, plus Samuel Maverick, had spent much of the Atlantic crossing huddled together, Baxter counseling Nicolls, detailing for the leader of the expedition what he would find once they sailed into the harbor in which Manhattan Island sat. If Maverick was Nicolls's guide to dealing with the Puritans of Boston, Baxter was his key to the inner workings of New Amsterdam.

Nicolls could scarcely have chosen better, at least in terms of familiarity with the place. True, Baxter was something of a roughneck, as was his brother Thomas, also a onetime resident of the Dutch colony, who had set aside his work as a carpenter (he supplied the lumber from which the original wall at Wall Street was built), turned pirate, and preyed on ships in Long Island Sound. But George Baxter knew New Amsterdam intimately. Like Maverick, he'd been one of the earliest settlers of the New World: he seems to have been part of the first migration of Puritans to Boston. In time he found the theocratic regime too rigid for his taste and moved to the Dutch colony, where he put himself forward to Willem Kieft as someone who could manage his correspondence with the English. He built a house in New Amsterdam, and after Lady Deborah Moody emigrated in 1643, he crossed the East River and joined her English-speaking settlement at Gravesend.

When Stuyvesant took over for Kieft, he kept Baxter on as his "English Secretary." Stuyvesant put considerable trust in Baxter. When he traveled to Hartford in 1650 in an attempt to establish a boundary between New Netherland and the New England colonies, he not only brought Baxter with him but made him one of the negotiators. (The results of that negotiation are reflected to this day in the Connecticut–New York border as well as the division of Long Island between Suffolk and Nassau Counties.) Baxter in turn repaid the trust. He was at Stuyvesant's side when he led a Dutch squadron in pushing out a Swedish incursion in the southern part of New Netherland, and twice when Stuyvesant's authority was questioned, Baxter wrote letters on behalf of the people of Gravesend declaring their allegiance.

The relationship between Baxter and Stuyvesant began to sour in 1652, with the outbreak of the first Anglo-Dutch War. The English Parliament had passed the Navigation Act, which barred middlemen—that is, Dutch ships—from supplying the English market. The war directly affected the business of New Netherland. Meanwhile, Stuyvesant had just faced the challenge to his leadership led by Adriaen van der Donck, which had nearly resulted in his being ousted by the West India Company. He responded to the internal threat and the war with the English

by tightening his grip on power, including removing English colonists from his government.

Baxter reacted to this affront by joining with several other
English residents of the colony in drawing up a formal complaint.
Stuyvesant dug in his heels. Tensions rose, and in March 1655,
Baxter and two of his comrades ran an English flag up the flag-
pole on Gravesend common and proclaimed that they were no
longer the subjects of the Dutch Republic but rather of England
and its Lord Protector, Oliver Cromwell. Stuyvesant had him
arrested, and he spent the next year a prisoner in the fort in New
Amsterdam. He eventually made his way back to England.

Thus, when he learned of Nicolls's mission, Baxter was keen
to be a part of it. It was probably because of Baxter that Nicolls
had chosen Gravesend as his base. It's unlikely Baxter led him
to his own house in the village for his meeting; it seems that
Stuyvesant had had it confiscated. Perhaps the meeting place,
where the strategy for taking Manhattan would be hashed out,
was a tavern or the home of one of the other English inhabitants.

We can imagine Nicolls, Baxter, and Samuel Maverick stepping
out of the summer sunlight and into the gloomy interior of the
meeting place. And there, waiting for them, stood John Winthrop
Jr. The governor of the Connecticut colony was darkly handsome,
fifty-eight years old but still boiling with ambition. His eyes were
beady but piercingly intelligent: he was a man of some brilliance.
Nicolls had been machinating with Winthrop during the weeks
since he had had his tussle with the Puritan leaders of Boston, the
two men hopscotching letters from one nascent New World community to the next as they both traveled, each sussing out what
the other wanted and whether their ambitions could align and so
serve them both. Nicolls had it in mind that Winthrop would be
the key to what he was trying to pull off. Now at last he stood face
to face with the man. He was, Nicolls hoped, his secret weapon.

Chapter 12

THE ALCHEMIST

———

*R*ichard Nicolls knew John Winthrop Jr. The two had first met three years before, in London, in the heady days following the restoration of the monarchy.

In one sense they had been enemies: they were on opposite sides of the Civil War that had torn England apart. Winthrop was a Puritan from birth, the son (and namesake) of the revered longtime head of that hotbed of extremism, the Massachusetts Bay Colony.

Then again, they were both what you might call moderates in their respective camps. Nicolls had backed the Stuarts ardently, but he was not among the faction that wanted, once Charles was on the throne, to hunt down every former Puritan leader and haul him to the gallows. For his part Winthrop Jr. was not a carbon copy of his father, and that distance between the sensibilities of the father and the son was what Nicolls intended to exploit at their meeting in Gravesend. For all their differences the two had a good deal in common. Winthrop had been born in a village to the northeast of London that was not unlike Nicolls's hometown of Ampthill (minus the rabbits). Both hailed from the English gen-

try, a class that, while it didn't have the advantages of the aristoc-
racy, probably had at this time in history more flexibility, more
opportunities for smart young men to excel, which they both took
advantage of.

Winthrop's father was part of the wave of English subjects
who converted to Puritanism in the early part of the century.
People then had looked at the horror and turmoil through which
they were living—in 1603, about one-fifth of the population of
London died of the plague—and concluded that theirs was the
age in which human history was reaching a climax, heralding the
second coming of Jesus Christ. Their duty was to pave the way.
People differed on how that was to be done, which accounted
for the various strains of Puritanism. Hard-liners—both within
Puritanism and among Church of England adherents—were for
rooting out Catholicism, to the point of hunting down and execut-
ing not only priests but those who harbored them. This was the
branch of the sect that banned Christmas (on the grounds that it
was based on a pagan holiday), that infamously fulminated against
dancing, playing cards, kissing in public, wearing fancy clothes,
and the like. When H. L. Mencken later defined Puritanism as
"the haunting fear that someone, somewhere, may be happy," he
was referring to what we might call its extreme right wing.

Another strain—call it progressive Puritanism—took a verse
from the biblical Book of Daniel concerning "the time of the end"
("Many shall run to and fro, and knowledge shall increase") as
an injunction to study, travel, learn. In this thinking the Fall
of Man had to be countered by intellectual growth that would
restore humanity's dominion over nature. Some thinkers blended
this relatively reasonable-sounding Puritan philosophy with the
study of alchemy. John Winthrop Jr., while he was studying law
at London's Inner Temple, fell under the influence of alchemists
and became one of them. In so doing he created a fissure between
himself and his father and made himself a far more complex and
interesting figure.

The popular idea of alchemy today equates it with quack science. There are excellent reasons for this. European alchemists fused their approach to the study of the natural world with Christian mysticism; they tried to distill an "elixir of immortality" and harped on finding a "philosopher's stone" that would turn base metals, like iron or lead, into gold; they wrote in a secret code. Some were little more than magicians who used combustible powders and sleight of hand to win royal favor. But others were doing what we might call proto-science. They were studying chemistry and astronomy, improving navigation, refining metals. They labored at the cutting edge of discovery, were attuned to the profit-making potential of their work, and were regarded the way people today see leading computer and tech figures, as harbingers of the Next Big Thing.

In 1630 the elder Winthrop was called to lead the Puritan mission to found the Massachusetts Bay Colony. His son, though now twenty-four and perfectly capable of setting out in his own direction, chose to follow him there. Winthrop Jr. had a hungry mind and a lust for travel: he had already seen Venice, Amsterdam, and Constantinople. God was now calling him to America.

The younger Winthrop came to New England early in both the region's development and his own. He brought with him his faith, training in science and the law, and connections in English society and business. America was for him like a laboratory awaiting experimentation. He evolved and grew along with New England and, as time went on, exerted his will in the shaping of these English colonies. With one foot in the law and the other in science, with a roving, gregarious nature, a fiery sense of faith, and an eye for business, he became an American Renaissance man.

His fellow colonists came to know the alchemist in their midst and to rely on him as a medical doctor and healer: over the decades he supposedly treated one in every ten Connecticut settlers. He was also a skilled astronomer, who just before his meeting with Nicolls at Gravesend had brought the first telescope into the colonies and would use it a few weeks later to discover the fifth moon of Jupiter. And he would serve as governor of Connecticut for more than seventeen years. The key to understanding this New Englander who would come to have such a significant impact on the fate of Manhattan Island is to see all of his parts as interwoven. If you were a man of science who equated the study of nature with the study of God, for example, how would you react to a group of educated fellow New Englanders asserting that a certain hill in Maine had suddenly "leapt" into the air and deposited itself upside down in a river? Winthrop studied the evidence for the phenomenon (a landslide, according to later writers), ruminated on "natural causes," then concluded that as far as he was concerned, "The power of His Allmighty Arm is herein manifest to all."

Scholars of American history once chose to set the entire story of colonial New England within the frame of "freedom." In this reading the struggles against the Stuart kings of the 1600s set the course for the valiant war of independence of the colonists a century later against the Hanover king, George III. New England's early days, however, can just as readily, and perhaps more honestly, be seen through the lens of Christian hypocrisy: as a story of the murder and subjugation of Native Americans followed by endless factional strife—a story of bickering, backstabbing, recrimination, fulmination, excommunication, banishing, and decamping, followed by boundary disputes and more bickering. Throughout the 1600s every clash in the region, it seems, boiled down to differences in religious practices. There was a simple reason for this. New England, with its rolling green hills and sweetly flowing rivers, was in the eyes of the Puritans who sailed from England to the New World supposed to be the new Promised Land, yet Massachusetts Bay held the key to it. It alone had a

charter from the king, and its leaders wielded it as a scepter. The
colony set the laws, demanded obedience to its rulers, minted its
own coin, shielded itself from meddling by the mother country,
and decreed that only those who were members of its church and
followed its interpretation of the Bible would have a say in how
things were done.

Since most who made the voyage from England did so for
religious reasons, they arrived with strong theological opinions
of their own, which inevitably led to disagreements. Doctrinal
clashes with the mullahs of Massachusetts Bay begat splin-
ter colonies. Some—Connecticut, New Hampshire—would in
the fullness of time become American states. Others—Exeter,
Merrymount, Plymouth, Portsmouth, Providence, New Haven,
Warwick, Newport, New London—would be swallowed up or
would die out. The Puritans of Boston, in their insistence on hege-
mony, bullied everyone, breakaway English colonies and local
tribes alike. Besides nearly exterminating the Pequot and stealing their land, they extorted the other major tribes of the region,
forcing the Narragansett and Mohegan to pay tribute in the form
of wampum, and used the leverage to gain control over the tribes'
fur trade and lands.

In 1645, John Winthrop Jr. had the temerity to leave the home
colony and start a settlement of his own. In doing so he positioned himself in the middle of the political crisis that was then
engulfing New England. Winthrop had become intrigued by the
possibilities—both scientific and financial—of extracting metals
from the New England soil. On learning that a mine in Connecticut
contained traces of silver, he engaged speculators and alchemists
in England to back him in founding a colony around it. The name
he gave his settlement—New London—signaled his grandiose
expectations for it.

Winthrop's settlement irked many of his fellow New
Englanders, among them, it seems, his father. One source of
mistrust was his practice of alchemy, which a faction of hard-

line Puritans seemed to view as dabbling in the diabolical. In addition, alchemists were known to be dangerously tolerant. Winthrop had recruited some fellow alchemists from England to come to the New World, men who like him professed a degree of toleration of other Christian sects. When they experienced the Massachusetts Colony's repression, one of them, Robert Child, spoke out, formally demanding the same rights that they enjoyed in England, such as the right to vote. This moderate alchemist was fined 200 pounds and thrown in prison. When he got out, he fled back across the Atlantic. The case reverberated around New England and damaged Winthrop's reputation.

Another problem was that Winthrop had purposely situated his colony right next to a Pequot village and involved the Pequot intimately in its community. The anger this engendered may have had something to do with shame: since 1637, when New Englanders, led by John Endecott in Boston, had decimated the Pequot in war, most of the remaining members of the tribe had become slaves of the Puritans, who also confiscated their lands. Winthrop's father, in his famous "city on a hill" sermon, had humbly instructed his followers that their duty was "to love mercy, to walk humbly with our God." By proposing to treat the survivors of the massacre more or less as equals, Winthrop Jr. seemed to be underscoring the breathtaking failure to live up to that dictum and to be offering an indictment of the power arrangement by which Boston's leaders enriched themselves. Winthrop's closeness with the Pequot village also unsettled people because of a prevailing Puritan belief that the Native Americans were physically inferior to Europeans—witness the ease with which smallpox had swept through their settlements—and that proximity to them could expose the English to disease.

Other tribes, too, were roiled by Winthrop's move. Shortly after his settlers began arriving and setting up rough homesteads, aided by the local Pequots, three hundred Mohegans descended on the place with war whoops and flying arrows. They didn't kill, but slashed the Pequots' wigwams to pieces, stripped people naked and drove them into the river, and broke into homes and stole valuables.

The raid was meant to terrorize, and it did. Winthrop, who had been in Boston at the time, had thought he had a handle on tribal politics. When he got back and surveyed the damage, he reported the matter to a newly formed commission, the United Colonies of New England, looking to that body to make things right. A hearing was held, but to Winthrop's shock the commissioners—all Englishmen, of course, and fellow Puritans—sided with the Mohegan and against Winthrop. They expressed sympathy for the Mohegan position—that Winthrop, in befriending the Pequot, had usurped the right of the Mohegan to control the vanquished people as their tributaries—and ruled that the Connecticut colony should take over jurisdiction of New London.

Nevertheless, Winthrop persisted in his political ambitions. He had charisma and shimmering intelligence; his self-confidence seemed unshakable. And for all his other tendencies and inclinations, he was a born politician. He spoke with authority, and people wanted to follow him. His bedside manner as a physician likely healed more people than did his potions (e.g., "powder of sea-horse pissle"); likewise, his political savvy mended fences. In time, most of his enemies came around. In 1655 the Connecticut and New Haven colonies began competing for him, making offers to lure him to join them. He made his choice, and in 1657 he was elected the governor of Connecticut, its leaders having swung from openly distrusting him to believing their fortunes could best be advanced by giving him the reins of power.

Winthrop was as ardent in his faith as any of his fellow Puritans, but in his tenure as chief magistrate he strove to

John Winthrop Jr., alchemist, medical doctor, governor of Connecticut, and a central player in the negotiations that determined the fate of Manhattan Island, shown here at about age twenty-nine.

restrain the excesses of the sect. Example: Connecticut was hit with witchcraft paranoia decades before the infamous Salem witch trials. Thirty-four people were tried as witches in New England between 1647 and 1663; in Connecticut a total of fifteen were found guilty and put to death. Walter Woodward, in *Prospero's America*, his biography of this mercurial figure, notes that in all four of the cases that came up in Connecticut during Winthrop's tenure as chief magistrate of the colony, the accused was exonerated. Winthrop did not achieve this feat by wielding reason over superstition, however. He believed in magic and witchcraft, but he thought these ideas were misunderstood by the masses; a sophisticated awareness of the occult, he reasoned, showed that the accused in these cases had not wrought evil. Precisely because of his own perceived mastery of the dark arts, because he was seen as a kind of Christian magus, the population supported his verdicts and went along with his push to raise the bar on finding evidence of the Evil One operating through humans. Thanks to Winthrop, witchcraft as a criminal charge all but died out in Connecticut.

Winthrop's tenure as governor proceeded relatively smoothly until May 29, 1660, when, on the other side of the Atlantic, Charles Stuart rode in procession across London Bridge and brought his whinnying steed to a stop before the Banqueting House—the very spot where, eleven years before, his father had been executed—and there, amid the undulating cheers from a vast crowd, extended one long and elegant hand downward so that one by one the members of Parliament, many of them former enemies who had sought his death, could kneel and kiss it.

With the return of the Stuart name to the throne of England, Winthrop's political situation—and that of all of New England—became a puzzle in desperate need of a solution. In the decades since the first settlers had arrived, New England had become intimately associated with Puritanism, and the Puritans' main enemies had long been the Stuarts. That remained the case in the colonies even after Parliament, with the blessing of the new king, passed the Act of Oblivion, which pardoned all who had fought against the royals during the civil wars. This was a genuine olive branch, which the New Englanders all but trampled on. An exception to the Act of Oblivion had been made for those "who gave Judgement and assisted in the said horrid and detestable murther of our said late Soveraigne." They were to receive the death penalty. The two runaway regicides who turned up in Massachusetts were not arrested for their crime but "were entertained by the magistrates with great solemnity, and feasted in every place," as

Nicolls and his fellow commissioners later reported. In defending the decision not to turn the men over, the magistrates of Boston argued that their colony's charter gave them the power to make their own decision in such matters.

The harboring of regicides was representative of the position of New England as a whole in this new era. In England people had spent the previous couple of years getting used to the idea of a return to monarchy. Puritan ministers who had previously fulminated against the corrupt ways of the Church of England and the Stuarts had rewritten their sermons as political power had begun to shift and become more nuanced. Life, after all, was complicated. But in the relentlessly plain meetinghouses of New England, unadorned even by crosses, religion—and politics—continued to be viewed as black and white.

The extra complication for Winthrop and for the governors of the other New England colonies besides Massachusetts Bay lay in the fact that Boston was the only one that possessed a royal charter—which meant it was the only New England colony with legitimacy. A scramble thus ensued. Suddenly, people were cobbling together old paperwork—bits of parchment adorned with signatures and marks made by Native people; anything, really, with a wax seal pressed onto it—and preparing arguments that they, too, deserved a colonial charter. And at the same time, they attempted to maintain their Puritan bona fides—to keep the monarchy at arm's length. It was a complicated dance they were trying to execute.

Winthrop made a simpler calculation than others did. He embraced reality. No sooner did the news from London reach Hartford than he penned an extravagant and obsequious letter to his "Most Dread Soveraigne." Though "seperated by soe vast an Ocean," he hastened to hail "soe great a Monarch" as "the glory of ye whole earth" and "to prostrate ourselves by an humble Address at our soveraigne Princes feet." He took pains to describe for His

Majesty the great work being done by his subjects who resided along "ye great faire River of Conecticut."

Meanwhile, Winthrop's successes as governor had fed his ego, with the result that his political ambitions had swelled since the days he had launched his New London settlement. While John Endecott and the leaders of Massachusetts Bay were wringing their hands as they tried to figure out how to do the least to appease the new king and still ensure that they might continue their autonomous rule, Winthrop saw almost at once that the return of monarchy provided him with an opportunity.

So he acted. He would travel to London himself to state his case for a Connecticut charter. While he was working with the other leaders of his colony to prepare, he found himself importuned by William Leete, the governor of the neighboring colony of New Haven. Leete wanted him to represent his colony as well at court: as Leete put it to one of his colleagues, he hoped Winthrop would "cast the skirt of his garment over us." Winthrop—who by this time had a plan in mind to swallow up the neighboring colony—led the man on, assuring Leete before he set sail that he "may be pleased to command me what your occasions require." But when Leete traveled to the town of Guilford to hand Winthrop the documents in support of his colony, Winthrop's vessel had already sailed. Leete hurried to New Haven, the next port of call, but again no Winthrop. Then to New London, and finally Saybrook, chasing through all the main ports of the region to no avail. Leete could do nothing more than write Winthrop expressing his annoyance, muttering, "I was wholly disappointed."

Winthrop gave the man the slip—in much the way he was outmaneuvering all of his fellow New England leaders—and was on his way, full of audacious hope and ideas for how he could paint a picture for King Charles that would distinguish Connecticut from its more rabidly Puritanical neighbors.

He was not, however, heading directly to London. Of all places, he was making for New Amsterdam.

Quite possibly the most consequential bit of politicking Winthrop undertook in this journey of ambition was vis-à-vis Peter Stuyvesant. His relationship with Stuyvesant went back to the late 1640s and the early days of the Dutchman's time on Manhattan. Their go-between had been none other than George Baxter, who accompanied Nicolls on his mission to take the Dutch colony and who conducted him to the Gravesend meeting place. At one point—back in 1650, when Winthrop was disgruntled with his New London efforts and before he took the post of governor of Connecticut—Stuyvesant, through Baxter, had tried to woo Winthrop to settle on Manhattan. (Baxter extolled the "privilidges wee inioy under this govermt" and took special pains to note that "Libertie of conscience according to the custome of Holland is graunted vnto all.")

Stuyvesant had had run-ins with the New England colonies, of course, but, politics aside, he rather liked their governors. Or at least he wanted to. His own colony, thanks to that famed "libertie of conscience," contained such a mishmash of peoples that it made it bloody hard for a man to rule. While the Dutch Republic had an official policy of religious tolerance, Stuyvesant himself was more of an old-school bigot, having tried to bar Jews, Quakers, and Lutherans from settling (and being overruled in each case). He admired his colleagues in New England for the purity of their settlements and once complained that his was "peopled by the scrapings of all sorts of nationalities."

But Stuyvesant found the hard-liners in Boston a bit too much; the younger Winthrop was closer to him in sensibility. Winthrop was a godly fellow, a proper, Catholic-hating Protestant, but he knew how to engage on an issue without harping on Scripture at every juncture, how to study real-world situations and search for a practical solution. And while Stuyvesant was hardly a man of science, he found that this business of poking and prodding into the natural world, of which Winthrop was so fond, stirred his interest. He admired and respected Winthrop, and Winthrop seemed to feel much the same about him. Over the years they had developed a friendship of sorts.

Yet Winthrop was an Englishman, and he had heard that the Stuart regime was turning its gaze toward the Dutch province. In his growing ambition Winthrop dared to imagine a colony of Connecticut that would one day extend southward, swelling in size to swallow the Dutch colony whole.

He wrote Stuyvesant in June 1661, asking about the possibility of hitching a ride to Europe on a Dutch vessel. It might be useful to get a look at the Dutch capital to garner some intelligence he might proffer before officials in London. After all, he would be asking the Council for Foreign Plantations for much; it would be smart to have something to offer in return.

Stuyvesant zipped off a reply to Winthrop's request, showing no suspicion at all; he could scarcely have exhibited more eagerness to assist. Yes, he said, there were indeed three Dutch vessels in port at Manhattan preparing to leave for Europe in a convoy: "I did speacke pryvately with the master and marchant of the bigest ship called the Trowe, which I thincke will bee most convenient for your honnor." As a bonus, he added, the master of the *Trouw* spoke good English. Stuyvesant assured Winthrop he would hold all three ships in port to give him time to get to New Amsterdam. He looked forward to Winthrop's visit and signed himself "Your honnors reall friende & servant, P. Stuyvesant."

The welcome of a "reall friende" was extended once Winthrop arrived at New Amsterdam. Stuyvesant blew off 70 pounds of gunpowder—which he might have rued three years later when facing down Nicolls's convoy with a low stockpile—on salutes to the Connecticut governor. He proudly showed his English colleague around town. Stuyvesant had been to Hartford and knew what a rough little outpost it was. New Amsterdam by contrast was a cosmopolitan village, bustling, with gabled houses, laborers hoisting cargo onto ships, the streets crawling with commerce and mischief, people gabbling in a variety of languages, all of it neatly defined by the newly constructed wall at the northern end. The fort was centrally located at the tip of the island, but it was plainly inadequate to defend the place.

Winthrop took note of everything. Then, after receiving yet another saluting flourish of cannon fire from the shore, his vessel left the island and the harbor, heading for Europe.

———

Winthrop spent the next two years in London. He became a regular at Whitehall, where he would likely have first met Richard Nicolls—introduced by a mutual friend—in its twisty corridors, between stints of bowing to the bewigged and ruffled men of power. He joined Samuel Maverick and Thomas Breedon in lining up to petition the Council for Foreign Plantations. If he had been wary of how his petition for a charter would go down, he breathed more easily at the realization that among the members of the council was William Fiennes, aka Viscount Saye. Saye was a wizened, rabbit-faced, slow-moving man of eighty, but Winthrop knew him from thirty years earlier, when as a vigorous and strident Puritan, Saye funded one of the many would-be New England colonies—this one was to be called Saybrook after Saye and his business partner, Robert Greville, Lord Brooke—and hired Winthrop Jr. to set it up. (It was subsequently engulfed by Connecticut.) While a flinty partisan, during the Civil War, Saye had kept a channel open to Charles II in exile, hoping for a way to reconcile the two sides. In putting Saye on the new council, the king and his brother James sent yet another signal of rapprochement to the New Englanders.

Saye turned out to be too ill to attend the council sessions, but he wrote advising Winthrop on how best to move his case forward. Meanwhile, when he was not advocating for his colony, Winthrop threw himself into the work of another organization newly created by the Stuarts. The Royal Society would seem a natural home for the alchemist, and indeed he was admitted as one of its early members. Here, in a stately room ringed with benches that faced a central table with a green cloth covering, he befriended Robert Moray, its first president, whom Richard Nicolls had been close with since their time in The Hague, as well as Robert Boyle, one of the founders of the field of chemistry, for whom Boyle's law is named. He would likely have met Isaac Newton at the society's meetings as well. Winthrop, Boyle, and Moray, along with Samuel Hartlib, another great promoter of scientific inquiry, became close enough that they afterward maintained a lively correspondence, sending one another presents ("I heartily thank you again for ye barrel of Cramburies"), scientific information ("discovery of Minerals & ye Singularities about Salt-Works, & ye Separating the fresh Water from the Salt in a speedy easy way"), and updates on politics.

After many delays Winthrop submitted his petition to the Council for Foreign Plantations on February 12, 1662, explaining that "by reason of the late sad times," his fellow colonists had not previously had the opportunity to request a charter: "May it therefore please his Majesty to confirm to petitioners the like powers, liberties, and privileges to his colony of Connecticut as were formerly granted to the other plantations of New England."

Two weeks later the Privy Council ordered "Mr Mentrope" to attend. Winthrop could easily swallow his pride at having his name mangled because two days after his appearance a warrant was issued to prepare a bill for a royal charter for his colony.

In April, lo and behold, the deal was done. And it was such a deal as could scarcely be believed. Winthrop must have gone dizzy reading the official language. He had thought he was cunning in his suggested wording, proposing a southern boundary that swallowed much of New Netherland and a westward bound-

A depiction of the Royal Society in its early days.

ary that engulfed the New Haven colony. But the king had gone
one better. He had not merely granted Connecticut a charter,
which meant that it was at last an official entity, with a good deal
of independence in how it ran itself and with as firm a status as
Massachusetts Bay; more than that, he had allowed Connecticut
to encompass Long Island, Manhattan, and other parts of New
Netherland and had set its western boundary at "the South Sea."
In the parlance of the day, that meant the Pacific Ocean. In one
go, Charles and his advisers (whose knowledge of North American
geography remained hazy) had turned Connecticut into a conti-
nentwide monstrosity, stretching like a snake across the future
states of Pennsylvania, Ohio, Indiana, Illinois, Iowa, Nebraska,
Wyoming, Utah, Nevada, and California, and turning Winthrop
into—well, the brain of a less pious and humble man might con-
jure up a term like emperor or potentate.

Representatives of New Haven and Rhode Island were also in
London by this point, making their own petitions, and as soon as

they heard about the Connecticut charter, they erupted, protesting that it all but obliterated their grants. After much wrangling the government presented Winthrop with a somewhat altered but still gargantuan parcel (which nevertheless did subsume New Haven, turning it into a mere town). He sailed for home in the spring of 1663, with the precious document snug in his travel chest.

Not long after this, Richard Nicolls was summoned to Whitehall. The outlines of what would become his mission to America began to take shape. In the short time since Winthrop had left London, Edward Hyde, the Earl of Clarendon, had taken it upon himself to try to comprehend the whole jigsaw puzzle of America. He, Charles, and James, no doubt with significant input from George Downing, then decided to rework their whole approach. They would send Richard Nicolls at the head of a royal commission that would attempt to solve their problems with the Dutch of New Netherland and the Puritans of New England in one go. In preparation for this the king made his stupendous land grant to his brother, which included not only New Netherland but a swath of territory wending northward as far as Maine.

The language of the duke's charter was vague enough that no leaders in New England could be sure that their territory had not suddenly been royally swiped from them and gifted to the Duke of York. Back in Hartford, Winthrop first heard rumors, then got more information confirming that the rumors were true. He conferred with leaders of other New England colonies. This was like an earthquake: they were all suddenly on unstable ground. The Puritans of New England had had two fears. One was that King Charles would pull the rug out from under all of them and reorganize New England into one entity under his personal control. The other was that the Duke of York, who was known to be a Roman Catholic in all but name, would become involved, and thus they would become pawns of the devil incarnate: i.e., the pope. Now those two fears seemed to be merging and coming true.

As for Winthrop, the charter he had worked toward for two

years had been amended. As more news arrived, the new shape of his colony was clarified for him. He wouldn't have Long Island or Manhattan—or Nebraska or Wyoming. His territory would no longer cross the American continent. What he was left with was, well, Connecticut. Worse, if things went according to plan, his neighbor to the south would no longer be the Dutch colony, with which, after all, he had forged a working relationship, but rather a swaggering, power-hungry, and quite possibly Catholic royal who would never stand for semi-independent Puritan jurisdictions nearby. The Stuarts were upsetting the political geography of North America like spoiled children upending the board of a game they were determined to win at all costs. What could he do?

What, finally, *would* John Winthrop do? That was the question occupying Richard Nicolls's mind as he sat across from Winthrop in Gravesend. It had been a year since they had last seen each other in London. Then, Winthrop had been on fire with all he had attained. This was a different man before him now—but how different? Was he still the realist, the gentleman scientist, whom Nicolls had gotten to know in London? Or had the government's new plan, including the drastic trimming of the ambitious leader's continent-sized colony, sent him back into the Puritan camp? Was he going to play cat and mouse with the government of His Majesty, Charles II, as the Bostonians seemed determined to continue doing? Would he use his newly won charter as a shield that he could hide behind as he allied with Massachusetts Bay and machinated against the monarchy?

In contrast to Robert Holmes, who had moved in on Dutch targets along the West African coast with guns blazing, Nicolls had approached his assignment coolly, starting his investigation of the situation in America while he was still in London. That included getting to know Winthrop there, learning from him about the different varieties of Puritans in New England. Nicolls appreciated that Winthrop, while subscribing to Puritan beliefs, had nevertheless worked adroitly to distance himself from the hard-liners in Boston. How fully Nicolls could rely on him, use him, remained an open question, but the fact that Winthrop was here at Gravesend was promising. Before leaving Boston at the start of his American sojourn, where he had been rebuffed in his request for aid against the Dutch, Nicolls had moved to plan B, composing a letter to Winthrop informing him that "we intend with the first winde to Set Saile for the Manhatoes," and posing a request: "Wee Earnestly desire you to give us your advice and Assistance . . . and that you would meete us on the west end of Long Island."

And here he was.

It's a good bet that the Gravesend meeting took place in a tavern. There were many in the Dutch colony, and official business was typically conducted in them. If so, then near the start of their meeting Nicolls would have placed on the table at which they sat with their glasses of brandy or rhenish wine (alcohol being among the few pleasures the Puritans allowed and indeed indulged in) an envelope on which was written,

For Mr WINTHROP, in New England.

Tearing it open and unfolding the paper, Winthrop discovered the letter was from his acquaintance in London, the Royal Society president, Robert Moray. "MY WORTHY FRIEND," he began:

> It is no small satisfaction to me that My Noble friend Mr. Nicolls hath done me the favor to undertake to deliver you two lines by which I may give you a testimony of the respect I bear you, & engage you in some measure to acquaint me with the conditions of your health, & what other matters you judge will not be unwellcome to me. I owe him much upon many accounts; but

I put a great value upon this favor of his. And I know no better
way how to acquitt myself towards him in this conjuncture then
to intreat you may in all things apply & open your self to him,
as you would do to the most vertuous person you know, if my
strongest conjurations weigh with you. You know him to be a
very worthy person, & may be perswaded of all the good offices
he can do you. This is purely upon the score of kindness that
I give you this trouble. For Hee being trusted so eminently by
his Maijesty in the affaires of these parts, I have not the least
doubt of your respect to him in that regard, or that you will
be wanting in any thing wherein you can be usefull towards
the advancement of His M^ties service. And I dare say he hath
great confidence in your abilities & vertue, & will be glad to put
obligations upon you. But I would be glad that my interposition
might not onely encrease that confidence, but settle between
you such a friendship as, upon further acquaintance, you may
have the same kindness for one another that I pretend to from
either of you. This will be to me such a satisfaction as litle can
be added to it, unless it be the happiness to receive from you
some occasion to make known to you with how much sincerety
& reality I am,
My worthy friend,

Your faithful humble Servant,
R. MORAY

It was Moray who had introduced Winthrop and Nicolls in
London. ("I am not a litle proud that I had some litle hand in your
acquaintance," Moray wrote to Winthrop later.) Moray's friendship with Nicolls predated his acquaintance with Winthrop,
and was deeper. They had been in exile together, had soldiered
together. Before sailing for America, figuring that this moment
would come, Nicolls had asked Moray to assist him in his deal-
ings with Winthrop, and Moray proved very willing to do so,
writing later to Nicolls, "I do much applaud your usage of him."

In imploring Winthrop to look on Nicolls as nothing less than "the most vertuous person you know," Moray was pulling out all the stops in the name of the Stuart cause, which was Nicolls's cause. And it didn't hurt to add that putting himself at the service of the crown would be in the best long-term interest of both Connecticut and Winthrop himself. Moray's message for Winthrop, reduced to its essence, was, Do what Nicolls asks of you; you won't regret it.

Alas, we have no record giving details of the Gravesend meeting. We don't know how Nicolls presented his thoughts about what was to come vis-à-vis the Dutch, how aggressively or cagily he delineated the role he had in mind for Winthrop, or what Winthrop said in response. We only know what happened next.

Chapter 13

THE DELEGATION

———

New Amsterdam, the 29th of August, 1664. By now everyone knew the name of the man in charge of the English squadron in the harbor, and all knew that whatever was going to happen was imminent. Everything was in worried movement: pigs, chickens, children, rearing horses, women big in their blowsy aprons and skirts, men brandishing muskets, spades, pikes, rowboats, wheelbarrows, drums, hammers.

People weren't just confused and afraid; they were crowded and getting hungry. Two weeks earlier Simon Gilde had anchored the *Gideon* and rowed himself, his crew, and 290 sick, bedraggled, and starving Africans ashore. Stuyvesant had been looking forward to this shipment and the expansion of his nascent slave trade, but the timing was terrible. Fortunately, it was summer—the new arrivals could sleep in the courtyard of the fort—but there had been food shortages lately; 290 starving captives added to a population of 1,500 was a huge extra headache.

Stuyvesant dictated directives, and messengers darted out of the fort. Several ran north up the island to the ferry, crossed the East River, then sped off—by means of waiting horses, surely—for

Breuckelen, Maspeth, Boswijck, Midwout, New Amersfoort, and away out to Vlissingen,* the settlements at the western end of Long Island (except for Gravesend, which was under occupation), two, four, six miles distant, with orders: all capable men were to cross to Manhattan to help defend the capital.

Back came the messengers, across the river, down the shore, and sweatily heaving into the fort and Stuyvesant's office again, all with the same answer: that the men of those places "could not leave their villages, wives and children a prey, whilst aiding to defend another place, not knowing what might happen to them from the English."

Stuyvesant did the same with the garrison at Esopus, a hundred miles to the north, sending a vessel upriver with a note informing the officers there of "the very distressed and anxious state" of the capital and opining that if "the principle place" were lost then "the whole country is lost." He therefore ordered that all the soldiers be shipped "immediately to this place." The messenger was ready to fly out the door with the order in hand when Stuyvesant thought of something else and added a postscript: "The Sergeant must be instructed and ordered, to keep a good look-out, while coming down and if an opportunity offers, send ahead a native, to find out, whether any strange vessels are in his way. If he hears of any, he can land his men and come down through the woods or as best as he can."

In the letter Stuyvesant dictated next, to La Montagne, his trusted lieutenant 150 miles to the north at Fort Orange, and the rest of the magistrates there, he adopted a different tone. It seemed a lifetime ago that he had been among them, albeit briefly, attempting to sort out trouble with the Mohawks before getting word of the English ships in the harbor, but in fact it had been little more than a week. "Difficult, on account of my indis-

---

*Brooklyn, Maspeth, Bushwick, Midwood, New Amersfort, and Flushing, to give these communities the names by which they are known today.

position, was my departure from your honors," he began; "more difficult and troublesome were my arrival and return here, on last Monday, on account of the rumors of the four English frigates, one of which showed herself on the following Tuesday in the bar near the *sant punt*. Yesterday, being Thursday, another three joined and together they sailed up until the bend of Nayack [i.e., Gravesend], where they remain at anchor up to the present time." He estimated the strength of the enemy for La Montagne, then added, "You can easily consider in what a frightening and worrisome state we find ourselves, without hope of any relief."

As if the administrator in him couldn't help it, he allowed himself a brief burst of business-speak: "Therefore this serves mainly as a warning for your honors and all friends especially and, among other things, mainly not to send down any beavers or peltries for fear and consideration that they might fall into English hands." Then he got to his real purpose, and interestingly he didn't make it an order but rather framed it as a plea for help: "It is desirable, and even highly necessary that we would be assisted by your honors with some aid in men and powder if there is any hope or means of transporting and bringing them here in time and immediately." He knew that there wasn't any such "hope or means": for one thing, it would take the better part of two weeks for word to get back upriver and any help to come from Fort Orange. He and La Montagne were cut off from one another, each on his own. And there would be no help from Esopus or the nearby villages.

At least he knew what resources he would have to fight with. And he would fight if need be.

And yet Stuyvesant and Nicolls were alike in seeing the destruction of the city as a worst-case outcome. Stuyvesant had expended some effort to learn what he could of the Englishman out there in the harbor. He guessed that Nicolls felt as he did: that the leveling of the city would hurt Nicolls's own cause. If so, that meant Stuyvesant still had moves to play.

Cornelis van Ruyven, his secretary, had some command of the English language. Huddled together, they composed Stuyvesant's first direct communication with the commander of the English fleet. Or rather commanders—for he chose to begin with the diplomatic vagueness of the plural: "Right Honorable Sirs . . ."

―――――――

Eight or so miles to the south, Nicolls, back aboard the *Guinea*, was issuing commands. He completed his blockade of the entrance to the harbor, with men and vessels now occupying both the Long Island and Staten Island sides of the channel. He directed that soldiers ride off to the communities scattered across the western end of Long Island—all those villages to which Stuyvesant had just appealed for aid—with orders. Dutch farmers were to stop sending goods to Manhattan. English residents of the area were to grab pikes and muskets, renounce any allegiance to the Dutch, and join his forces as loyal subjects of Charles II.

A short while later, inhabitants of those towns gathered around their central squares, where the English riders had dismounted and hammered up a piece of paper, and read at the top of it, "A Proclamation to publish the designe of the Commissioners; By his Majesties Command." Below this Nicolls explained his intention—"to expell or reduce to his Majesties obedience, all such Forraigners, as have without his Majesties leave and consent seated themselves amongst any of his Dominions in America"— and warned that the purpose of the proclamation was essentially perfunctory: "to cleare Ourselves from the Charge of all those miseryes, that any way may befall such as live here, and will not acknowledge his Majestie for their Soveraigne, whom God preserve." In other words, I'm only giving you this notice so as to save myself trouble later.

The veteran soldier in Nicolls, who had seen armies inflict horrors on civilian populations, wished to instill a healthy fear in the inhabitants but at the same time to balance this against the promise of humane treatment. Therefore his men tacked up alongside the proclamation a list of "Ordinances to be observed by all Officers and Souldiers." They were calculated to get the attention of a would-be occupied people. In the event of their taking the colony, none of his forces, he declared, "shall blaspheme God, and if any doe, he shall be punished by death." Any soldier who swore or cursed would be fined. None would be allowed to "do violence to the person of any, not in Armes against us whether Christian or Indian." Any English soldier guilty of rape ("ravishing any woman") would "suffer death." Likewise, any of his soldiers who were guilty of plundering locals would "Suffer death for it."

Suddenly Nicolls's shipboard flurry of orders was interrupted. A small boat appeared on the horizon, heading toward them. It had sailed out from New Amsterdam. Nicolls could not see the city, with its red-tiled roofs glinting in the summer sun, but the vessel, its sails full in the warm breeze, must have made for a pretty picture.

As they drew near, Nicolls surely had both George Baxter and Samuel Maverick at his side on the deck of the *Guinea*, whispering into Nicolls's ear, alerting him as to who each of the approaching men were.

The little boat pulled alongside. Amid the unsteady chop and the late summer heat, the newcomers clambered aboard the flagship. Nicolls learned that they formed a cross-section of the local hierarchy. The oldest and longest-residing of them, a ponderous man of the cloth with the equally ponderous name of Johannes Megapolensis, had assisted Stuyvesant from the time of his arrival in the colony and was a stalwart supporter of both the West India Company and the Dutch Reformed Church. He was sixty-one as he stood on the deck of the *Guinea*, but Nicolls would have found himself confronting not so much an aging cleric as a tough and tenacious pioneer who had lived for years far to the north, preaching among the Mohawk, learning their ways.

The Megapolensis family was closely tied to Stuyvesant's administration and his world. The minister's daughter, Hillegond, was married to the man who had penned the letter they now carried, Stuyvesant's secretary Cornelis van Ruyven. And his thirty-year-old son, Samuel Megapolensis, was also of the delegation Stuyvesant had sent. He too was a minister and had a degree in medicine as well.

Also hoisting himself aboard Nicolls's vessel was Johan de Decker, an attorney who had arrived on Manhattan nine years earlier as a supercargo—in charge of the cargo of a vessel. The directors of the company in the home country had recommended him to Stuyvesant as "a young man of sound judgment" who merited "a higher and more powerful position." Stuyvesant made him a member of his council and he had grown in the position.

Maybe the most formidable member of the delegation to the English was Paulus Leendertsz van der Grift. He had come to the colony as a career military officer and ship's captain; jumped quickly into local politics, becoming one of the nine men opposed to Stuyvesant's rule; but eventually, as the two sides in that now long-ago dispute came to an understanding and a new kind of alliance formed, joined Stuyvesant's inner circle. He was currently one of the two *burgemeesters*, or mayors, of New Amsterdam.

So here they stood, on this wooden deck, as on a stage encircled by the arena of the harbor: the bluff and capable Dutchmen who had sailed out to parlay; the Englishman Baxter who had once been one of them, not just an inhabitant of the Dutch colony but a member of its hierarchy; and his fellow Englishman Samuel Maverick, a New Englander of wealth and power who had been in New Amsterdam many times and was well known to all. Now they were squared off. Were angry words of betrayal and recrimination exchanged? Probably not. Nicolls was in charge, his soldiers were everywhere, his ships and their cannons were ranged around them. This wasn't a barroom. It was international diplomacy.

Then again, Baxter for one was a hothead who had been longing to get back at Stuyvesant for tossing him in a jail cell where he stewed for an entire year. There was history between these men: long, tangled, clotted years of shared experiences, social and familial and business. And now that tangle of relationships was to play out at the level of international politics.

Probably one of the Dutch emissaries, whoever had the best command of the vexing syllables of the English language, began by reading aloud Stuyvesant's words, requesting—nay, demanding, sir—to know on behalf of their superior "by what order or pretence" this English vessel had sailed into their jurisdiction "without giving any notice to us." Nicolls was further informed that his appearance in the harbor, not to mention his belligerent actions, "hath caused much admiration in us"—"admiration" in the seventeenth century meaning something like "astonishment." They could as well have added "confusion" or "consternation," for England and the Dutch Republic were not presently at war with one another. An aggressive act on Nicolls's part would have colossal impact, reverberating across the Atlantic. Then they got to the point, demanding to know "the occasion of your arrival here."

We might suppose that a decorous series of stiff bows and salutes accompanied the flourish of concluding pleasantries: "well wishes to your health . . . to pray that you may be blessed in eternity." Following which, the missive they carried was handed to Nicolls to be read carefully:

Right Honorable Sirs.
Whereas Wee have received Intelligence that about 3 dayes since, there arrived an English man of Warr, or Friggott in the Bay of the North-River belonging to the new Netherlands, and since that, three more are arrived, by what Order, or pretence, is yet unknowne to us, and having received various reports, concerning their arrivall, upon this Coast, and not being apt to entertain any thing of prejudice intended against us, Have by Order of the Commander in Chief of the new Netherlands

thought it convenient and requisite, to send the Worshipfull the
Bearers hereof, (that is to say), The Worshipfull John Decker,
one of the Chiefe Councill, The reverend John Megapolensis
Minister, Paule Leender vandergrift, Major of this Towne,
and have Joyned with them, Mr. Sam Megapolensis, Doctor
in Physick, whom by these presents I have appointed and
thus Ordered, that with the utmost respect and civillity, they
doe desire and entreate of the Commander in Chiefe, of the
aforesaid men of Warr, or Friggotts, the intent and meaning
of their approach, and continuing in the Harbour of Nayac,
without giving any notice to us, or first acquainting us with
their designe, which Action hath caused much admiration in
us, having not received any timely knowledge of the same,
which in respect to the Government of the place, they ought,
and were obliged to have done; Werefore upon the consideracon
aforesaid, It is desired and intreated from the Generall of the
aforesaid men of Warr or Friggots, as alsoe from Our before
deputed Agents, whom we desire your Honors civilly to treat,
and to give and render to them the occasion of your arrivall
here, upon this Coast, and you will give an opportunity (that
after Our hearty Salutes, and well wishes of your health) to
pray that you may bee blessed in eternity, and alwayes remaine,
Right Honorable Sirs,

Your Honors affect. Friend and servant,

P. Stuyvissant

By Order and appointment of the Governor and
Commander in chiefe of the Councill of the N: Netherlands.
Dated in Fort A in
New Netherlands the 19/29th
August 1664.   COR. RUYVEN, Secret.

Up to this point, Richard Nicolls's actions were those of a
soldier carrying out orders. He was methodical: in his voyage, in
the visit to Boston and the warning he gave to the officials there

as he delivered the king's message, in his preparations here in the harbor.

But here we see a shift. Nicolls may have been caught off guard by this preemptive diplomatic strike. Stuyvesant had supposedly gone off, away up north. Nicolls may have hoped the capital city would be leaderless and that he could push past whatever caretaker government Stuyvesant had left behind. But here were his emissaries, delivering words on his behalf. The letter contained a clever balance of diplomatic nicety and reproach, informing Nicolls that the English "were obliged to have" shown respect to the Dutch authorities hereabouts. These were bluff, capable men standing before him, who had faced the hardships of a mostly wilderness continent. They seemed fairly fearless.

Nicolls knew that New Amsterdam was a different kind of place than Boston—savvier, more worldly and supple and creative. These weren't Puritan bullies. They were men of finance, and they had built not only lives and wealth here, not only homes, but a way of being—a structure, we might say, for a new kind of society: unusually mixed, connected to other parts of the world, in which individual residents could help finance shipments and earn profits. It was complex, intricate, delicate, and valuable. And they weren't going to simply hand it over to him. Their demeanor and their presence, right down to the edginess in their words, suggested that just around the tip of Long Island the Manhattanites might be ready for him, with cannons loaded. Were they really willing to risk all?

Nicolls had his instructions, but he knew that in terms of how to get the job done, the duke had told him he would "leave it to your skill & dexterity." The next move would be his alone.

Chapter 14

THE EFFUSION OF CHRISTIAN BLOOD

The Dutch gentlemen left the letter with Nicolls, made their bows, and offered their parting salutations. The summer sun set over the Staten Island shore. The *Guinea* rocked in the current. Night fell. A gibbous moon lit the sky.

Nicolls deliberated on Stuyvesant's letter. His instructions from the Duke of York and the Earl of Clarendon were both clear and vague: "A great end of your designe is the possessing Long Island, and reduceing that people to an entyre submission and obedience to us . . . that the Dutch may noe longer ingrosse and exercise that trade which they have wrongfully possessed themselves of." "Long Island" was, again, shorthand for the Dutch colony. What was crystal clear in the order was the objective: "that trade"—the Dutch way of doing business, which dazzled and confounded the English.

Nicolls must have repeatedly cast his eye into the near future, tracing several trajectories. In one, the matter came to open conflict, and he was the loser—through what guile he could not guess, but he had gotten to know the Dutch quite well in his time on the

Continent, including their martial prowess. In this scenario he limped back home, or else to New England, to make repairs and try to salvage what he could of his mission with the Bostonians.

In the other scenario he was victorious and reigned here as the leader of a new English colony, which would actually be owned by the Duke of York, brother to the king. If the victory came through arms, if it were a battle as violent as those of the last war between these two nations, if he employed tactics as merciless as those of his doppelganger on the African coast, Robert Holmes, his chief task in office would be to rebuild this place. But reconstructing houses and wharves would be the least of it. His hope was to take what had been built here. One didn't accomplish such a thing by force. One negotiated, discussed, cajoled, offered inducements. While he knew something of the Dutch in Europe, he was learning that the people of this place had fashioned their own way. Maverick, Winthrop, Baxter—he had been quizzing these men who had experience here. Whatever made it work, he wanted that formula. And it wasn't a formula that could be written down. It existed within the experience of the members of this polyglot community.

He wanted more than anything to effect a peaceful transfer. The age-old irony in such situations was that the only way to obtain a peaceful transfer was to brandish a genuine threat of force. The day after receiving the Dutch emissaries, he began to craft his reply:

Col. Nicolls his Answer and Summons.
To the Honorable the Governor and Chiefe Councell at the Manhatans.
Right worthy Sirs.

I received a letter by some worthy Persons intrusted by you, bearing date the 19/29 August desiring to know the intent

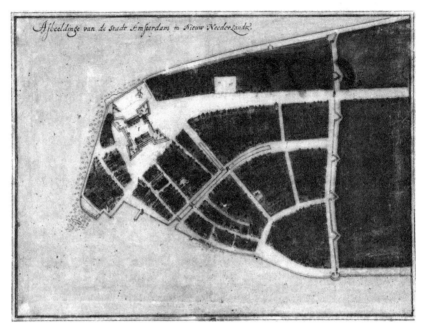

The so-called Castello Plan depicts New Amsterdam just before Nicolls arrived: as a small but thriving entrepôt, or global port, with docks, canals, gardens, and a windmill. About 1,500 people lived in its 300 or so houses.

of the approach of the English Friggotts, in returne of which I thinke it fit to let you know, That his Majestie of Great Britane whose right and Title to these parts of America is unquestionable, well knowing how much it derogates from his Crowne and Dignitie, to Suffer any forraigners, how near soever they be allyed, to usurp a Dominion, and without his Majesties Royall consent, to Inhabit in these, or any other his Majesties Territoryes, hath Commanded me in his name to require a Surrender of all such Forts, Townes, or places of strength, which are now possessed by the Dutch, under your Commands.

Was that plain enough? No. It needed more steel. He added,

And in his Majesties Name, I do demand the Towne, Scituate upon the Island commonly knowne by the Name of Manhatoes with all the Forts there unto belonging, to be rendered unto his Majesties obedience, and Protection into my hands.

He was probably ready at this point to make certain promises, but it wasn't time to lay them on the table. Instead, he would close with only the most modest one. He would let the inhabitants live, even while warning of dire consequences in the event of resistance:

I am further commanded to assure you, and every respective Inhabitant of the Dutch Nation, That his Majestie being tender of the effusion of Christian blood, doth by these presents confirme and Secure to every man his Estate, life, and liberty, who shall readily submitt to his Government, And all those who shall oppose his Majesties gracious intencon, must expect all the miseryes of a War, which they bring upon themselves.

That was it. Enough. Now finish quickly: "I shall expect your Answer by these Gentlemen . . ." He named four men as his emissaries to deliver the letter, including his fellow commissioner George Cartwright and three military captains—Robert Needham, Edward Groves, and Thomas Delavall—noting that he expected them to be treated

with such civillity, as is due to them, and your selves and yours shall receive the same, from
Worthy Sirs

Your very humble Servant
RICH NICOLLS.

Dated on Board his Majesties
Shipp, the Guyny riding before
Nayck, the 20/30 August 1664

There—done. He handed it to Cartwright and the others, and off they went.

———

In New Amsterdam at about the same time, a dozen or more men filled the building formerly known as the City Tavern, now City Hall. Factor in agitation, fear, summer heat, the customary clothing (linen shirts and coarse wool pants), and an enclosed space, and you have to reckon the place must have stunk of them. The windows looked directly onto the East River and the Breuckelen shore opposite. Nicolls had sent a troop of soldiers marching overland from Gravesend to the ferry on the Long Island side. From City Hall the leaders of New Amsterdam could see them massing there.

The assembly included Van der Grift, the ex-soldier who was one of the city's two mayors and who had been with the party delivering Stuyvesant's letter to Nicolls. He was bluff and resolute but normally a rather reticent man. His co-mayor, Cornelis Steenwijck, on the other hand, an active man with hard, intelligent eyes and an angular nose, spoke up regularly in official gatherings, whether as an attorney representing a client, as a merchant defending his business, or in carrying out his office. Also here was Pieter Tonneman, the *schout*, or sheriff, and Isaack Grevenraat and Christoffel Hooghland, New Amsterdam's two aldermen, as well as the men who had held these offices previously, in addition to "some principal burghers and inhabitants of the city."

Van der Grift began by informing the assembly that he and the other representatives had been aboard the *Guinea* and met face to face with Colonel Richard Nicolls, who had told them, in answer to their frank inquiry concerning his intentions, that he had come to "free this place and bring it under the obedience of his Royal Majesty."

We can imagine a deep roar at this: of anger but not of surprise. Van der Grift acknowledged that they were outmanned and outgunned. Nevertheless, he formally proposed that if the English attacked, they should fight back. Steenwijck seconded the motion. Those in the room were together on this. They were afraid, certainly, but committed. The officeholders voted unanimously—to fight.

Outside the building the city was on war footing. Groups of ten to twelve armed, able-bodied male residents of the city, the "burgher guard," made the rounds. Inside the fort, a few minutes' walk from City Hall, Stuyvesant and his council—the provincial council, that is, as opposed to the city council—were carrying on some regular business. They registered the paperwork on the "cargo" that had arrived two weeks earlier: the 290 "*stux Negros*" ("head of Blacks") that were the company's first direct shipment from Africa to New Netherland.

At some point the meeting was disrupted by the appearance of two young soldiers, boys really, who came stumbling into the fort with the news that they had been shot at. They were probably babbling excitedly. However other councilors may have reacted to them, Stuyvesant was instantly and intently interested. He had them enter the council chamber and made Van Ruyven take a formal statement from them. Accordingly, Martinus Haeck, twenty-one, and Hendrick Jansen, nineteen, both sailors on the ship *St. Jacob*, "at anchor before this city, and, at the request of the aforesaid honorable lord director general and council," declared that at about seven o'clock that morning, at the command of their skipper, they rowed to Gowanus Bay together with two of their shipmates. There, they were met by a shallop with six oars—Englishmen from Nicolls's force—who, when they saw that the Dutch sailors were trying to elude them, rowed after. It

was clear to Stuyvesant what was going on: the English were trying to stop communications, to keep New Amsterdam guessing
about his movements. The chase lasted an hour, and when the
men in the shallop saw that the Dutch sailors were pulling away
at last, they fired four shots "that fell in the water at the side of
and behind" their boat. The Dutch sailors made it back to their
ship unharmed. "If requested," Stuyvesant made sure the two
young men stated at the end, "they will confirm everything with
a solemn oath."

Stuyvesant was thinking ahead. He could already imagine
future proceedings—intergovernmental proceedings, perhaps,
between English and Dutch negotiators, or a panel within the West
India Company or the Dutch government at which he was made
to defend his own conduct. The story these sailors told was something of value. He had evidence that the English had fired first.

It must have been about this point that George Cartwright and
the other emissaries that Nicolls had sent appeared with a letter
from Nicolls containing his response to Stuyvesant. Stuyvesant
opened it and didn't like what he read.

———

Nicolls didn't like it either when he saw his little delegation returning to the *Guinea* far too quickly. He must have feared the worst
from this—that Stuyvesant had rebuffed them outright, torn up
his liberal offer, and sent them back with a curt message defying
him to attack.

But no, that wasn't quite it. The message that Cartwright
brought back was one of diplomatic fussiness. Stuyvesant noted
that Nicolls had not signed his letter, rendering it null and void.
To the contents themselves—the threat and offer that Nicolls had
painstakingly crafted—he had nothing to say. It was unofficial. He
was therefore returning it.

We can envision Nicolls emitting some soldierly manifestation of exasperation. This punctiliousness was an indication of the kind of fellow he was dealing with, surely, but he didn't waste time trying to parse it. He signed the original letter, then dashed off another to accompany it:

> These to the Honorable the Governor of the Manhatoes.
> Honored Sir.
> The neglect of Signing this inclosed Letter, when it was first brought to your hands, by Colonell Geo: Cartwright, was an omission which is now amended, and I must attribute the neglect of it at first, to the over hasty zeale I had dispatching my Answer to the Letter I received from you dated 19/29 instant, I have nothing more to add, either in matter of Forme, then [sic] is therein expressed, only that your speedy Answer is necessary to prevent future inconveniences, and will very much obliege.
>
> Your affectionat humble Servant
> RI: NICOLLS.

The crowd at City Hall was swelling. Everyone could see straight across the East River; more and more Englishmen were gathering there in answer to Nicolls's summons. For that matter the ferry was right outside the door: they could see, plain as day, the messengers going back and forth across the East River. They were able to follow as Nicolls's letter, now duly signed, made its way back to the fort. The representatives of the city government then sent a delegation of their own to the fort—following the letter, as it were. These men told Stuyvesant that they were aware of the letter's contents: they knew, they said, that in it Nicolls "claimed this place and its fortification in the name of his Majesty of England, voluntarily or otherwise by fire and sword, and if the place would be surrendered voluntarily that they would keep life, state and freedom; if not, that they would have to bear all misery and distress that would happen to them." They requested that Stuyvesant give them an "authentic copy" of Nicolls's letter so that they could show the people of the town, who were in a state of great agitation.

Stuyvesant refused.

This stunned them. Until now the Dutch—those who represented the city of New Amsterdam on the one side and Stuyvesant and his council as the authorities of the colony on the other—had been acting more or less in concert. Over the years Stuyvesant, who early in his tenure in the colony had been at odds with the merchants of New Amsterdam, had realized that the future of the city lay in working together. He had become one of them. Now the old, domineering, pigheaded Stuyvesant seemed to be back. A fracture had formed in the Dutch ranks.

The next day was Sunday, so everything came to a halt. People went to church. The service started at nine in the morning and, especially if there was cause for a lengthy sermon, which this situation surely merited, could last two hours. Afterward, there wasn't a whole lot to do: drinking was forbidden on Sundays (though people routinely ignored that law), as were farming, building, hunting, fishing, playing games, riding in boats or wagons, gathering fruit, and trading with the Native people. But you could sit and talk. You could argue with one another.

The leaders of the community debated the situation before them. So did everyone else. I think about Dorothea Angola and Catalina Trico and how they spent that Sunday. Dorothea would likely have ridden southward for services at the church in New Amsterdam, maybe with a wagonful of family members. We might imagine her afterward back at home, sitting with her children and grandchildren and maybe with the families of Pieter Santomee and Anthony Portuguese, who lived on either side of them, looking out on their acreage, discussing what was to come, what they could do, and whether they would lose what they had worked so hard for.

Years earlier Catalina and her husband, Joris, had bought

land across the East River. Just as Dorothea lived among freed Blacks, this was a community of Walloons: people like her. It was called Waalbocht, or Harbor Bend.* If she had decided to stay here through this period, she and her family were now cut off from New Amsterdam by Nicolls's embargo of Manhattan, in which case they too would have hashed things out with their neighbors.

Few in the colony held much love for Stuyvesant—he wasn't that kind of leader—but most knew how hard he had worked over the years to win support from the company and the Dutch government for their community. It was public knowledge that he had appealed repeatedly to Amsterdam for help—in dealing with the English to the north and with the Esopus people upriver—only to be told to figure it out himself. In fact, not long before, the directors had informed him he should make do with even fewer soldiers so that the colony would not be such a drain on the West India Company. If the company couldn't be bothered to protect them, where did that leave the people of New Amsterdam?

The Sunday deliberations gave Stuyvesant much to think about. When Monday came, he needed more time. He and Van Ruyven sat down and crafted a short note to Nicolls:

Sir

Even now we received yours of the 20/30 August by your Deputyes Capt. Willm Hill, Robert Needham, and Matthias Nicolls, concerning which (if it please God) we shall fully Answer you to morrow, mean time we Salute you, and commend you to the Proteccon of God.

Stuyvesant next met up with Simon Cornelisz Gilde, the skipper of the *Gideon*, the vessel that had brought the large shipment of Africans into port. Having studied both the tides and the situation vis-à-vis the English, Gilde had concluded that he should set sail at

---

* Today both the neighborhood and the bay it sits on are called Wallabout.

once, heading for Europe, departing New Amsterdam along a tricky course that would take him up the East River and through Long Island Sound. Stuyvesant handed him a letter, sealed with wax and addressed to the "Honorable, Wise, Prudent, and Very Discreet" directors of the West India Company in Amsterdam. Outwardly to his own "subjects" here in the city he remained steadfast and defiant, but to his bosses in the home country his analysis revealed another side of his thinking, which showed that he had spent the Sabbath canvassing the inhabitants of the town for their feelings:

> As the bearer of this, Simon Cornelisz Gilde, has just informed us that he intends to quietly go through the Hellegadt the coming night, along the East River through to thus escape the approaching violence and attack of the English frigates that arrived 5 or 6 days ago on this North River, these few lines must just serve as information of our very dangerous and troublesome situation. . . . Long Island is gone and lost. This capital was summoned and claimed last Saturday and again today. Lack of soldiers, ammunition of war and provisions, added to which is the despondency of the citizens, who are completely without expectation and hope of any help, and in fear that, if they would offer resistance and were attacked by the threatening English, who daily receive much help from New England, they would, together with their possessions also lose their lives, wives, and children—it is clear from all circumstances that this place will not resist long.

Throughout these tense days, Stuyvesant seems to have gone back and forth in his thinking about the steps he would take. He was trying to defend a decision that he was afraid he would have to make: to surrender the colony. He went on to talk about the disheartening discovery that most of the gunpowder supply in the fort was spoiled. He speculated that in the event of a fight the outcome would be "total ruin and loss."

Gerhard ter Borch the Younger, *Guardroom Interior with Soldiers Smoking and Playing Cards*, circa 1640. West India Company soldiers had to bide their time while Stuyvesant and Nicolls maneuvered.

But if he was signaling that he would surrender, he was also looking ahead and laying out next steps, imploring Amsterdam to send reinforcements, which "needs to happen with a sufficient force of soldiers and ships within 6, 7, or 8 months or otherwise it is to be feared, and it will also follow, that in a short time they will get the country so full with people and occupy it with strongholds that after tarrying long there will be little hope to win it back unless with a great force, unless accommodation and boundary settlement could be realized with the king."

The letter was never sent. Nicolls fielded more men along the East River. Stuyvesant, seeing this, ordered Captain Gilde to remain in port rather than risk trying to slip past them.

Before long the delegation from the city council appeared at the fort to restate the demand they had made on Saturday, that they be given a copy of Nicolls's letter. With them came four men who had been chosen by the residents of the town who were gathered at City Hall. Stuyvesant gave them the same answer and added a remarkable explanation for why he would not give up the letter: it "would not be taken very well by the principals in the fatherland because the community by receiving and reading the same would lose courage," and as a result he, Stuyvesant, would eventually "be charged with surrendering." Stuyvesant was trying to protect himself from official censure in the home country, and at the same time, he was trying to maintain what little enthusiasm there was among the inhabitants for fighting the English.

The delegation pushed yet again and finally Stuyvesant relented—somewhat. He wouldn't give them an official copy of Nicolls's letter, which would have had potential ramifications in the home country where it could be seen as relinquishing his authority to a lesser body, but he allowed them to make an unofficial one and translate it into Dutch.

But he still didn't like the townspeople getting this news. The men bent over a table while one of them picked up a pen and carefully copied out the letter, then handed the original back to him. Before they left, Stuyvesant warned them of "disasters that might result" from their action.

Chapter 15

WHITE FLAG

———

Stuyvesant owed Nicolls a response. He proposed to write a letter that would be delivered to the *Guinea* by Cornelis van Ruyven and Dr. Megapolensis. The members of the city council, their trust in Stuyvesant shaken, demanded to send their own representatives as well. They selected *burgemeester* Cornelis Steenwijck and former *schout* Jacques Cousseau.

Stuyvesant had to be holding in his mind a range of outcomes. There was the possibility that by feigning news from Europe, he could bluff Nicolls into sailing away. That was unlikely to work, but he would try. If on the other hand Nicolls attacked him outright, he would defend, never mind the odds. He was caught in a vise: surrender and be charged with abandoning his colony or fight and see it all destroyed. But he believed the situation was not black and white, that between the extremes of destruction and capitulation there was the possibility of manipulating words in such a way as to give himself room to maneuver—to try to work out a future for his people and what they had built.

This was a political chess match—a game he relished, though he had not always been especially good at it. He had a tendency to lapse into twisty legalese when he got excited, and he couldn't resist doing so now. "Honorable Sir," he began, and plunged into the arcane matter of territorial claims. He made a point of indicating to Nicolls that the Dutch had laid the foundation for their claim to this portion of the continent with the "purchase of the lands of the Native Princes and owners of the country (though Heathens)." Thirty-eight years after the purchase of Manhattan Island, here he was attempting to put that event into play in international relations.

Regarding Nicolls's claim "that his Majesty hath an indisputable right to all the lands in the north parts of America," Stuyvesant drily observed that this was something "which the Kings of France and Spain will absolutely disallow, as we absolutely do deny." The Dutch government, Stuyvesant went on to say, had granted the territory of New Netherland to the West India Company in 1621 "with as much power, commission and authority, as his said Majesty of England hath given, or can give to any colony in America." And the States General, the governing body in the Dutch Republic, "absolutely declare" the inhabitants of the colony to be under their jurisdiction, whereas "the unsoundness of your first supposition (that the title of his Majesty of Great Britain to these parts of America is indisputable), is as manifest and palpable as the brightness of the sun at noonday."

He then launched into a discourse on the roots of Dutch claims to the North American colony, which rolled on for several long and twisty paragraphs. It's worth noting that when they delivered the letter to Nicolls, Stuyvesant's emissaries didn't just hand it over but read the entire thing aloud, so we can imagine, as the minutes went by, Nicolls, standing on the deck of his ship, leaning or pacing, huffing, staring off, scratching himself, exchanging meaningful gazes with Samuel Maverick and George Baxter. Or maybe Nicolls stood ramrod straight the whole time, stiff with the dignity of his mission, as Stuyvesant's words, the ponderous clauses and subclauses, droned on:

Moreover it is without dispute . . . Touching the second subject
of your letter . . . in the years 1614, 1615, and 1616 . . . Besides
what hath been menconed . . . Consequently . . . it is not
probable . . . under my government . . . And there is less
ground . . . which makes us think it necessary . . .

Eventually the poor fellow who had been tasked with reading
the letter aloud reached its substance. Stuyvesant referenced the
articles of peace that were in effect between the two countries and
declared that because of these, as well as his above-referenced justifications for the Dutch claim, "We cannot imagine . . . that his
said Majestie of Great Brittaine would give a Commission to molest
and endamage" the inhabitants of the Dutch colony. Therefore,
Nicolls's mission was null and void. Essentially, Stuyvesant was
telling Nicolls there had been some mistake and that if he sailed
back home, he would learn this for himself.

He ended with a smart little parry to Nicolls's letter: "Touching
the threats in your Conclusion, we have nothing to Answer, only
that we feare nothing but what God (who is as just, as mercifull)
shall lay upon us." Then he brightly wished the Englishman "all
happynesse and prosperity."

The last words must have hung in the sea air for a spell.
Stuyvesant may have thought he was leaving an opening for the
next round of discussion. Nicolls, however, didn't take it that way.
He had hoped they were proceeding through diplomatic niceties
toward a peaceful outcome, but as he listened to Stuyvesant's
tortured sentences, he came to a different conclusion: that
Stuyvesant was backpedaling.

Nicolls shifted abruptly. He was a soldier. He had orders. It
was time to act.

A rarity for Nicolls: he let his temper take over. He didn't
bother with a written reply but instead barked his response to
the messengers. Stuyvesant's lengthy arguments concerning his
country's rights and claims, he told the four Dutchmen, "did not

enter into the matter." The only part of the letter to which he felt obliged to pay attention, he said, was the conclusion, in which Stuyvesant declared he had no choice but to defend the island. Nicolls's answer, therefore, was that he "must and should take the place, refusing henceforth to permit any parleys." Steenwijck and the other representatives, once they were back in the fort and making their report to Stuyvesant, informed him, presumably with alarm, that Nicolls had "renounced all his previous reasonable offers." They told Stuyvesant that Nicolls's position was that since Stuyvesant was clearly not of a mind to work toward a constructive outcome, he had no choice but "to attack the place by force, declaring himself innocent of the mischiefs and bloodshed."

While the Dutch delegates were still on Nicolls's ship, they had tried to find a way to limit the damage. They told Stuyvesant that they "asked when we would speak with each other again." Nicolls didn't reply. They asked again. They suggested that they should perhaps come back "in a friendly manner" to make a fresh start at negotiations. Nicolls fairly spat at this. They told Stuyvesant that he replied that "it would be a brave messenger who would dare to come aboard his ship to request an agreement when he would be with his ships near the fort." Yet again Megapolensis, Van Ruyven, Steenwijck, and Cousseau tried to talk Nicolls down, asking what he would need in order to avoid bloodshed. Nicolls calmed slightly, replying that "if a white peace flag would be put out of the fort," he would take that into consideration. Otherwise he would attack "at the end of twice twenty-four hours."

Nicolls must have been in a black mood as he made preparations to do what he most assuredly did not want to do. Men from the nearby villages on Long Island, together with the soldiers who had sailed into the harbor with him, were massed on the East River shore with their pikes and their muskets. If he was to invade, he wanted more men. He dictated a warrant to be delivered to the magistrates of the communities farther out on Long Island—Jamaica, Hempstead, Middleborough, and Vlissingen—to raise every able-bodied Englishman to join his army for an attack on the island of Manhattan. To this end he sent two soldiers— John Coe and Elias Watts—on horseback with "liberty to beate their Drums."

He also sent men off to the nearby village of New Utrecht with orders to conscript the wagons of the farmers there. Soldiers loaded them up with arms and ammunition and off they trundled the four or five miles to the Breuckelen ferry, where the growing army stood ready to cross the river.

As the waters of the bay rocked him in his cabin, Nicolls wrote out a formal warrant to Hugh Hyde, captain of the *Guinea*, who was probably standing right there at his side, "to prosecute (with the advice of the Captaines under his Command,) his Majesties Claime and Interest by all wayes, and meanes, as they shall think most expedient for the speedy reducing of the Dutch." This was no trifling formality. It was a necessary and sober step in declaring a hostile act against a foreign power. In effect it could be read by the Dutch government as an act of war, a document with global consequences. The warrant tells us, too, that Nicolls's actions in front of the Dutch representatives hadn't been mere theater. He was genuinely preparing to fight.

The next day, with all preparations for battle taken, Nicolls gave the word, and the convoy made sail. All four frigates weighed anchor and glided through the Narrows and into the Upper Bay. Within an hour or so the sails were visible from New Amsterdam. Likewise, Nicolls and his shipmates could now see plainly the red-tiled roofs of the city, the gables, the walls of the fort, the windmill, and before it the *Gideon* sitting at anchor in the East River.

At Captain Hyde's orders two of the English ships, with cannons trained on the city, anchored just off the tip of the island— within easy sight of Stuyvesant's own house, a high stone structure that stood out prominently on the waterfront. The other two made the most aggressive move yet, brazenly sailing straight by the town and the fort, daring Stuyvesant to take a shot at them. They came to a spot on the west side from which, as Captain Hyde clearly knew in advance, the heart of the little city was fully exposed. One of the inhabitants later wrote home, "They had put all their cannons on one side, having orders and intending, if any resistance were offered, to pour a full broadside into this open place and so take the city by assault giving up every thing to plunder and massacre."

Having provoked his opponent into battle formation, Stuyvesant now determined to adopt the same posture. The town was openly against him in this. A perilous split had formed, with Stuyvesant and the 150 West India Company soldiers at his disposal determined to fight and the townspeople together with most of their leaders opposed. The prominent figures of New Amsterdam—the official magistrates and principal businessmen—tried to talk Stuyvesant out of his course of action, but he pushed them aside.

Two things then happened in rapid succession on the Dutch side. As a protest against Stuyvesant's sudden militaristic turn, the townsmen on drill suddenly stopped their rounds. When the soldiers saw this, they reacted by withdrawing into the fort. Stuyvesant stumped into the courtyard after them. They probably took approving note of the fact that he now had a sword at his belt. One of his advisers, Nicasius de Sille, was at his side. The colony's chief financial officer, who wrote poetry on the side, was seemingly an odd choice for a supportive comrade at arms, but de Sille was indefatigable in his loyalty, and presumably he'd been nearby.

Without bandying words Stuyvesant asked the men how they felt: were they ready to fight for "the fort and the fatherland"? The soldiers let out a unanimous cry of "*Ja!*" Posterity has decided that this showdown was one-sided, that the Dutch couldn't possibly win. But the professional soldiers actually under Stuyvesant's command thought otherwise. They had taken stock of the Englishmen along the Breuckelen shore and weren't impressed. Most of the men Nicolls had summoned locally weren't professional soldiers but farmers carrying whatever weapons they possessed. From Manhattan the Dutch soldiers could easily make them out—their lack of uniforms, their postures, everything indicating amateurs. "Poorly armed . . . and inexperienced" was how two of the Dutch soldiers later summed up the English forces. The same two men avowed the Dutch soldiers' faith in Stuyvesant, saying that, as they stood there arrayed about him in the courtyard, "there were none among all of them who would leave him." Their job was to fight, and they had in him a superior the evidence of whose sacrifice in the line of duty—in the form of his wooden leg—was readily apparent. They would follow him into battle.

Building on the moment, Stuyvesant, emboldened by their energy as they were by his, gave them a *Henry V*–style pre-battle speech, ending with, "I shall precede as a father before his children, and if I fail you, just kick me aside!" De Sille echoed this, and all the warriors cheered.

The next image we get of Stuyvesant, he's standing on the battlements of the fort, his heavy face set, his long wisps of hair whipped by the constant breeze, gazing out at the English vessels with defiance. The cannons sit nearby, manned and ready. One nod from him, one kiss of flame to touchhole, one blast, and it would begin.

In the midst of this sudden escalation, what must have seemed like an apparition appeared on the water: a rowboat, a cluster of men in it, and, praise God, one of them holding aloft a white flag.

John Winthrop Jr. hadn't planned on being part of this particular delegation. He was supposed to be in the background at this stage, kept in readiness for when they reached the negotiating table. Nicolls may have ordered him to climb in at the last minute as tensions flared. It's necessary to unpack the source material here to try to determine what changed the course of events, causing Nicolls—who had insisted it should be the Dutch who proffered a white flag but who had also come of age fighting against extremism and knew the folly of pigheadedness—to try one more time to get his opponent to see reason.

Two other interventions had occurred probably just before this, which at first blush may seem unrelated, but they were surely of a piece. On the one hand we have the father-and-son team of ministers, Johannes and Samuel Megapolensis. Both men climbed up to join Stuyvesant on the ramparts of the fort. Stuyvesant, a West India Company soldier tells us, was now openly itching for a fight, behaving "as if he wanted to go to the gunner to order him to fire." Along with the rest of the townspeople the two ministers saw this as disastrous. Both knew—as of course Stuyvesant did as well, if only he would regain his reason—that a return to negotiations was essential. The people of New Amsterdam must have watched from below en masse as the three men spoke, gestured, harangued.

Meanwhile, a less obvious peace mission slipped past the fort, made for the ferry, and crossed the East River to the English army. A notarial record preserved in the Amsterdam City Archives tells us that some of the soldiers in the courtyard saw a pair of women, Hillegond van Ruyven and Lydia de Meyer, heading off; knew what they were up to; and interacted with them. The exchange was heated. A soldier must have taunted them, calling them weak women and weak townspeople, accusing them of attempting a peace mission while they, the soldiers, were unafraid and ready to fight. Whereupon Hillegond replied sneeringly, "Now the lousy dogs want to fight, now that they've got nothing to lose, and we stand to lose everything we have here."

The quote shows grit, as does her willingness to undertake such a mission in the first place. And we can also surmise that, while it was against Stuyvesant's wishes, the mission had other important backing, for Hillegond was both the daughter of Johannes Megapolensis, who was trying to talk Stuyvesant down, and the wife of Stuyvesant's trusted secretary. The logic of this back-door diplomacy was that, as women, they would not be viewed as either combatants or official representatives.

Suddenly, then, there was plenty going on behind Stuyvesant's back among his most loyal officials. And old man Megapolensis— who had devoted more than two decades of his life to New Netherland and was deeply enough embedded in its dense inter-play of peoples that he was conversant in the Mohawk language— was at the center of this effort. So much so that he committed himself and two of his children to the task.

We don't know who the two women met with once they crossed to Long Island, whether they were taken to Nicolls himself or per-haps met with some of the English residents of the colony, who in turn communicated their message to Nicolls. But while her father and brother were working on Stuyvesant, Hillegond was delivering a crucial message: that the people of New Amsterdam had analyzed the situation and saw that their interest lay not in fighting but in talking.

A leader in battle spends a good amount of time trying to figure out what is going on in the minds of the opponents. Nicolls now knew the Dutch were by no means united: in fact, if these women were to be believed, most of the town wanted to work things out with words. Nicolls decided to trust them.

And so the rowboat appeared. Why a rowboat? Why not send messengers across to Manhattan via the ferry? Nicolls's ships were in position, the men on them with orders to be ready to fire. He himself was on the *Guinea*. He needed to send a signal to them as well as to Stuyvesant. The white flag was meant for both sides.

And why Winthrop? Because he was the trump card, and this was the time to play it. Nicolls knew that Stuyvesant had known Winthrop for fifteen years or more. Stuyvesant was no fool: he understood power and had probably calculated that Winthrop's best move, in terms of furthering the cause of his colony of Connecticut, was to join with Nicolls. But there was also a history between Stuyvesant and Winthrop that had built to friendship over time. The "Your humble servant" salutations in their early letters had elided in recent years to "Your most affectionate friend." Seeing Winthrop's face coming into view as the boat approached the shore gave him pause. Stuyvesant had spent years developing the system on Manhattan together not only with the merchants of New Amsterdam but with men like Winthrop. Winthrop had relationships with many of the city's leaders going back at least a decade. His presence on the water just now was a reminder that the community Stuyvesant oversaw was bigger than New Netherland itself. It depended on its trade network, which extended to the Caribbean and to Europe and included people in the New England colonies. It was only a year earlier that Stuyvesant himself had openly expressed his desire to Winthrop that the Dutch and English colonies could live together in peace, and Winthrop had responded that he hoped there was "the like reall disposition in all the English of this wildernesse" and promised "my best indeavours" to "promote the same."

One might surmise that saying such things then had been an act on Winthrop's part. But Winthrop had seen value in maintaining relations with the Dutch colony despite the testy relations between the home countries. He didn't know which way things would fall, whether the Dutch would find a way to rebuff the Stuarts and keep their North American colony. Besides, Winthrop had had his own extravagant ambitions—which extended all the way to the Pacific Ocean—and pursuing them had meant navigating his little colony between the greater powers of Massachusetts Bay, New Netherland, and the Stuart government in England. When the plan fell apart, when Charles and his advisers decided to drastically trim the boundaries of the colony for which they had granted Winthrop a charter, he may have pondered joining a Puritan confederation led by Boston. Despite paying lip service to the hated Stuart government, the Massachusetts Puritans remained largely independent of the English regime. But Winthrop had never been a dyed-in-the-wool Puritan. He may have shared a native language with the leaders of Boston, but in sensibility he was more naturally allied with the New Amsterdammers. He was a man of science—political and natural—and following his political instincts meant, ultimately, letting himself be guided—and pressured—by Nicolls.

The rowboat came up to the wharf, next to the main warehouse of the West India Company. Hundreds were gathered there now, ranged along the shore from the fort up past the ferry. Winthrop and his five fellow emissaries clambered out of the boat—teetering, leather boots sounding on wooden planks—and, the crowd parting before them, were led a few paces northward to the tavern of Hans Dreper, on the corner looking out over the East River and the canal. Stuyvesant came hustling over from the fort, along with his council members. Steenwijck and Van der Grift, the *burgemeesters*, joined them to complete the ad hoc Dutch delegation.

We can suppose that Hans Dreper quickly supplied all with drink: he was known for being an amiable host. Probably Stuyvesant ordered soldiers to keep the populace out. The meeting began with a polite round of compliments and bows, then everyone made speeches. Nicolls's representatives were all New Englanders: he intended this to be a conclave at which the leaders of the New England colonies strategically threw their weight behind him, showing the Dutch that on the English side Puritans and Royalists were united. Nicolls's representatives told Stuyvesant that they were ready to offer the Dutch fair conditions but that if they couldn't reach an agreement, they would have to excuse themselves "from any mischief that may follow."

Of the six in the English party, the one that really mattered to Stuyvesant was Winthrop. Before the meeting broke up, he

handed Stuyvesant a letter. It had Nicolls's seal on it, meaning its
contents met with his approval, but when Stuyvesant opened it,
he saw that it was written by Winthrop. In it the Connecticut governor made a point of telling Stuyvesant that he had come not of
his own volition but "upon the command of the Right Honorable
Colonell Richard Nicolls, Commander in Cheife of his Majesties
Forces now arrived heere." He then essentially reinstated the
terms that Nicolls had offered Stuyvesant and then withdrawn:
that if his inhabitants submitted to English rule, Nicolls would
allow them to "peaceably enjoy whatever Gods blessing and their
owne honest industry hath furnished them with." He added that
he "thought fitt to give you this freindly advertisement, that I
understand his Majesties command concerning this businesse is
urgent"; that Nicolls had under his command "very considerable
forces, exceedingly well fitted with all necessaries for warre, with
such ingeneeres and other expedients for the forcing the strongest
fortifications"; and in addition had ordered New Englanders to
augment the ranks of his soldiers. "My serious advice therfore to
your selfe & all your people, as my loving neighbours and freinds,"
Winthrop went on, "is this, that you would speedily accept his
Majesties gracious tender" and so prevent "a needlesse warre."

And there was more. Winthrop said that Nicolls was offering
an additional concession—that "any of your freinds in Holland
that will come over hither, shall have free liberty to inhabite &
plant in these parts under his Majesties subjection, and to transport themselves in theire owne country ships." This, he promised
his friend, would mean that he would "find little alteration" in his
circumstances.

This was a remarkable addition indeed. Nicolls was telling
Stuyvesant—telling the whole population of New Netherland—
that not only were they themselves invited to continue conducting business as they had, but their way of life could continue
along the trajectory they had been following.

This new concession may not have been so new. Nicolls

may have been mulling such an offering since London. And as he learned more about what the Dutch had done here, an idea had taken shape—of a kind of joint future, if such a thing could be imagined by both sides, which frankly would be especially difficult given that both knew an English takeover of this Dutch possession would likely touch off another war between their respective countries. At any rate it would be the hint of a solution to the problem facing both men: a blending of two rival European empires on an island tucked into a harbor on the edge of North America. Under English rule but employing Dutch ingenuity.

Stuyvesant didn't read the letter in the tavern but waited until he was back at the fort in his council chamber. There, he declaimed it aloud to both his colonial council and the two *burgemeesters*. The latter left, hustled back to City Hall, and returned a short while later with word that the city council wanted to see the letter. As before, Stuyvesant refused—"for reasons." There was an argument. Tempers and voices rose. These were big, powerful men who had everything on the line, who could easily veer into violence. Steenwijck and Van der Grift became "greatly disgusted and dissatisfied."

Whereupon Stuyvesant tore up Winthrop's letter.

Later, describing the incident for the directors of the West India Company, Stuyvesant suggested that in consultation with his council "it was resolved to destroy the aforesaid letter, in order thereby to prevent its communication." A premeditated fit seems unlikely. Stuyvesant had a history of losing his temper, especially when his authority was challenged. Whether he tore up the letter in a rage or through a deliberate decision, he was clearly feeling undermined by his countrymen at the very time when it was vital to provide a united front. Disloyalty—to the company, the country, to him—drove him to distraction.

What Stuyvesant had been going through over the course of these past several days, what he was still going through, was a struggle regarding loyalty—not just the loyalty of his "subjects" toward him but his own loyalty. Where did it lie? He was duty-bound to serve both the West India Company and the Dutch Republic. He knew perfectly well that as far as his superiors across the Atlantic were concerned, that was all that mattered. That duty required him to defend the place against foreign invasion.

But there was a third entity to which, he was coming to realize, he owed loyalty as well, and that was this city, and by extension the island of Manhattan and the whole of New Netherland, from Beverwijck way up north to the settlements along the Delaware River in the south. Ten thousand people called it home and had participated in building this new kind of community, rangy and exuberant, often ugly in its morality yet undergirded by faith and leavened by the still novel and exotic force called tolerance or toleration. Here, in the New World, where people were just a bit freer and less encumbered by tradition than in the homeland, that combination of forces had fashioned a different kind of system and settlement. This wasn't the Dutch Republic. It was unlike Winthrop's Connecticut. It was a far cry from Boston or Plymouth. What did he—and the other leaders and, for that matter, all the inhabitants—owe to this place? If it was to continue, if this paradoxical kind of city, with its mishmash of peoples, faiths, and languages and its remarkably efficient approach to business could somehow be preserved through all of this, might that be a kind of victory?

Chapter 16

"THE TOWN OF MANHATANS"

<hr />

Negotiation is arguably the oldest human art. Anthropologists say there is evidence extending back two hundred thousand years of people weighing the use of brute force against other factors in attempting to obtain their aims. If either Richard Nicolls or Peter Stuyvesant was looking for a model for how to resolve their conflict, they had a plethora of examples in the recent past. Both men were mindful of what would become one of the most celebrated negotiations in history. The Peace of Westphalia, which was signed in 1648 after the involvement of hundreds of negotiators stretching across the whole of Europe, had simultaneously ended the Eighty Years' War and the Thirty Years' War, ushering in the modern era of sovereign states—i.e., independent entities not beholden to the Catholic Church or the Holy Roman Empire—and shaping the political world right up to the present.

More recently and closer to home, Stuyvesant himself had conducted rather skillful negotiations of his own, with the Esopus to the north of Manhattan for a peace that both sides hoped would last and with the governors of the New England colonies to determine a boundary. In each case he had armed himself with information about his adversaries, knew what their positions were and what each might be willing to compromise on. He learned how the Native people bargained and about the role of gift-giving in their negotiations. He knew a thing or two about pushing forward and stepping back. Harder for him to maintain was the trick of keeping his emotions at bay. Nicolls, meanwhile, had played a role, albeit a minor one, in the stratagems and negotiations that brought the Stuarts back onto the throne of England.

Yet another momentous set of negotiations, which bore directly on the standoff between Nicolls and Stuyvesant, was the one that resulted in the Treaty of Westminster of 1654. That agreement ended what became known as the First Anglo-Dutch War. So complex and deep-seated were the issues that the negotiators had actually begun meeting before the war commenced. Those issues grew out of England's civil war and the beginning of the reign of Oliver Cromwell and included the boundary that Stuyvesant had negotiated with the New England governors, which London refused to endorse. The events unfolding between Nicolls and Stuyvesant would bring that decade of peace to an end.

It may not be a coincidence that so many consequential negotiations were conducted in this period. The Dutch thinker Hugo Grotius had a generation earlier outlined the conditions for when war was justified and when it was not. It was the age of Descartes and Locke, the advent of modern philosophy, the dawn of science, a time when people were championing the use of reason over received wisdom and the divine rights of kings. The seeds planted in this generation would result in the democratic movements of the next century.

Each of these negotiations had far-reaching results. In none of them was the outcome a foregone conclusion. In most, there was a preliminary period in which the parties had to decide whether negotiation was even possible, whether it was in their interest to sit down with the other side. That was what Stuyvesant and Nicolls had been doing up to this point. The two men had been testing one another. Even now Stuyvesant, always a gutsy combatant, pushed to the very brink of violence: he waited the full period of "twice twenty-four hours" before responding to Nicolls. Everyone on both sides of the river must have been in a state of swelling anxiety as the hours went by. Was the lack of a response the message? Was the pugnacious Dutch leader saying, "Bring it on"?

With just an hour left in Nicolls's ultimatum, a team of inter-mediaries left the fort and crossed the river. This time Stuyvesant sent De Decker, Van Ruyven, Steenwijck, and Cousseau out to the *Guinea*.

Yet again, the peroration that was read out to Nicolls began with "the just right and possession" of the Dutch to Manhattan and New Netherland. This time Stuyvesant threw in, as if it might meaningfully scramble the situation, some "News from Holland" that he expected Nicolls to believe had somehow gotten past the English and reached him in the fort: "The King of Great Britain, and my Lords of the Said States, are at this hour agreed upon" the matter of territorial boundaries in North America. With this in mind he hoped that Nicolls might have "given time that we might attend an Answer from our Masters." But, he went on, since the latest word from Nicolls was that he would attack, Stuyvesant was obliged once more to say that if an assault was mounted, he and his soldiers would defend.

Such then, he suggested, was the situation they were faced with. The English would attack; the Dutch would defend. And there would be, Stuyvesant assured his opponent, "a great deale of blood spilt."

But then came that tantalizing, critical, stop-you-in-your-tracks word: *however*. As howevers go, this one altered not only the course of the confrontation but of history itself.

All of this backing and forthing had been, in essence, a pre-lude to negotiation. Through time immemorial, parties have jockeyed thus as they have pondered the same elemental questions. What do I want out of this? What does my opponent want? What happens if we don't negotiate? If we do, can I be sure the agreement will hold?

Nicolls hoped right from the start to move from threats to negotiation. It took Stuyvesant longer to get to the same place, but he was there now. What pushed him finally was the confrontation with his townspeople over the past two days. At the height of the confrontation Stuyvesant had agreed to allow de Sille to reassemble the pieces of Winthrop's letter that Stuyvesant had torn up. When the puzzle was completed, Nicholas Bayard, Stuyvesant's twenty-year-old nephew, copied out the message and translated it from English into Dutch. As Stuyvesant knew it would, it reinforced the New Amsterdammers' determination to negotiate terms. The townspeople then drew up a remonstrance aimed squarely at him. It was a form of democracy in action: the people exerting their will en masse. They implored him to avoid "misery, sorrow, conflagration," not to mention "the dishonor of women" and the "murder of children in their cradles." They diplomatically insisted that he "adjust matters according to the conjuncture of the time" and negotiate based on the terms of the offer that had been made by "so generous a foe." The letter was signed by ninety-three leading inhabitants of New Amsterdam. The second signature in the long list was that of Stuyvesant's own son, Balthazar, who was seventeen.

Some scholars believe that Stuyvesant's bluster during this period was essentially an act, a formal piece of theater to provide cover for himself, to show the leaders in the home country that he had been ready to fight but, faced with a mutiny, had no choice but to back down. But such reasoning requires reading a great deal into the records. While Stuyvesant was certainly aware of the personal and political ramifications, it seems reasonable to let his actions speak to his motivations, at least for the most part. He kept changing his tack based on the circumstances—and, when he couldn't help it, he lost his temper. He wanted more than anything to keep the colony that had been entrusted to him. He saw increasingly that that was not likely. Yet he kept trying until every conceivable option was exhausted. Then, finally, with a pain in his heart, he moved to plan B: if not to keep the place in name, then to keep it in spirit—to preserve what he and others had created here.

However. Whichever of the Dutch officials read the letter aloud to Nicolls as they all stood around on the deck of the *Guinea*—perhaps it was Steenwijck, as the highest ranking among them—coming to that word must have caused a twitch in the features of the listening Englishman:

> However, in regard that we make no doubt, that upon your assault and Our defence, there will be a great deale of blood spilt, and besides, its to be feared, greater difficulty may arise hereafter, Wee have thought fitt to send unto you Mr. John de Decker Councellor of State, Cornelius van Riven, Secretary and Receiver, Cornelius Steenwicke Major and James Cousceau, Sherriffe, to the end of finding some meanes to hinder, and prevent the spilling of innocent blood, which we esteeme (My Lord) not to be your intention, praying you that you will please to appoint a place and hour, and send, or cause your Deputyes to meete there, with full Commission to treat, and seeke out the meanes of a good accommodacon, and in the meane time, to cause all hostillity to cease.

He signed it:

> Your thrice affectionate Friend and Servant.
> P. Stuyvisant.

"To appoint a place and hour"—that was the magical formulation toward which all the threats and counterthreats had been building. Nicolls must have expelled a great sigh of relief at this about-face, this crystal indication that his employment of Winthrop had worked. He wasted no time in replying, positively but with an important caveat:

> You may easily believe, that in respect of greater difficulties which are ready to attend you, I should willingly comply with your proposicon, to appoint Deputyes, place, and time, to treat of a good accomodacon, but unles you had also given me to know, that by such a meeting you doe intend to treat upon Articles of Surrender, I do not See just cause to deferr the pursuance of his Majesties Commands.

Stuyvesant had moved past the stage of feints and delays. He swiftly acknowledged that agreeing on "Articles of Surrender"—"Articles of Transfer" in the eventual Dutch formulation, which had a less military and more businesslike connotation, as if this were a corporate merger—would indeed be the intention of the meeting. Nicolls promptly sent three men to Manhattan, where they conferred with Stuyvesant, Steenwijck, and Van der Grift on procedure.

As the Englishmen rowed back to the *Guinea*, all of New Amsterdam watched and wondered exactly what was transpiring. Suddenly a cannon fired from the fort, probably startling more than a few people in the city. But it was an "honor shot," the first of seven ceremonial blasts signaling an important event.

Stuyvesant called his council into session. Surely what consumed them was the next step in this intricate dance—the negotiations with the English—but the topic is utterly absent from the surviving minutes. Much else that occurred during the next forty-eight hours wasn't written down. This isn't surprising. Throughout history secret negotiations have greased the machinery of international relations. In the twentieth century the Camp David Accords were reached after thirteen days of back-channel talks. During the Cuban Missile Crisis, secret messages were conveyed between the two governments that were officially not speaking to one another by a cast of characters that included a French journalist and the novelist Gabriel García-Márquez.

There are many reasons for such secrecy. Populations might balk if they knew what negotiators were offering. Foreign powers might be riled up to enter the fray. The Treaty of Westminster, which had ushered in the present peace between the English and the Dutch nations, had included a secret clause, negotiated directly by Oliver Cromwell and Dutch leader Johan de Witt, by which the Dutch agreed to bar the four-year-old Prince of Orange, heir to the title of stadtholder, or steward, from playing a future role in politics. Forces in the Dutch Republic were outraged when they eventually learned of the deal, but it got the parties to an agreement that held for ten years.

So no negotiations were recorded in the minutes of this day's council session. Instead, another quietly remarkable piece of business was logged. Eight of the city's African residents—Ascento Angola, Christopher Santome, Peter Petersen Criolie, Anthonie Criolie, Lewis Guinea, Jan Guinea, Solomon Pietersz Criole, and Basje Pietersen—marched into the colonial council chamber. The record refers to them as "half slaves," a term that was occasionally employed in this era before slavery was fully institutionalized, and in this case was a reference to the fact that, though "owned" by the West India Company, the men had been working their way toward freedom. A year earlier they had come before the council to petition for release from servitude, arguing that they had done enough to warrant it, only to be told by Stuyvesant to come back once repairs to the fort were completed. They had also been informed on that earlier occasion that they would have to wait until a shipment of "new Negroes for the Company" had arrived, workers who could replace them. Now they were back, with updates: they had done the requested work on the fort, and the Africans from the *Gideon* were in New Amsterdam. Besides which, they said, they were especially anxious to have their case reviewed in light of the "arrival of the English ships." If new bosses were to take over, they wanted to have something in writing that would prove their status.

The council granted their request. After years in the service of the West India Company, now, at this precarious moment and with a wholly uncertain future, they left the room as free men.

On Saturday, the sixth of September, six Englishmen came ashore on Manhattan. Presumably they met their six Dutch counterparts outside City Hall, then all twelve rode two-and-a-half miles north and dismounted before the country house of Peter Stuyvesant. It was quiet up here, the house perched high on a promontory above the East River, with only Stuyvesant's farmland and the farms of several freed Africans surrounding it. Everyone marched inside. We can imagine them sitting heavily around a table, the clunk of tankards, the staccato of preliminary conversation. In keeping with tradition neither of the two commanders was present.

The English delegation consisted of Robert Carr, George Cartwright, Connecticut magistrate Samuel Willys, Thomas Clarke, John Pinchon, and John Winthrop Jr. Stuyvesant's representatives were Nicholas Varlet, who was Stuyvesant's brother-in-law; Hillegond Van Ruyven's brother Samuel Megapolensis; *burgemeester* Cornelis Steenwijck; former *burgemeester* Oloff Stevensen van Cortlandt; Jacques Cousseau; and Johan de Decker. Many of these men had been part of the various delegations going back and forth between New Amsterdam and the *Guinea*. They had been intimately involved in the ongoing discussion, took part in the behind-the-scenes debates, witnessed the two sides coming to the brink of violence. They knew their respective leaders' minds well and had a sense of the opposing leader.

Up until now Stuyvesant had changed course repeatedly, had

twisted and shifted, tried everything he could to keep charge of the colony he had sworn to defend with his life. He had threatened that he would force Nicolls into military action. But in doing so he would have lost the most valuable of the many things he was trying to protect. In the end he was a Dutchman. Societies have their proclivities, and he and his colleagues were representatives of a culture whose very origins were tied to the value of negotiation and compromise. When, in the Middle Ages, the first Europeans migrated en masse to the waterlogged region now known as the Netherlands, they learned that if they were to make such a forbidding land a home, they would have to band together to build dams and dikes. They created "water boards" to whose authority all would submit; they agreed that every inhabitant would pay a special tax for the upkeep of the infrastructure that kept them dry. A polder is an area of land reclaimed from the sea. The "polder model" is the Dutch term for their characteristic approach to problem-solving: sitting down and talking, talking, talking, until everyone feels that they have gotten at least some of what they wanted.

The polder model shaped Dutch politics in the seventeenth century. The ideal that educated people in the country espoused, *de ware vrijheid* ("true freedom"), referred to a culture of open debate in a republic of rational-minded merchants and traders. Richard Nicolls had learned something of this culture during his stay in The Hague and had deepened his awareness of it as he studied what the Dutch had created on Manhattan. Stuyvesant himself, with his temper, may not have been the likeliest representative of the polder model, but he showed in the end that it was in his nature.

Probably few of those present at Stuyvesant's country house knew Nicolls's own backstory, but his motivations become clear when the trajectory of his life and career is taken into consideration. He had been raised in an era awash in religious terrorism and extremism and in a family that had resisted those forces. Everything we know of him, all of his writings and actions, makes him out as a man of moderation.

Today when we think of the Stuart cause in the English civil wars, it is mostly in terms of the preservation of the institution of the monarchy. Richard Nicolls certainly was loyal to the Stuart brothers throughout his life, but loyalty to the crown was only one element of what English people like him—Royalists—championed. They were fighting for a return to normalcy. They were exhausted by fanaticism, zealotry, fundamentalism. Two generations had grown up in the cross fire of competing religious ideologies, each of which believed its brand of Christian truth was the truth and that all others needed to be fought, persecuted, destroyed.

But if it was an era of religious intolerance, it was also the era of the rise of natural science and political science, when Galileo and Newton, Locke and Hobbes, Descartes and Spinoza and Grotius were puzzling out other pathways to truth, grounded not necessarily on one type of religious faith but on, as Descartes said, the mind and its "good sense." After years of fighting actual battles against religious extremism, Richard Nicolls, in London, had lived in the midst of people like chemist Robert Boyle, the architect and astronomer Christopher Wren, and his friend Robert Moray, first president of the Royal Society; he may well have known Isaac Newton. These were men who penned scientific papers based on observation and reason. Life had taught Nicolls two main lessons: to abhor extremism and to value reason. From everything he had gleaned about it, this little Dutch outpost in the New World was a society grounded on common sense and business.

Thanks to the negotiations that were held over the two days since Stuyvesant's "however" letter, the details of an agreement had been worked out by the time the twelve men sat down at Stuyvesant's bowery.* They had only to put it down on paper and sign the thing.

---

* The Bowery, which refers to a street and neighborhood in Manhattan, is a corruption of the Dutch *boerderij*, or farm.

The document they formulated is so congenial in its terms that it indeed reads more like a corporate merger than a treaty of surrender. It is essentially a bill of rights, which the English guaranteed to the inhabitants. It contained twenty-three articles. The people of the former New Amsterdam were to continue living as "free Denizens and enjoy their Lands, Houses, Goods, Shipps, wheresoever they are within this Country, and dispose of them as they please." More remarkably, the agreement provided "that any people may freely come from the Netherlands, and plant in this Country, and that Dutch Vessells may freely come hither, and any of the Dutch may freely returne home, or send any sort of Merchandize home in Vessells of their owne country." This made it clear that Nicolls wanted not only the island, not only the people of New Amsterdam, but their connections. He wanted these to invigorate the new entity.

The agreement contained protections that the Dutch negotiators had pushed for: "No Dutchmen here, or Dutch Shipp here, shall upon any occasion be prest to serve in Warr, against any Nation whatsoever." And "The Townesmen of the Manhatons shall not have any Souldier quartered upon them."

Religious liberty was a relatively easy point to hash out since the two sides felt the same on the matter: "The Dutch here shall enjoy the liberty of their Consciences, in Divine Worship, and Church Discipline."

Where the negotiators most likely locked horns was on the matter of the political arrangement of the new city. Nicolls had not been given authority to allow the inhabitants to continue governing themselves. But the Dutch pushed hard on this, and Nicolls relented. In fact, though he didn't appreciate it at first, doing so was necessary if he wanted their system to continue. The municipal government that Stuyvesant and the other leaders in New Amsterdam had pushed for a decade earlier was what set the place apart from other colonial outposts. In a wildly dangerous and unstable world, it provided enough stability to encourage merchants and investors to bet on Manhattan.

So Nicolls agreed: "All inferior civill Officers and Magistrates shall continue as now they are," and "the Towne of Manhatans, shall choose Deputyes, and those Deputyes, shall have free Voyces in all Publique affairs, as much as any other Deputyes."

In addition, Stuyvesant won a concession that he had been especially desirous of including: that "if at any time hereafter the King of great Brittaine, and the States of the Netherland doe Agree, that this place and Country, be redelivered into the hands of the said States . . . it shall immediately be done." He had reason to believe that this agreement, however peaceably reached, would lead to war in Europe, and once that war was over, there was every likelihood that Manhattan would become Dutch again.

Together, these articles had a single purpose: to reassure the inhabitants of Manhattan. The message to them was clear. *Don't go anywhere. Stay here. Keep your shops open. Keep the ships coming and going. Nothing will change.*

Over time, of course, things did change, but slowly, incrementally. The remarkable thing about this transfer-of-power document, about the English takeover of Manhattan and the Dutch colony of New Netherland, is that by the time both sides sat down together at Stuyvesant's country property, they wanted much the same thing. What mattered to most of the population of Manhattan was that they be allowed to remain on the island that had become their home, to keep their property and business, and to go about their lives as they had. This was what Nicolls most wanted too. Historians have noted the remarkable concessions Nicolls made, both in the back-and-forth with Stuyvesant during the harbor standoff and in the final surrender negotiations. But what he gave was also in alignment with his objectives. He wanted not only the territory but the society that had developed there. He wanted the secret sauce, and they knew the recipe.

What was in the secret sauce exactly? It involved a new way of

The agreement negotiated in the late summer of 1664 was called Articles of Capitulation or Articles of Surrender in English, but a Dutch broadside used the milder term *overgaen*, meaning "transfer." The Articles were in essence a bill of rights for the people of the former New Netherland.

doing business, which included financial methods that had been pioneered in Amsterdam; the curiously diverse population and its equally diverse trade network; and the political stability to ground it all.

This is why the last years of New Netherland are so relevant and why the documents in the New York State Library translated by Charles Gehring and Janny Venema are so vital. Thanks to the publication of those records, which has unfurled one volume at a time over a period of more than four decades, supplementing and adding detail and perspective to the material published earlier, we can now see New Netherland more or less as its inhabitants saw it and as Richard Nicolls came to see it; we can appreciate why Nicolls wanted to keep it intact. The merchants of New Amsterdam, with Stuyvesant as middleman between them and the West India Company, had devised a newfangled approach to Dutch capitalism, and the results were evident. New Amsterdam had doubled in size in the past decade. The trade on which it had been founded four decades earlier—in furs—continued thanks to the unending demand in Europe, but merchants had also developed a vigorous tobacco industry, which linked to the English in Maryland and Virginia and to Europe. In the years leading up to Nicolls's arrival, in fact, more consistent production coupled with greater demand in Europe had resulted in what Dennis Maika has called a "tobacco frenzy," which would of course go on for centuries. And in recent years these merchants had likewise begun to develop slavery into what would become—thanks in no small part to steps Nicolls would soon take—an elemental part of New York's rise. Surely the groundwork laid by the Dutch with regard to a slave trade was especially appealing to the English, given the work that Nicolls's doppelganger had begun in West Africa. It would have been, for them, part of what made Manhattan so attractive.

Through these documents we can see New Amsterdam as if we were accompanying Richard Nicolls on his first stroll through its streets. Its people were no longer content with the primitive lives of the generation that had founded the colony. They had built solid and elegant homes, outfitted with wainscoting and tongue-and-groove flooring and stocked with silver, crystal, and brandy for entertaining; good-quality paper and ink to write their letters; elegant furniture made by European craftsmen; stockings and lace; thimbles and needles; "French scissors" and "Venetian pearls." Just in the few months preceding Nicolls's appearance, eleven big cargo vessels had arrived from Europe, their holds packed with goods.

From the time he was chosen to lead his mission, Nicolls had been studying the Dutch colony. He had learned from people like George Baxter, Samuel Maverick, and John Winthrop Jr. how it functioned. By the time he sent his delegates to Stuyvesant's bowery, he had a very good sense of its value.

And the leaders of the colony—Stuyvesant, Steenwijck, Megapolensis, and the others—had a sense of what Nicolls's mission was. They knew English politics: they grasped perfectly well the deep philosophical division between the Stuart government and the Puritan governments of New England. They may not have known a great deal about Nicolls's own history, but they understood that he was the Stuart representative and that he was tasked with solving the puzzle of North America, which had two components, one of which involved gaining some kind of mastery over the New England colonies.

And although we are focusing our attention on the two leaders, largely because they are the ones who left the most records behind, we should keep in mind that nearly everyone in New Amsterdam took part in this resolution of the conflict. The residents of the city appreciated what they had created and knew, from years of disappointment, that the West India Company was not going to support it. As Van Ruyven, Stuyvesant's secretary, would later write, the leaders of the colony had appealed to the home country for assistance "not once, nor one year, but for several years and by almost every ship." Everyone in the colony knew that they had built something of value, that the English wanted it, and that their supposed overlords, the West India Company directors, sitting in their headquarters on the Brouwersgracht in Amsterdam, had consistently ignored their appeals for aid, believing to the end that their outposts in the Caribbean and South

America would eventually yield higher profits and therefore that that was where their money should be invested. So the people of New Amsterdam took matters into their own hands.

The standard view that American history has of the English taking of Manhattan distorts this picture by forcing a particular type of Anglocentric frame on it. It probably relates to the fact that many early American historians were themselves descendants of the English Puritans who settled New England. Those pious gentlemen—for they were all men—crafted narratives in which their forefathers were the heroes. This meant lionizing (and sanitizing) the Puritan project in America—indeed, making it synonymous with the American project. And once Nicolls had his victory, it meant relegating the Dutch colony of New Netherland to a dismissive paragraph or two, telling a semicomic story in which cartoonlike Dutchmen muddled around in North America for a few decades, with fat bellies and clay pipes, not sure what to do with the valuable real estate they had somehow landed on, until the English relieved them of it and started New York on its journey. As Dennis Maika has elucidated this misreading, "The story goes like this: New Netherland was a colony in decline when it was rescued by the English in a surprise attack in 1664, its Director-General, Peter Stuyvesant, unable to defend it. The city of New Amsterdam surrendered without a fight, suggesting both resignation to the inevitable and just a hint of Dutch cowardice."

The reality is more complicated and more meaningful for us today. Ultimately, it was Stuyvesant, his councilors, and the people of New Amsterdam together with Nicolls and the other English officials in his squadron who, through the give-and-take of their negotiations in the harbor, crafted the idea of creating a kind of hybrid colony, which would maintain the features of its Dutch predecessor but move forward under the flag of England. Their idea was all the more remarkable because, in Europe, these two nations were enemies on the verge of open warfare. It was remarkable too that this transfer happened without the loss of a single life.

Not everyone was pleased with the outcome. A Dutch minister reported that several of the English soldiers complained to him that they had "come here from England hoping for booty; but that now, since the matter turned out so differently, they desired to return to England." On the other hand, some English residents of New Amsterdam saw the discussions that led to an agreement as a sign that "God had signally overruled matters, that the affair had been arranged by negotiations; else nothing but pillage, bloodshed and general ruin would have followed."

Think ahead to what this mixing of two of Europe's most vibrant colonizing powers would develop into. Think of the energy inherent in this new Anglo-Dutch formulation. Maybe the most remarkable short-term feature of the Articles of Transfer is that it gave New Amsterdam's inhabitants the status of denizens within the English empire. In one stroke they were able to trade within both the burgeoning English and Dutch empires. It set the city on a course of global power.

What transpired in the late summer of 1664 involved the work not only of Stuyvesant and Nicolls but also Hillegond van Ruyven, Lydia de Meyer, Margaret Hardenbroek, Dorothy Angola, and Catalina Trico: the women of the colony who, denied overt political power, worked behind the scenes to bring it about. Other leaders included John Winthrop Jr., who was not an inhabitant of either New Amsterdam or New York. What all of these people had engaged in was both a complex power play and an instance of intellectual puzzle-solving, one that involved European governments and American colonies, but most of all the people of Manhattan themselves.

———

Nicolls stood on the deck of the *Guinea*, perhaps with his arms folded and a feeling of satisfaction spreading inside him, as a small vessel rowed up to the ship. The signed document was brought on board and delivered to him. He approved it, put it together with a copy of his commission and the patent by which the king had granted the territory to his brother, and sent the packet off across the river.

The next day was Sunday. After church service everyone hurried over to City Hall and gathered outside to hear the proclamation read aloud. There were several steps up to the front door of the building; the reader probably stood up there to be seen and heard, with the people gathered below and spread out along the waterfront. It was a moment of catharsis for the inhabitants and a turning point in the development of what they had created. Every one of them knew from experience, better than we do today, that there is no certainty in human affairs, that at any moment plague or shipwreck or a sudden attack could end everything. But now they had a sense that they would continue.

By mutual agreement, at eight o'clock the next morning, Stuyvesant was standing on the Manhattan shore by "the old mill," where he received the packet of documents. He read out another proclamation, which began sweepingly, as if, in looking around at his boisterous, recently anxious, and now cautiously hopeful little community, he was gesturing toward a bright future: "To all People, health!" He asserted formally that "wee the governor Generall and Council of the New Netherlands do consent to the Articles . . . and we have hereby ratified and confirmed them, and do Acknowledge this to be Our Act and deed, and shall do all things therein contained."

Two hours later he led his loyal soldiers, fully armed, out of the fort. The fighting men clambered into boats and rowed out to the *Gideon*, which still lay in the harbor. If the mood among the townspeople was one of relief, the soldiers were still fuming, still itching for a fight. (So uncertain was Captain Gilde of their mood that he had taken the extraordinary step of removing all the gunpowder from the ship's holds and having it sent ashore for safekeeping.)

A short while later Nicolls stepped onto Manhattan Island for the first time. He walked past the West India Company warehouse, the warehouse of *burgemeester* Van der Grift, the house of Cornelis Steenwijck. Turning right, he saw before him Fort Amsterdam. He marched through its gate—beneath the chamber from which Stuyvesant had run the colony for the past seventeen years—at the head of two companies of English soldiers, men who had crossed the ocean with him for this purpose.

The two *burgemeesters* came in and formally pronounced Nicolls their new leader. Officially his title now was deputy governor, the actual governor being the new owner of the province, but James had given him full power so that in fact he would function as governor.

Nicolls announced some changes in nomenclature. The military post would now be called Fort James. As for the city, the Dutch had known it as New Amsterdam for the past thirty-eight years, but that was finished. As recently as two days earlier Nicolls's representatives had referred to it as "the Towne of Manhatans." No one had instructed Nicolls on what to call it, so he decided himself. He later told his royal patron that his idea had been to "comprehend all the titles of your Royal Highness" in naming various parts of the colony. Since James was the Duke of York, the Duke of Albany, and the Earl of Ulster, Nicolls presumably considered New Albany and New Ulster as possibilities for the city. Then he made up his mind. As he later informed James, "I gave . . . to this place, the name of N. Yorke."

He ended up bestowing Albany on the colony's second city, which under the Dutch had been called Beverwijck. There was also some discussion of lending a variation of that title to the area of the mainland across the Hudson River from Manhattan, in which case history would have come to know it as Albania. Eventually, however, they decided on New Jersey.

The Dutch city of New Amsterdam, occupying the southern tip of Manhattan Island, became the English city of New York in 1664. The area grew into the Financial District of New York City, shown here in 2017.

Part Four

THE INVENTION

Chapter 17

REMAINING ENGLISH

---

*T*he previous chapters of this book have been working toward a particular notion: that New York was an invention. The *Encyclopedia Britannica*, to pick one standard source, defines invention as "the act of bringing ideas or objects together in a novel way to create something that did not exist before." That is precisely what the people involved in this saga did. And what did their invention consist of? New York is often thought of as the archetypal modern metropolis. Two features of such a metropolis stand out. It is pluralistic—not made up of one dominant ethnic group but rather built around, and deriving energy from, its diverse population. And it operates on free-market principles, as a laboratory for economic experimentation, providing (theoretically) unbounded opportunity for its inhabitants.

New York came into being not organically but through a purposeful act, which involved the stitching together of two cultures and traditions into something new. The Dutch had developed New Amsterdam to be an entrepôt—a port city with pretensions to global trade. Richard Nicolls, as the representative of relatively tolerant and pragmatic factions within England, came to see that rather than crushing New Amsterdam and starting over, it would be in his interest to make a deal with his Dutch nemesis, one that might benefit both of them. The pluralistic and capitalistic features of New York had their origins in the Dutch colony, and both of those elements of the city were reconfigured and invigorated when the Dutch and English strains merged.

As with, say, the light bulb or the computer, the invention of New York rested on earlier ideas. It required a willful steering of forces in a particular direction, as well as a will on the part of the inhabitants to be steered in the new direction. And, as with the light bulb and the computer, nobody who played a role in the invention of New York could comprehend what it might lead to. In fact, as with many potentially useful inventions that fall by the wayside for lack of nurturing, New York seemed to most of its inhabitants likely to vanish before it was a year old.

Johan de Witt had one of the most brilliant minds of his age. He wrote the first textbook of analytic geometry and devised the first accurate actuarial tables. He was also the Grand Pensionary of Holland, more or less equivalent to Prime Minister of the Dutch Republic. In October 1664 he was busy leading a nation that was in the midst of not only an unprecedented economic boom but a golden age in art and one of the first European experiments with a republican form of government.

De Witt was not the sort of person who shied away from complexity—his mathematical work had been praised by the likes of Isaac Newton—yet even he must have struggled to manage his emotions on this autumn day. The English had been increasingly belligerent toward his country of late. Through the swashbuckling efforts of Robert Holmes, they had attacked and taken Dutch holdings on the West African coast. De Witt was well aware of English jealousy toward his nation and of the increasing yearning for war among those close to the Stuart government. He knew the English were goading him.

De Witt was a careful, methodical man. He did not want war. That was why he was at this moment sitting opposite George Downing, the English ambassador, in the Binnenhof, the castle-like government complex in The Hague. The two statesmen were equally brilliant, yet physical and temperamental opposites: Downing bloated, regal, and with a tendency to pompously display his intellect; the Dutchman fine-boned and with a monk's dourness. Downing was probably anything but diplomatic just now. As the main proponent of the idea that a war with the Dutch would propel England toward empire, he wanted to irk the man.

De Witt likely detested Downing as much as everyone else did, but we can imagine him dispassionate in their discussion, determined to maintain propriety. Then, whatever the point was that De Witt was in the process of making, he was interrupted by an aide handing him a hastily scribbled note. It was from several of the directors of the West India Company. They had traveled to The Hague with alarming news. Apparently, they were at this moment standing outside the meeting room, saw who De Witt was with, and felt he had to be informed at once of developments. De Witt read the note:

> Honorable and Strict Lord, The Directors of the West India Company, granting themselves the honor to come and speak with you and noticing that Your Honor is in conversation with the Lord Downing, considered it necessary to interfere so as to inform you that we have with express letters received the news that New Netherland has been completely conquered by the English on the 7th of August [sic] and that the city of New Amsterdam has been renamed New York.

Perhaps Downing guessed at the note's contents and sneered with satisfaction at the remarkable coincidence that the Dutch leader was receiving it while face to face with the man who had orchestrated the provocation. Maybe De Witt broke his calm demeanor and raged; maybe he kept his cool. We don't know. We do know that the Second Anglo-Dutch War, as it would become known, began formally on March 4, 1665.

Downing's spies in the Netherlands had convinced him and the Stuart government that if England showed enough force, the Dutch would buckle after the first battle of a naval war and ask for terms. For all its vaunted global trading empire, the Dutch military was modest in size. The country's population was only one-sixth of England's. The Dutch had shown the way to empire, but they could be toppled. This, Downing had pressed to his comrades in Whitehall, was the moment for the big push.

It looked at first like Downing was right, that the war would

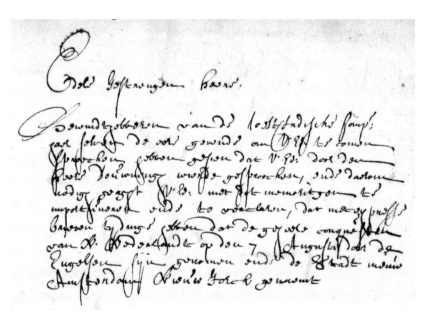

Hastily scribbled note from West India Company directors to Dutch leader Johan de Witt, who was at that moment in a meeting with English ambassador George Downing, informing him that New Netherland had been taken by the English.

be over quickly. In the Battle of Lowestoft, off the coast of Suffolk, the Dutch put everything they had into the water: more than a hundred ships and twenty-one thousand men. And the English fleet crushed them.

But De Witt didn't back down. He too had spies, and those close to Charles's court told him that the English government was bankrupt: goading the Dutch had been in a sense an all-in bluff. De Witt initiated back-channel negotiations with Louis XIV, which resulted in France, England's longtime enemy, coming into the contest on the Dutch side. The war quickly escalated into a transatlantic slugfest, ranging from western Africa to the Caribbean, a furious fight for control of slaving posts and for the dream of future wealth—involving sugar, tobacco, cotton, and salt—that would rely more than ever before on the labor of captive Africans.

Even before the formal start of the war, De Witt sent a message to Michiel de Ruyter, one of the greatest naval leaders of the age, summoning him into action. De Ruyter had fought pirates in the Mediterranean and faced down Spanish and English squadrons in the Caribbean. He was a national hero. But he may have read the orders with a sigh. He had been at sea since he was eleven years old, was famous for the discipline and loyalty he instilled in his men and the zeal with which they performed, but the truth was he didn't like fighting, preferring to be home in Amsterdam tending his garden. Though he kept trying to retire, one Dutch leader after another had called on him, and now De Witt wanted him to undo the actions of the two Englishmen—Nicolls and Holmes—who had caused the Dutch such damage.

De Ruyter dutifully followed orders and made for Africa with a fleet of twelve warships. The first post he attacked was Gorée, retaking it from the English. In the ensuing weeks of bloody battle, rivaling Robert Holmes in its precision and lethality, De Ruyter got back all but one of the forts Holmes had captured. When word reached London, people who had been led to believe the Dutch would succumb quickly were stunned by the efficiency of his attack and the extent of the setback to England's hopes. Samuel Pepys recorded in his diary that among the merchants he met at the Royal Exchange that morning, "I hear fully the news of our being beaten to dirt at Guinny, by De Ruyter with his fleete . . . it being most wholly to the utter ruine of our Royall Company, and reproach and shame to the whole nation."

But De Ruyter wasn't finished. Before the English could begin to plot a countermove, he turned his fleet westward, toward Manhattan.

In the immediate aftermath of the English takeover, life in the former city of New Amsterdam continued much as it had been before. These were late summer days of harvesting crops, feeding animals, guiding wheelbarrows from the dockside, getting bread from the baker, sitting down of an evening with a glass of beer or brandy to reflect on what had just happened. Willem Doeckles and Anneke Ryzens walked up the steps of City Hall and announced their intention to marry. Geleyn Verplanck bought Francis Browne's house. Pieter Claessen denied that he had been in a fight with Herman Meinderson despite the testimony of several eyewitnesses. Albert the Trumpeter—a military bugler— accused Daniel Tourneur of stealing his hog.

Richard Nicolls went to work as governor at once and was methodical from the start. He sent his fellow commissioner Robert Carr with a contingent of soldiers south to take command of the Dutch outpost on the Delaware River and George Cartwright and another contingent north up the Hudson to take Fort Orange from Johannes La Montagne. He put out word that all ship captains in the region were to appear before him in order to report "whence they came, and whither they are bound, together with the Contents of their lading." He stopped all payment of levies to the West India Company.

The steady approach of De Ruyter's fleet hung like a storm cloud over New York's early days. First, ships arriving from Europe brought news that the feared Dutch admiral had taken back the African posts. Then, from London, Nicolls received a frank warning: "De Ruither being sent thither with twelve shippes of warre." Everyone on Manhattan—Dutch, English, African, Native American—could look around and see that Nicolls's rule was upheld by a mere four ships and a few hundred men. What Nicolls and Stuyvesant and their representatives had achieved with their ornate negotiations was about to be undone. It seemed a foregone conclusion that Manhattan was going to become Dutch territory again.

In the midst of the ordinary activity, the members of the city council of the former New Amsterdam, which continued to function as if nothing had happened, decided they had to explain the recent turn of events to the directors of the West India Company in Amsterdam. This involved a tricky bit of positioning. They, along with the other residents of the former Dutch city, having pushed for this outcome, now, as a result of the negotiations, expected to keep their property and maintain their lives as before. With any luck, in other words, this would all work out well for them. Because of that outcome, on the other hand, the West India Company had lost its entire colony. That wouldn't necessarily matter so much to the people of New York, except for the fact that if De Ruyter succeeded, all would revert to Dutch control and the company would be in charge again. It was felt necessary, therefore, that the council should go on the offensive in conveying the story of what had transpired. While appropriately servile, the letter had to cast a measure of blame: "We, your Honors' loyal, sorrowful and desolate subjects, cannot neglect nor keep from relating the event, which thro' God's pleasure thus unexpectedly happened to us in consequence of your Honors' neglect and forgetfulness of your promise—to wit, the arrival here, of late, of four King's frigates from England."

Indeed, the Dutch residents of New York had mixed feelings

as De Ruyter's fleet approached. Some were ebullient. Those who fancied that being connected to England's rising empire would be good for business were dismayed. Others worried that they had escaped one naval onslaught only to be faced with another. Nicolls put men to work renovating the fort, preparing for the coming storm. His new city council met. Thomas Willet, an Englishman whose ties to the Dutch colony went back twenty years, was chosen as the first mayor. The council was a mix of English and Dutch: Cornelis van Ruyven, Stuyvesant's former secretary, was one of its members. Willet noted for those gathered in City Hall that Governor Nicolls had offered to contribute two thousand planks to repair fortifications and was asking all residents to do their part to resist the coming storm. Cornelis Steenwijck replied that he would do whatever was asked of him, making it clear that some of the Dutch were willing to support Nicolls's government. Others were noncommittal or defiant. In trying to sell them on the idea of pitching in, Mayor Willet put forth a novel idea: that the Dutch weren't being asked to fight against their own country but rather to defend their city. It was an interesting argument, suggesting that New York existed somehow on its own, without firm attachment to any nation.

It never got put to the test. De Ruyter didn't make straight for New Netherland. He sailed first to the Caribbean to inflict damage on English possessions there. For all his aversion to war he did whatever was asked of him with single-minded energy, in this case attacking Barbados, Monserrat, Nevis, and Saint Kitts, and in the process capturing more than a dozen English ships and three hundred prisoners.

But his vessels were beaten up in the bloody encounters. On sailing up the North American coast, De Ruyter made a decision that would alter history. He knew by now that war had been declared in Europe and concluded that he was needed there. Rather than slip into the future New York Harbor and subject his battered fleet to another round of fighting, he sailed past it and put into port at Newfoundland to effect repairs, then made for home.

The centerpiece of the two-year bloodbath that was the Second Anglo-Dutch War, the so-called Four Days' Battle, has been jauntily called "the greatest sea fight of the age of sail." In fact, it was an appalling contest, with nearly two hundred ships arrayed in the North Sea in "line of battle" formation, essentially two miles-long columns of vessels traveling in opposite directions, separated by a few yards of blood-dyed water, blasting relentlessly into one another. Thousands were killed. Hundreds of men burned alive as their ships, towers of wood and sailcloth, went up in gigantic plumes of flame and black smoke. When the smoke cleared, the Dutch declared themselves the victors.

Abraham Storck's depiction of the Four Days' Battle, the bloodiest naval encounter of the Second Anglo-Dutch War.

In England people smarted at the loss, but they had other calamities to deal with as well. The first year of the war coincided with the return of the bubonic plague to London, which arrived with unimaginable intensity. By the time it subsided the next year, an estimated one hundred thousand people had died. At virtually the same time, in September 1666, the Great Fire of London rampaged through the English capital, destroying more than thirteen thousand houses in four days.

But Charles and James kept throwing everything they had at the Dutch. Downing pulled every lever he could think of, including trying to engineer a coup against De Witt. Just weeks before London burned, James sent Robert Holmes back into action, on a daring raid into the northern estuary of the Netherlands where the Dutch fleet anchored. Holmes caught them off guard and burned 140 ships and a small village to boot.

The Dutch pounded back. De Ruyter's fleet yet again countered a move of Holmes's, conducting a raid on English warships that were laid up in and around the Medway River in southeastern England, setting them afire, capturing the royal flagship, humiliating King Charles, and at last forcing England to negotiate terms.

People on Manhattan, English and Dutch alike, awaited the results of the Treaty of Breda, the agreement by which the war was officially ended, with the same expectation: that the victors would demand the return of their possessions. But the envoys sent to Breda didn't see it that way. The Dutch had the upper hand in the negotiations, and they used their advantage to press England on what mattered most to their economy: curtailing its Navigation Acts, which had been aimed at restricting Dutch trade. Once they achieved that, the Dutch negotiators were willing to allow *uti possidetis*—a principle of international law by which both sides would keep what they had gained in war—to apply to the agreement. The Dutch would maintain control over the spice-rich island of Pulau Run in the East Indies and Surinam in South America, which was making money from its sugar plantations.

And New York would keep its English name and affiliation. For the Dutch rulers, the East Indies, the greatest source of national wealth, remained their focus. New Netherland was profitable for the private firms that invested in it from bases on Manhattan and elsewhere, but from the vantage point of the nation's leaders it had been decades of bother. James's advisers, meanwhile, wanted to keep Manhattan and the rest of what had been the Dutch colony, which was crucial to their long-term strategy of countering the Puritans in New England and creating one contiguous stretch of North American colonies.

New Yorkers were stunned when the news reached them. Some were pleased, feeling that at last their new city could look

The 1667 Treaty of Breda is often mischaracterized as the occasion of a fateful and lopsided "swap" of territories: England getting New York and the Dutch the tiny island of Run in the East Indies. In fact, as this engraving suggests, the negotiations to end the Second Anglo-Dutch War were vast and complex, involving dozens of negotiators and territories around the globe.

toward the future without this uncertainty hanging over it. A leading Dutch resident of the colony—Jeremias van Rensselaer, the son of one of the founders of the West India Company—expressed what was probably a general feeling when he wrote to his mother in the home country that "we did not have the least idea here that the country would remain English."

But Van Rensselaer wasn't one of those who looked forward to a free-trading future as part of the rising English empire. The Dutch people where he lived, far up the Hudson River, in and around the city that the English had renamed Albany, were more conservative and inward-looking than the cosmopolitans on Manhattan. Up here they had hoped for a return to the old ways. In writing to his mother, Van Rensselaer rued the fact that he had just built a new house, suggesting that he might decide to return to Europe rather than live as a New Yorker. But in the same letter he insinuated that when all was said and done he would likely remain, as indeed most of the residents would do. "Now," he added peevishly, "it seems that it has pleased the Lord that we must learn English."

Chapter 18

MERGER

———

*A*t just eighteen years of age Richard Nicolls had made the difficult decision to break with most of the population of his hometown and county and side with England's monarchy in what became a horrific civil war. He had personal reasons for doing so: his family had been intimate with the royal family since he was born. But being a Royalist wasn't only about supporting a king. Like others, Nicolls deplored the proliferation of restrictive religious sects. He became a lifelong advocate of toleration.

Nicolls was also connected to the founders of the Royal Society, people who believed in the primacy of reason and in what we would call science. By the time he sailed to North America to try to take Manhattan, everything in his past had established him as a conduit for these forces. He opposed the Puritan rule in Massachusetts not only because those leaders defied the Stuart government but on principle. In the confrontation with the Dutch on Manhattan, meanwhile, he found enough common ground to hash out an agreement that would allow features of the system they had created to remain in place. He promised to merge the pragmatic tradition in English culture with the similar tradition that he found in New Netherland.

Once Nicolls was in charge of New York, two questions presented themselves. Would he indeed lead the population toward that merger? And would the inhabitants of Manhattan Island do their part to make the merger work?

Things didn't seem promising at first. A month after the takeover Nicolls asked the leaders of the city to gather in order to swear an oath of allegiance to the government of King Charles. Nicolls considered this the fulfillment of their side of the bargain. He had given them, in the Articles of Transfer, a guarantee of their rights. He expected loyalty to England in return.

When Nicolls arrived at City Hall, he looked around in confusion. The city council and the *burgemeesters* were here, but where was Stuyvesant? Where was Cornelis van Ruyven? Where were the ministers of the church? One of the Dutchmen informed him that they hadn't understood that they should be present since they were not official leaders of the city. Nicolls said they certainly were expected—he wanted every person of influence to sign the oath—so someone ran off to get them. A short while later, when all were assembled, Nicolls read the oath they were to swear to. It contained the line "and I will obey all such commands as I shall receive from his majestie, his Royall Highnesse James duke of Yorck, and such governours, and Officers as from time to time are appointed over me."

The assembly erupted in protest. Demanding that they swear such an oath, they informed Nicolls, was in violation of the Articles of Transfer, which gave them the right of self-government. A debate ensued. Nicolls eventually left in exasperation.

That was on a Friday. The following Tuesday the two *burgemeesters* met with Nicolls, who was in an even worse mood. Over the weekend word had swept through the town that he intended to break the transfer agreement.

The uproar throughout the city had become so great that

Nicolls felt the need to issue a public declaration to be read out in the streets reasserting his commitment to the agreement: "Whereas there is a false and Iniurious aspertion cast upon the Oath of Obedience to his Matie his Royall Highnesse the duke of Jorck . . . I do think fit to declare that the Articles of Surrender are not in the least broken or intended to be broken by any words or expressions on the said Oath."

This calmed the Dutch leaders. The *burgemeesters* reiterated that they couldn't sign the oath as it was written, but they suggested a simple addition: "conformable to the Articles concluded at the Surrender of this place." Nicolls agreed to it.

The meaning of the little episode was clear: the former New Amsterdammers took the merger idea seriously. So did Nicolls, in fact, but his situation was complicated. Throughout the whole of his time on Manhattan he found himself in the classic position of the diplomat, trying to mediate between the locals and the home country. On one side he had the Duke of Clarendon, with whom he was in regular correspondence about the need to make New York into an English city obedient to a monarch, as well as the Duke of York himself. On the other were his new constituents, who were determined that their agreement with him, including the right to self-government, be upheld. To Clarendon he complained that "Democracy hath taken so deepe a Roote in these parts" that it would be difficult for him to institute "Kingly Government." Then again, after a dinner in his honor following his arrival, hosted by Johannes van Brugh, a leading merchant, he felt that these pragmatic Dutch were indeed the kind of people he could work with. His tenure as governor would in effect be an attempt to answer one question: how could the city be both Dutch and English?

The church suggested one answer. The Dutch ministers made room in their Sunday schedule so that the minister Nicolls had brought with him could conduct an English-language service between the services in Dutch. Religious freedom was likewise an area where the two groups were more or less in agreement. Nicolls was actually prepared to go further than the supposedly tolerant Dutch had gone. Stuyvesant, motivated by his own prejudices, had had a special loathing for those who professed Lutheranism and had made it known that they weren't welcome on Manhattan. Nicolls countermanded that, ruling that Lutherans "may freely and publiquely exercise Divine worship, according to their Consciences."

He pleased his new constituents too when he appealed to London to grant New York special status as a trading port. The war was still on at this point; no ships from Europe were coming to Manhattan, and England was enforcing its draconian Navigation Acts against Dutch shipping. Nicolls asked that the Duke of York grant "a Generall Liberty for some Terme of yeares to the better Encouragement of this Place, that shipps of any Nation may Import or Export into or from hence all sorts of Merchandize whither they please." The merchants of the city could not have asked for more.

Nicolls went to work too on relations with the Native peoples of the region and in a way that pleased his townspeople. He traveled upriver to meet with several Esopus sachems and agreed to a treaty that extended the peace Stuyvesant had worked out with them the year before. Nicolls understood that the traditional gifts exchanged on such occasions carried great meaning, and he impressed the Esopus by offering forty blankets, twenty pounds of powder, twenty knives, six kettles, and twelve bars of lead. He also acceded to their custom that required treaties to be regularly renewed. The agreement established a peace in the lower Hudson Valley that lasted for the next hundred years. Of course, throughout that time, Europeans were steadily buying up Native lands.

Nicolls also sent George Cartwright upriver to Fort Orange to negotiate a treaty with the Seneca and Mohawk, two of the most important nations of the powerful Haudenosaunee confederacy. The confederacy had had mostly good trading relations with the Dutch. The sachems who strode into the fort to meet with Cartwright—Ohgehando, Shanarage, Soachoenighta, and Sachmackas of the Mohawk, and Anaweed, Conkeeherat, Tewasserany, Aschanoondah, and Sachamackas of the Seneca— understood power. They comprehended both that the English had taken over New Netherland and that these English were different from those of the New England colonies, with whom they had had much trouble. Cartwright probably had some Dutch representatives with him, perhaps even Stuyvesant himself. It was important for the survival of New York that the Haudenosaunee knew that Nicolls intended to carry on relations with them in the same manner that Stuyvesant had.

Thanks to the foundation the Dutch had laid, they had an agreement in short order—sealed in writing for the benefit of the English and with wampum to satisfy Haudenosaunee custom. The English would continue to provide manufactured goods to the Haudenosaunee "as heretofore they had from the Dutch," and if someone from either the Native or English domains attacked a person from the other, they would be punished. The Haudenosaunee leaders further asked the English not to give aid to three Algonquian tribes with whom they were at war and that the English arbitrate a peace treaty between the Haudenosaunee and the Lenape peoples whose territory lay to the south. Most of all, the Haudenosaunee wanted to "have free trade as formerly." The English agreed.

This was not a treaty between a dominant European power and a cowering Native people. They were more like equals who had respect for one another and wanted to do business with the other. In the next decade this treaty would form the basis of the so-called Covenant Chain between the English and the Haudenosaunee. The Covenant Chain established English and Haudenosaunee territories and brought peace between these two powers in North America, in some cases at the expense of their mutual enemies. Such a strong alliance with the dominant

confederation of Native peoples gave the English a basis for dealing with the Lenape and other Indigenous tribes of the region,
which helped Dutch traders and those of other nationalities in
the colony as well. It helped New York to prosper over the course
of the next century.

———

Nicolls had known before he ever left London that slavery would
be among the projects he would be taking on were he to capture
Manhattan, but he must have been surprised at how quickly he
found himself in the role of overseer of a nascent industry. The 290
Africans from the *Gideon* had been processed in New Amsterdam
while he was still anchored off Gravesend. By the time he was on
Manhattan, 72 of them had been purchased by a tobacco dealer
and taken overland to the Delaware River, and most of the rest
had been sold at auction. One final "lot" remained when Nicolls
took up residence in the fort. Nicolls issued a ruling. His concern
wasn't for the fate of the human beings that were about to be sold
but rather that the West India Company not see any money from
the sale. All payments, he decreed, whether in "Goods or Beaver,"
would be held by him until the finances were sorted out, and "no
discount (as to the said Negroes) be Allowed of upon any pretence
of the West India Companyes Debts, or any other, till I shall give
further Order therein."

As Nicolls was dealing with this matter, a visiting Englishman
from the Massachusetts colony by the name of Thomas Mathews
appeared before him with a complaint. Shortly after the takeover his "Negro Servant" had run away. A leader couldn't tolerate
such things; newcomers had to feel that the new city was a place
of law and order. In an effort to accommodate the man, Nicolls
created a template of sorts for American enslavers of later centuries, putting out a warrant for the escapee, complete with a
detailed description:

The Negroe is a lusty young fellow about 20: years of Age, hee was cloathd in a red wastecoate, with a sad colour'd cloath Coate over it, a paire of linen breeches, somewhat worne, and a grey felt hat, but no shoes or stockings.

Not long after, Peter Stuyvesant appeared in Nicolls's office. He came not on behalf of the West India Company or the people of the town but rather with a problem of his own, which mirrored that of Mr. Mathews. Stuyvesant complained to the man who had replaced him that, perhaps seeing a chance at freedom in the period of the changeover of governments, four of his own enslaved Africans had fled from his farm. Nicolls obliged Stuyvesant as he would any other resident and issued a warrant for their return.

At the same time, it was unclear to the Dutch on Manhattan whether the English would view the legal status of freed Africans the same way they had. Several months after the takeover Stuyvesant and his former secretary, Van Ruyven, got together and, as if they were still in office, quietly forged several documents, complete with seals, confirming the land patents that had been granted to freed Africans. Stuyvesant had himself granted some of these people their freedom in the New Netherland period and awarded them land; others had been freed by his predecessor, Kieft. The most logical explanation for this extraordinary action was that he had personal relationships with these people, didn't trust that the English would uphold their property rights, felt it would be wrong for them to lose what they had been given, and decided to make sure they would keep their land by manufacturing paperwork.

Nicolls discovered the ruse and took the remarkable step of having Stuyvesant and Van Ruyven arrested. He made the charges misdemeanors, however, pending an investigation. This may simply have involved asking Stuyvesant to come to his office to explain himself. The relationship between the two men was complicated, to say the least. They had led the way in the creation of this new city. Its success depended on its inhabitants buying into the invention. As in any society, mutual trust was the glue holding the place together. Each man wanted to be able to trust the other. If this forging of documents raised concerns in Nicolls's mind about what Stuyvesant was up to, in other ways the Dutch leader showed his trustworthiness and fulfilled his side of the merger bargain. He went so far as to write to the Duke of York to request that James formally ratify the Articles of Agreement, which he said would be for the "welfare and mutual benefit" of all New Yorkers. He declared to the duke that the Dutch of Manhattan were "now his Royal Highnesse most faithful and obedient subjects" and backed up Nicolls's request for free trading rights, asking that New Yorkers be allowed to continue to ship goods to and from Europe so that "the Inhabitants being plentifully supply'd, may chearfully follow their Vocations, and blesse God for the opportunity of Injoyment of all peace & plenty under the Auspicious wings of Your Royall Highnesse paternall care and protection."

Stuyvesant presumably came clean to Nicolls about what he had done with the land patents and why he had done it. Nicolls seemed mollified, and he concurred. He confirmed the patents for the property of the freed Africans, including that of Dorothea Angola and her husband, giving them some hope that they would have a secure future as free New Yorkers.

If that was one small, positive step for Black people in the city, the liveliness of the sale of the men and women from the *Gideon* also made it clear that Manhattan held great promise as a slave-trading center. Farms up the Hudson River needed workers, and the Chesapeake region to the south was becoming filled with tobacco plantations; tobacco was a demanding, labor-intensive crop, and planters were willing to pay good money for enslaved workers. Nicolls was all for turning Manhattan into a slaving hub: he showed no hesitation at mounting a trade in human beings. His problem was that the slavery business that Stuyvesant had pioneered in New Netherland had been conducted under the auspices of the West India Company, and the trade went through the Dutch-controlled island of Curaçao. Nicolls's own action in taking Manhattan had severed that connection.

Still, Nicolls did what he could to lay the groundwork for such a trade. He had engaged a capable lawyer named Matthais Nicolls (who was not related to him) as his secretary. This Nicolls, in 1665, took on the task of creating a legal code for the colony that mixed features of the English and Dutch systems. The Duke's Laws, as the New York code became known, officially recognized slavery, turning what had been an informal practice in New Netherland into a legalized institution. Enslavement would henceforth be a recognized state pertaining to people who were "judged thereunto by authority." The law stipulated that "a Record of such Servitude shall be entered in the Court of Sessions held for that Jurisdiction."

Of Richard Nicolls's many achievements—willing New York into being, creatively merging English and Dutch elements to forge a new sort of city, defining much of the political map of the eastern seaboard—it's possible to conclude that this tortured bit of legalese overshadows all the others in its future impact. Slavery would remain a minor element during Nicolls's term, but that was only because it took time for the Royal African Company and the Council for Foreign Plantations to focus their efforts in the Americas. The enslaved population of New York grew over the next couple of decades, to the point that in 1702 the colony felt the need to enact its first "slave code," an official set of rules restricting the lives of the enslaved and ensuring the rights of their enslavers. From that point, for example, enslavers were given legal permission to punish their human property as they saw fit, and enslaved people were forbidden from congregating in groups larger than three. More codes followed an uprising in 1712. By this time, as the number of Africans had swelled, white New Yorkers were not only fearful of the enslaved but of freed Blacks as well, over whom by definition they had little control. Giving the enslaved some form of freedom had been relatively common in New Amsterdam; henceforth enslavers wishing to do so would have to pay a prohibitive manumission fee of 200 pounds.

Americans today are slowly coming to realize that New York was a major hub of the slave trade. We may still associate the institution with the southern states, but it was so much a part of the economy and way of life of New York in the city's first century and a half that by 1730 some 42 percent of families in the city owned slaves. Even as it seemingly faced the changing times and passed an act for the gradual abolition of slavery in 1799, the state of New York did so with subterfuge and with every consideration for the enslavers. The act freed no one but rather ensured that children born of enslaved mothers would be free once they reached the age of twenty-five in the case of women and twenty-eight in the case of men. Ten years after the supposed abolition, 20 percent of the population of Brooklyn consisted of enslaved Blacks.

As the city became both the country's largest port and its financial center, its role in the cotton trade tied its economy tightly to southern slavery, such that by the middle of the nineteenth century New York was as much a hotbed of pro-slavery sentiment as anyplace in the South. At the same time, white and Black abolitionists made the city their base, and thousands who fled enslavement in the South sought refuge in New York. The city became a battleground. "Slave catchers" prowled lower Manhattan as Black abolitionists led meetings and edited newspapers with names like *Freedom's Journal* and *The Rights of All*. As the Civil War was about to break, journalist J. D. B. De Bow asserted what everyone already knew, that New York was "almost as dependent on Southern slavery as Charleston itself." If anything, attitudes among whites in the city hardened after the war, when stereotypes of Black people as slow-witted, drunk, and lecherous became commonplace. As in other places the end of slavery in New York didn't result in equality but in new forms of racism.

All of this later history traces back to Stuyvesant's "experiment with a consignment of Negroes" and Nicolls's legalization of slavery. If the idea of New York that was forged in 1664 contained within it the liberating concept of tolerance, it also contained both the seeds of intolerance and plenty of fertilizer to help them grow.

And yet, despite that nettlesome fact, do we still have to apply the word "tolerant" to Richard Nicolls? Calling someone tolerant who helped to establish the institution of slavery is absurd from our vantage point. But wrestling with history often involves such incongruities. The religious liberty movement of the seventeenth century, of which Nicolls was a part, limited though it was, was a step toward championing broader civil rights.

In his relations with his new colonists, Nicolls's tolerance stemmed from pragmatism. There were certainly tensions between the English and Dutch factions in New York in the city's early days, especially while the two home countries were at war. At one point during this time Nicolls declared that he felt his Dutch colonists paid only a "forc't Obedience" to King Charles and that they were "treacherous to the English Nation" in their hearts. Yet he also ordered his soldiers to treat all New Yorkers the same and not to "beget a prejudice in your mind against the Dutch." Given that there was a war on, he counseled his subordinates that "wee cannot expect they love us."

There was some grumbling among the Dutch when Nicolls convened a gathering of representatives of towns throughout the region at Hempstead, on Long Island, to announce his new legal code. Political offices were anglicized, the *burgemeesters*, *schouts*, and *schepens* becoming mayors, sheriffs, and aldermen. As with other matters, though, the code contained a mix of features from the English and Dutch systems. It was also pointedly non-Puritan, which certainly pleased the Dutch. Unlike the Massachusetts code, for instance, it said nothing about heresy or witchcraft. And it adhered to the freedom of conscience that both the Dutch and the English now running the government in London favored. As under the Dutch, however, the tolerance it offered was largely restricted to white Protestants.

Overall, the former New Amsterdammers were pleased enough with their new situation that they sent a flowery letter to the Duke of York, deeming themselves "fortunate that his Highness has provided us with so gentle, wise and intelligent a gentleman as Governor as the Honrable Colonell Nicolls," and voicing confidence "that under the wings of this valiant gentleman we shall bloom and grow like the Cedar on Lebanon."

Nicolls returned the favor, bestowing remarkable praise on his Dutch townspeople and their willingness to do their part to make the invention succeed. He predicted to his superiors in London that his non-English populace would in time "proove better subjects than wee have found in some of the other Colonyes"—a clear swipe at Massachusetts—and that they would "support this government better than can be reasonably expected from new comers of our owne nation."

Nicolls made a slew of other decrees that would set the features of the region. He decided that the city of New York would no longer be contained by the little triangle of sixteen streets that had made up New Amsterdam; ignoring the wall that had been the northern boundary of the Dutch city (which people were already calling Wall Street), it would extend up the whole thirteen-mile sweep of Manhattan Island. When John Winthrop Jr. arrived with a delegation from Connecticut, the two men sat down (after Winthrop first marched approvingly through the streets of New York and congratulated Nicolls on his success) and did their best to work out a boundary between New York and Connecticut. In King Charles's grant of territory to his brother, he had—inadvertently perhaps—included much of what had been western Connecticut, including its capital. The two governors came up with a congenial settlement: Connecticut would take back about thirty miles of what the king had bequeathed to New York, and New York would take the whole of Long Island. The overall features of their arrangement would hold, but the details would take some ironing out. Later the two colonies would begin a protracted legal battle over the boundary between them, which would only be decided in 1880. As far as Nicolls knew, however, the matter was settled.

But he was no sooner done with that business than he learned of a larger territorial problem: his entire colony was about to be split apart.

Of all people, it was Nicolls's noble patron and boss, the Duke of York, who was responsible for dramatically diminishing his own property. James had decided to reward two of his close friends, Lord John Berkeley and Sir George Carteret, for their loyalty to him during the civil war by carving off a piece of his colony and giving it to them. (Technically, he leased it to them, for "the summe of Tenn Shillings of Lawfull Money.") York still had little understanding of North American geography. He had never visited his territory across the Atlantic and never would. The land between the Hudson and Delaware Rivers seemed like it would make a nice gift, compact and well defined. Carteret had been the governor of Jersey and had kept that English Channel island a Royalist stronghold during the war. James thus thought that, as a name for this new territory, New Jersey had a nice ring to it. Suddenly what Nicolls was planning to call Albania, in the Duke's honor, simply ceased to be.

Nicolls had counted on exploiting this vast parcel in his effort to make New York succeed financially. The matter was so vital that he expressed his concerns directly to the duke, informing him (with some exaggeration) that "all the prooveable part" of

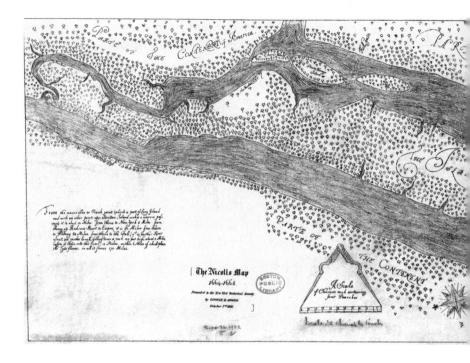

the colony was contained in this gift, not to mention "the faire hopes of Rich mines."

He slashed out another letter to the Earl of Clarendon. In nearly all of his communications with superiors, Nicolls was the model of a deferential, courtly officer. But here he unburdened himself. The "late Indenture made to My Ld Berkley and Sr George Carterett is to the manifest destruction of the Dukes Collony," he fumed. The duke's act, Nicolls told Clarendon, would make the work of attracting settlers to New York vastly more difficult. Further, Nicolls had planned that the colony would gain revenue from incoming ships that moored in the

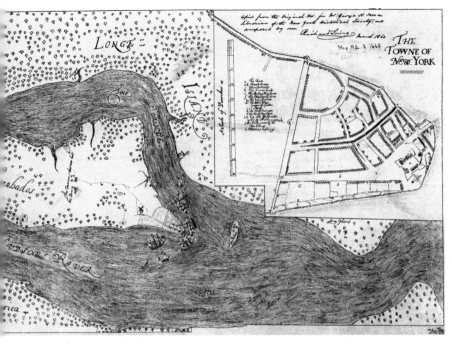

Shortly after taking charge on Manhattan, Richard Nicolls ordered a survey of the island and its surroundings to be sent back to London to aid in the military defense of the colony. Nicolls knew that his superiors in the home country had little knowledge of North American geography, hence the labeling of New Jersey as "Parte of the Contenent of America." This is a nineteenth-century copy of the so-called Nicolls Map.

harbor and the Hudson River. Now, any and all ships could dock on the "New Jersey" side and pay nothing. Nicolls pleaded to Clarendon; the duke had no idea how thoroughly he had crippled his own North American holding: "I humbly begg your L^dpp to take the whole matter into serious consideracōn, for if the Duke will improove this place to the utmost, Neither the trade, the River, nor the Adjacent lands must bee devided from this Collony, but remayne Entire."

But James had made up his mind. His loyal servant would have to redraw his maps, rethink his plans, and make do. New York would be New York. New Jersey would be . . . something else.

Defining and taking charge of New York was only half of the mission Nicolls had been assigned in London. He was still the head of the commission appointed to bring the New England colonies into line. These were very different tasks, but as far as the English government was concerned, it was all one project: to create a unified North America.

Over the next four years Nicolls and his fellow commissioners toiled at this assignment. Robert Carr, George Cartwright, and Samuel Maverick plodded through thick forests in February 1665, making their way from Manhattan into New England and then across frozen meadows from colony to colony, from one snow-covered village to another—"in all which we found bitter weather"—in their effort to rein in the Puritans. In most, they were "welcomed with great expressions of loyalty," they reported to Nicolls and to London. The leaders of Connecticut, Plymouth, and Rhode Island readily consented to Nicolls's demands: "that all administration of justice shall be in the king's name; that all householders shall take the oath of allegiance; that church membership shall not be considered in making freemen; that all persons of civil lives shall have liberty of conscience."

In Massachusetts, however, they ran into a wall. They wrote Nicolls in New York, telling him they needed him. Nicolls had hoped that by going to the other colonies first and gathering a chorus of loyal voices, his fellow commissioners would find the leaders of Boston softened. It wasn't to be. The situation he found on arrival was a repeat of his first visit to the city, before he ventured to Manhattan. The Puritans of Boston had amassed a great deal of power; they were unwilling to give it up and resisted demands to change. At the same time, however, maintaining their royal charter was vital: they weren't about to take the mad leap of declaring their independence from England and trying to exist as a lone entity in a hostile continent. Rather than open defiance, they employed an array of legalistic and theological doublespeak before the king's agents.

The commissioners sent reports to London detailing the intransigence they encountered in Massachusetts. Far from agreeing to follow the Stuart policy of supporting religious liberty, the Puritan government maintained its requirement that "freemen"—people with voting rights—had to be members of their church who were "orthodox in matters of fayth." The more time the commissioners spent among Bostonians, the more outraged they grew at the Puritans' aggressive intolerance, which showed in their reports: "They have put many Quakers of other provinces to death. . . . They have beaten some to Jelly, & been otherwayes exceeding cruell to others, & they say That the king allowes it in his letter to them. Indeed they have misconstrued all the kings letters to their own sence."

Nicolls's efforts to bring Boston to heel would fail as thoroughly as the plan to create a new Anglo-Dutch city on Manhattan would succeed. Long after Nicolls's time in America, the Puritan elders would continue to rebuff agents sent from London to rein them in. As a result the two regions of English North America would develop along sharply different lines. The unresolved conflict at the heart of Nicolls's mission, which would shape American culture for centuries, would not be between the English and Dutch of New York but between the merged, worldly, polyglot, business-minded New Yorkers and the religious sect centered in Boston.

Chapter 19

GOING DUTCH

———

*F*ive months after the creation of New York, a ship from the Dutch Republic sailed into the harbor carrying what Peter Stuyvesant had been expecting: a summons to return to the home country to face a formal hearing concerning his behavior in surrendering the colony. When he set sail, in May 1665, Judith, his wife, stayed behind. Their elder son, Balthazar, was on Curaçao. Stuyvesant took with him their younger son, Nicolaas, and a chest containing a veritable archive of the last few years of his administration as well as depositions and other documentation of his handling of the events of the previous summer. He knew he had hard work ahead of him.

Over the next two years he lived the life of a diplomatic shuttlecock, batted back and forth between the West India Company and the States General. Stuyvesant compiled a report that went on for dozens of pages, which amounted to a catalogue of excuses as to why he could not hold the colony. There was truth in it, but the underlying cause of his problems was that the two institutions that had controlled the fate of New Netherland hadn't given the colony the support it needed.

The West India Company sent Stuyvesant's defense to the government committee along with a scathing rebuttal. It countered every one of his points. To his charge that the fort lacked gunpowder, they flat-out lied, declaring that all requests for powder "were fully honored." They had little choice. Stuyvesant was shifting blame for the loss of the strategically and economically valuable North American real estate to the company; they had to defend themselves.

They pushed back even harder on the matter of Stuyvesant's failure to fight, arguing that "a capital fortress garrisoned by 180 brave soldiers ought not to have been surrendered without making some defence." There was something in this. It was what the Dutch soldiers on Manhattan had felt. But letting them fight would probably have resulted in the destruction of the city. Stuyvesant and Nicolls were in agreement that that was an unacceptable outcome. The directors' next point underscored that their priorities and his were different. To his lament that the inhabitants of the town had not wanted to participate in its defense, the directors blithely declared that the correct move was then to let the English attack rain down and simply "abandon the Burghers."

The company then put its finger on the crux of the matter: what had transpired in the harbor between Stuyvesant and his representatives and Nicolls and his negotiators. It charged that Stuyvesant and other officials in New Amsterdam had "wholly neglected" their duty to the colony and "surrendered it to the enemy without firing a gun, and sought out all means for the best terms, as soon as free possession of their private property was proposed, and did nothing towards offering the enemy the smallest resistance." Yes, that was precisely it. To create New York, Stuyvesant and the other New Amsterdammers had had to betray the West India Company.

Stuyvesant served up hundreds of pages of evidence: a detailed defense accompanied by sworn depositions and itemized inventories. The verdict could well have gone against him, as he could not refute the fact that he had given up the city. But geo-politics changed the dynamic. This courtroom-like drama played out against the backdrop of the Anglo-Dutch war. Once war with England was over and the negotiators in Breda had chosen to allow New York to remain New York, the whole matter suddenly became moot. Overnight, the officials relented. Stuyvesant was absolved. He was free.

What happened next speaks to Stuyvesant's own deepest feelings as surely as his decision to negotiate with Nicolls had. Those feelings had evolved over the years: from his rocky start in New Netherland two decades earlier, through the growth of the city and his own education in how to administer a colony, to the standoff and the decision to negotiate with Nicolls. He requested permission to return to Manhattan.

And so he did return, late in 1667. He spent his last years living in a city he had simultaneously lost, saved, and helped to create. Though he was never a beloved figure during his regime, public sentiment seemed to change upon his return, perhaps in acknowledgment of what he had done to preserve the place. He was known affectionately as "the General" and could occasionally be seen stumping around the fort and city hall, involving himself in a selection of municipal affairs and otherwise keeping to his farm and his tropical birds.

He died in 1672; Judith outlived him by fifteen years. Their descendants inherited the family farm and slowly developed it into what eventually became the East Village neighborhood of Manhattan. At some point in the early nineteenth century, people realized that a lone pear tree at the corner of 13th Street and Third Avenue was the last vestige of Stuyvesant's bowery. The city fenced it in to create a little memorial. People were still pluck-ing pears off of it until one day in 1867, when a horse-drawn wagon careered into the tree and it had to be cut down. One of Stuyvesant's descendants, a land developer named Rutherfurd Stuyvesant, who still owned this portion of the original farm, had a cross-section of the tree cut and donated it to the New-York Historical Society, where it stood on display as, simultaneously, a reminder of the bucolic Manhattan that once was and a victim of the urban grid.

Richard Nicolls spent a total of four years on Manhattan. Considering all he accomplished, it seems a remarkably short stay. When he wasn't laying the foundation of the city of New York and of much of the rest of the region, he somehow found time to travel the woods and meadows and waterways of the region under his charge and to engage in his hobby of investigating the natural world. He exchanged lengthy letters with Robert Moray of the Royal Society, who encouraged him to give reports on "every kind of minerall you meet with, be it earth, clay, sand, stones," as well as the plants, fish, and the "kindes of woods you have thereaway." A little coterie of transatlantic correspondents formed, including Nicolls, Moray, John Winthrop, and, of all people, Peter Stuyvesant, the purpose of which was "to consorte & cooperate" on matters relating to exploring North America "for the advancement of so universall a Benefit as the Scope of this Societie."

By the spring of 1666, however, despite all his achievements, Nicolls was deeply frustrated. His own royal patron—to whom he had devoted his life, for whom he had crossed an ocean, and whose province he had endeavored to start off on the best possible footing—had undercut his efforts by giving away half of it. Nicolls couldn't let it go: New Jersey simply drove him to distraction.

So did Boston. His second winter on Manhattan was seemingly without end. It began with the Hudson River freezing over in early November, effectively cutting the city off from much of the colony. By the beginning of April much of the river was still icebound. Shivering as he picked up his pen, he wrote to the Earl of Clarendon with great bitterness in his heart. The rulers

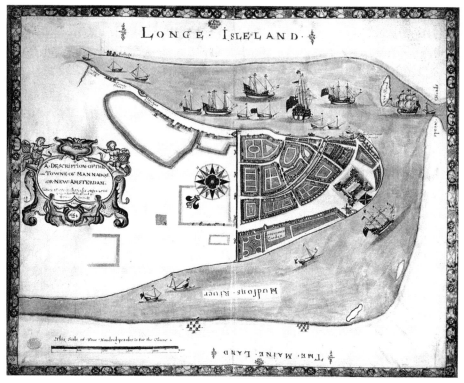

"The Duke's Plan" is an English map that may be better termed a trophy. After naming New York in honor of the Duke of York, Richard Nicolls apparently sent a drawing of the city to London, where an artist used it to make a handsome painting for the duke. That it was created shortly after the takeover is evident in the confusion about the new city's name. The legend calls it both "The Towne of Mannados" and "New Amsterdam." The artist apparently hadn't yet heard of New York. This is also the first time the Hudson River is so named.

of Boston knew that they had the better of him. He had gone to them with clear orders from London that they amend twenty-six of the articles in the "booke of the Generall Lawes & liberties" by which the Puritans governed their province, articles that set them up as practically an autonomous state, but he had no authority to enforce the orders, and the Bostonians knew it. He described for Clarendon the "shuffling sort of discowrse" they employed in order "to evade the discover of their hearts." They had rebuffed his commission in the most outrageous way, drowning the royal commissioners out with an actual blast of trumpets.

He was also close to personal financial ruin. Funds hadn't arrived to support all that he needed to do for the colony, so he had used his own money and borrowed from friends to the tune of 2,000 pounds—$500,000 in today's money.

Six months later things had not improved. The New Jersey business still rankled. He made a last desperate appeal to Clarendon to try to convince Carteret and Berkeley to swap the territory the duke had gifted them for another: the region called Delaware, which he argued was just as good. That way New York would once again have control of the whole harbor and river that was its heart.

But it was a futile hope, and he knew it. In the same letter he made an appeal on his own behalf: "I hope your Lordship will prevayle with his Royall Highnesse that I may bee recall'd, and some other fitt person sent in my place." It was one of several requests he would make for a transfer to the home office. There's no way of knowing what reasons he may have had besides his frustration. Was there a woman back home? In the will he made out several years later, one person stands out. He gave small amounts of money to a variety of friends and family members, none totaling more than 100 pounds, but to "Elizabeth Bennet, the daughter of the widow Bennet," he bequeathed the fairly enormous sum of 1,000 pounds—$250,000 today. Was she a love interest? Did they have an understanding? If so, and if his plan was to marry her on his return, that marriage never took place.

Finally, London granted his wish. They could hardly do otherwise. He had, after all, achieved everything that could possibly have been expected of him in bringing the Dutch colony into the English sphere. Any disgruntlement among the residents of New York about the merger remained minor. In the home country English officials would complain for years after about the pesky insistence of New Yorkers on having a direct role in their politics, which had been a feature of New Amsterdam and was one of the promises in the Articles of Transfer, but on the other major issue, the local desire to maintain free trading relations with the Dutch empire, well, what was good for them was good for New York and thus for England. It was true that Nicolls had failed in bringing Boston to heel, but no one within the Council for Foreign Plantations seemed to think that had been a realistic objective anyway.

The regret in New York and beyond when Nicolls announced that he would be leaving was seemingly genuine. John Winthrop, who had had his arm twisted by Nicolls to get his help in convincing the Dutch to negotiate, declared that "people not only of that colony, both English and Dutch, but of the neighbouring places also, are really sorrowfull at the report of his departure." There were dinners in his honor. A military band serenaded him to the ship. One of Nicolls's last acts was to pardon Stuyvesant and Van Ruyven for their fraudulent forging of patents for freed Blacks. Despite the problems he had encountered, he could sail away feeling, as he had written earlier to the duke, that New York was "the best of all His Majesties Townes in America."

And so, in the fall of 1668, he found himself back in London and in very familiar surroundings: wandering through room after room, from rickety to royal, of the patchwork palace at Whitehall. Once again he was Groom of the Bedchamber, except that now there was no definite article: he was one of several. Again he attended James, organizing meetings and events. When possible, he made his way back to Ampthill, where he bought a piece of land in the center of town, just opposite the church, with the idea of building a house. Perhaps he had plans to lead a domestic life, a life of retirement and ease.

He maintained an interest in how things were going in New York. People wrote him with news and updates. He had put in a word with the duke for Samuel Maverick, and as a result James gave his former commissioner the present of a fine house on Broadway, as the onetime Lenape trail, which under the Dutch had been the Herenweg, or Gentleman's Way, was now being called. Maverick had permanently sworn off Boston and henceforth would be an official New York resident. In 1669, Maverick wrote to thank Nicolls for his help in this and gave him the latest gossip. Improvements were being made all around town. Excellent cod-fishing banks had been discovered near Sandy Hook. And things were going well with the merger. "There is good correspondence kept between the English and Dutch," he informed Nicolls, "and to keep it the closer, sixteen (ten Dutch and 6 English) have had a constant meeting at each others houses in turnes, twice every week in winter, and now in summer once; they meet at six at night and part about eight or nine."

What's more, Cornelis Steenwijck was now the mayor of New York. There could scarcely be a clearer indication that the invention was succeeding than having a Dutchman and onetime *burgemeester* of New Amsterdam running the English city.

But Nicolls was no longer a part of it. The work he was engaged in now for the duke and the government once again involved the Dutch, but in a different direction. The year 1672 is to this day known in the Netherlands as the *rampjaar*: the year of disaster. England and France conspired to attack the Dutch Republic simultaneously, and by the end of it the Dutch countryside was a flooded mess and the nation was in economic ruin. The Third Anglo-Dutch War was supposed to begin with the Duke of York, as the head of the admiralty, organizing a huge naval blockade of the Dutch coast. Nicolls was among the thirty-five thousand English soldiers and sailors taking part. On June 7, in the midst of preparations, the English on their ships were shocked to see the horizon filled with Dutch sails: a surprise attack was in the offing. Instead of moving aggressively on the enemy, the English fleet had to fight a defensive action. The duke's flagship, the *Prince*, with James on board, saw intense action, taking two

Cornelis Steenwijck served as both *burgemeester* of New Amsterdam and mayor of New York, making him the living embodiment of the idea that the new city would be a merger of English and Dutch elements.

hundred casualties. More than three thousand men were killed in the Battle of Solebay, off the coast of Suffolk. Richard Nicolls was among them. He was forty-eight years old.

He was laid to rest in the church in his hometown of Ampthill. The lengthy Latin inscription on his tomb highlights what the friends and family members who buried him clearly understood to be his major achievement: "In the year 1664, being already mature in age and military science, he was sent into North America with a command. He restored the well-known Long Island and other islands to their true master, the Dutch being driven out, and the ensign of his lord adorned a province and strongholds well fortified." Embedded in the memorial is a cannonball—purportedly the instrument of his death, though how someone would have had the wits and foresight in the heat of battle to pick up this hot potato and save it is a question unanswered by the inscription.

Two months later, in New York, Peter Stuyvesant died, aged about sixty-two, of what cause we don't know. Perhaps the ultimate irony in the struggle between the two men, each of whom had firm ideas about the future of Manhattan Island, was that once he exonerated himself in the Dutch Republic, Stuyvesant, the supposed loser, sailed back across the ocean to live out his days there, whereas Nicolls ultimately showed that for him the creation of a new city had been just a job. He was an Englishman,

Richard Nicolls's tomb, St. Andrews Church, Ampthill.

in the service of his royal master. Nicolls may have been the winner of the confrontation in the harbor, but Stuyvesant was the one who showed himself, in the choices he made, to be both a New Yorker and an American.

The idea in this book that New York has a Dutch element in its makeup, which contributed to its uniqueness and its eventual success, may seem provocative to some. An even more provocative assertion, but one that is no less true, is that shortly after the establishment of New York, England itself became subject to an actual Dutch invasion, which would transform the country. The unwitting instigator of this invasion was none other than James Stuart, whose spectacular downfall would pave the way for an infiltration that few English people today are even aware of.

In 1668, as Richard Nicolls was boarding a ship to return to England, James privately converted to Catholicism, just as most English people feared he would. That fear had many layers, of which the top one was the belief that a Catholic who became King of England would turn the country over to the Vatican.

Despite the antipathy toward Catholicism and the danger his conversion thus put him in once it became known, James's yearning for the faith was genuine and deep, stemming from his Catholic mother. It both fed his commitment to religious toleration and limited that commitment: his desire, after all, wasn't so much to establish religious freedom for all as to make England a place in which Catholics could worship openly. In fact, he harbored a "Grand Design" of returning all of England to the Catholic faith. This impossible notion, the schemes associated with it, and combating those opposed to it, consumed much of the second half of his life.

James was so preoccupied with defending Catholicism that he doesn't seem to have noticed when, in August 1673, amid the war that cost Richard Nicolls his life, a Dutch fleet sailed into New York Harbor and retook his colony. This odd footnote to history bewildered everyone involved in it. The Dutch government hadn't authorized it nor had the West India Company. The fleet had been sent by the Dutch province of Zeeland as a freelance mission, to harass English possessions in the Atlantic and to try to squeeze some financial return out of the war for the province. Its commander, Cornelis Evertsen, had been given a menu of possible targets as far-flung as the Cape Verde Islands, Surinam, and New York. Evertsen decided he would have a go at all of them. He seems to have been surprised, on sailing into New York Harbor, when the official in charge of the fort on Manhattan abruptly surrendered the colony. Evertsen went about renaming everything—New York became New Orange; Albany was to be Willemstadt—and assigned a military captain named Anthony Colve to be the governor.

The inhabitants of New York didn't have much time to adjust to the sudden dissolution of their invention because, as it turned out, the leaders of the Dutch government had moved on from New Netherland. When the Treaty of Westminster was signed six months later, ending the Third Anglo-Dutch War, it reverted all captured overseas properties to the *status quo ante bellum*: both sides gave back what they had taken. New York was once again New York.

If James exulted in winning his property back, it was probably in part because New York was about to benefit from a recent development in London. The Royal African Company, of which he was the chief shareholder, now had a new charter, which authorized it to be more aggressive in exploiting that continent than it had been before. Once again English "adventurers," as they were chirpily termed, descended on what became known as the Gold Coast and the Slave Coast, requisitioned forts, and set up an English slave trade on a larger scale. The Royal African Company would go on to send more than 150,000 people into lives of slavery in America. Many of those people were subjected to being branded—on the shoulder or breast—with "DY," for Duke of York, before boarding a ship to America. Perhaps it was pride of ownership that sparked the idea in James: these people were *his*, and some of them were bound for *his* colony. And, indeed, they would help it to grow in power.

James's mad notion of returning England to its Catholic roots took a turn in February 1685, when his brother, King Charles II, died suddenly of an "apoplectic fit"—probably a stroke. Charles had no legitimate offspring to inherit the throne, so it passed to James—relatively peacefully, at least on the surface. But turmoil was brewing. In 1687, King James II issued a Declaration of Indulgence, a partial toleration of religion, which raised the hackles of the growing anti-Catholic movement. The next year, when his second wife—Mary of Modena, a Catholic—gave birth to a son, it set in motion James's downfall. The baby represented nothing less than an assurance that the throne of England would remain in Catholic hands far into the future.

By the time of the birth anti-Catholic noblemen in England had built a coalition bent on toppling James from the throne. Their strategy for doing so put a remarkable cap on the rivalry between the English and the Dutch that occupied the whole of the seventeenth century and that provides the spine to the story that this book tells. Secret missives crossed the English Channel, and answers came back the other way. As it happened, James's elder daughter, Mary, a Protestant, was married to the Dutch Prince of Orange, Willem. Had James's wife not given birth, Mary might have been next in succession. Now, thanks to that link to the royal family, seven English noblemen issued an "invitation" to Willem to invade their country and take the throne.

The so-called Glorious Revolution of 1688 is oddly named, and characterizing the decisive action in it as an invitation, as English history has done, is a case of spin-doctoring on a historic scale. The idea for it came not from England but from the Continent:

from Willem, his advisers, and a small band of English noblemen in exile. Willem paved the way for a Dutch takeover of England by engineering what historian Jonathan Israel has called "one of the greatest and most decisive propaganda coups of early modern times," arranging to have Dutch publishers secretly print and distribute thousands of copies of a declaration to the English people in which he decreed that James had "overturned the Religion, Laws and Liberties" of England and that he, a Dutch prince, had been asked by English officials to establish "lawful authority."

In November 1688, more than four hundred ships carrying twenty-one thousand soldiers crossed to England and landed on the Devon coast. Once there Willem announced that he had come to free English Protestants from Catholic tyranny. English leaders who were opposed to James had prepared the way, and Willem's army met little resistance on its two-hundred-mile procession to London. Dutch troops took over the city, manning Whitehall Palace and other official locales, and indeed would remain stationed in England for years. James fled London and the Dutch army and spent much of his last eleven years wandering or on the run. In February 1689, Willem and his wife became William and Mary, King and Queen of England.

This peaceful invasion was made possible by the same thing that made the invention of New York possible: an infusion of Dutch ideas. Over the previous decades, despite the bitter rivalry between the two nations, a parade of Dutch thinkers, painters, craftsmen, cartographers, mathematicians, and politicians had entered England and profoundly influenced English life. And the segment of English society that Richard Nicolls epitomized—pragmatic, curious, tolerant of the new and the other—had welcomed these foreigners and absorbed this flow of influences. The founders of the Royal Society were directly influenced by Dutch scientists. John Locke, the great English political philosopher, wrote his *Two Treatises of Government* while living in the Dutch Republic. The great "English" artists of the period who depicted and worked for the English royal family—Anthony van Dyck, Peter Lely, and Peter Paul Rubens—were actually from the Low Countries.

What's more, after Willem became King William, George Downing, the odious but brilliant English ambassador to The Hague, who had worked for years to transplant Dutch financial methods to England, finally succeeded in doing so. When the Bank of England was established in 1694, it capped a transformation of the English system of finance along Dutch lines. Methods the Dutch had long used to finance their government and build their empire became English. The success of the British Empire that was to come, many historians assert, rests in no small part on this Dutch base.

The English historian Lisa Jardine, in describing in her book *Going Dutch* the scope of English borrowings from the Dutch during this period, employs the same term I have used here with regard to the creation of New York. She calls it a merger. After asserting that the Glorious Revolution was nothing less than "an invasion," she notes that "by 1688 England and Holland were already so closely intertwined, culturally, intellectually, dynastically, and politically . . . that the invasion was more like a merger."

By the late 1680s, then, many people in England were familiar with "Dutchness." They accepted Willem—or rather, William— and they were willing to believe that he had come to save them from the tyranny of King James. In fact, Willem's motive was entirely different. England had been a main adversary of his country and so had France. The French were at that time preparing to invade his country; had England done so as well, the Dutch nation might have been annihilated, its provinces divided up by others. Taking up the cause of the English forces that were arrayed against James and using it as cover for an invasion became for Willem a brazen maneuver to avoid ruin by turning the tables on the English.

There is thus an enormous irony in James's downfall. He had wanted in the worst way to get at the Dutch, and not only took their North American colony but stamped it permanently with his name, only to have a Dutch nobleman trump him in colossal fashion, taking his crown, his country, and virtually everything that mattered to him. If New York became a merger of Dutch and English elements on American shores, the Glorious Revolution fused Dutchness and Englishness in England itself and in ways that English history has never truly come to terms with. Put another way, if the Dutch city of New Amsterdam became English in 1664, a quarter of a century later England itself became, in a sense, Dutch.

Chapter 20

THE MYSTERY

———

*W*hat is the source of New York's mystery? Why do people admire the city? Why does it attract and inspire? The deepest mysteries are unsolvable, but this book suggests that a possible answer to this one lies in the city's origins—its DNA, we might say. New York had two parents. Like all offspring, it grew up to have its own identity, but it continued to have support along the way. The parent nations were generally at odds with one another, but each was powerful, and the New World port became a node on the trading circuits of both empires. That fact nurtured it, helped it grow, and reinforced its nature as a global city.

The way those parents came together was important, too. The merger—as opposed to a hostile takeover—allowed for many voices to be involved as the city developed. The merger created a template for pragmatism—for reason and moderation in a world riven by extremes and fundamentalisms.

Some might scoff at the suggestion that reason and moderation are the right words to apply to the culture of New York. Putting this in context may make the point. We might think of American politics as having two wings. One is defiantly moralistic, harps incessantly on the country's Christian origins, and insists that these should be the guiding principles in settling issues of the day. We can look to the Puritan settlement of New England as the source of this strain in American politics. When the Puritans arrived, they saw America as the Promised Land and believed they had God's blessing to settle it. As the leaders of the "New Israel," they, and American leaders who followed them, believed that Europe was the corrupt old world and that they had a mission to establish on the American continent a base of righteousness. This strain of thought runs through all the great political issues the country has grappled with. It has been used to justify slavery, to combat women's suffrage and the civil rights movement, to oppose abortion, to champion Donald Trump.

While volumes of scholarship have been devoted to the Puritan element in American politics, the source of the other wing of political thought has been harder to pinpoint, partly because it is so diverse. It sees itself as secular, reason based, rooted in the Enlightenment. It is a messier tradition. I think there's good reason to look to New York as its source. From its Dutch beginnings New York has always been pluralistic. Out of that pluralism came the city's tradition of factionalism, which in turn made it an ongoing breeding ground of ideas. The first political parties in the country's history came into being in New York in the 1730s, as did the concept of freedom of the press. Kenneth Jackson and David Dunbar, the editors of *Empire City*, a collection of writings about New York, ask, "Is it a coincidence that the American Communist Party, the National Association for the Advancement of Colored People and the gay rights movement all started in the city?" They might have added as well modern liberalism (Franklin Roosevelt's New Deal grew out of his time as governor of New York) and conservatism (both William F. Buckley's *National Journal* and the neoconservative movement were born in New York).

To this day the United States is in a tug-of-war between religious tribalism and secular pluralism. I think there's a case to be made that that struggle goes back to the seventeenth century, to the settlement of the Puritan colonies and the invention of New York. That invention paved the way for a society based on pluralism and capitalism. Its texture was evident to newcomers in the decades after New York came to be. When William Byrd, a gentleman of Virginia, traveled to the city in 1685, he wrote his brother a description that, with some adjustments in spelling, would seem perfectly appropriate for the New York of two or three centuries later: "They have as many Sects of religion there as att Amsterdam, all being tolerated, yet the people seem not concerned what religion their Neighbour is of, or whether hee hath any or none." In 1692, Englishman Charles Lodwick, who had taken up residence in the city, wrote home that "our chiefest unhappyness here is too great a mixture of nations, and English the least part." Maybe he got the hang of it. Two years later Lodwick became the mayor of New York.

Thinking beyond America's shores, isn't the combination of pluralism and capitalism the glue that holds all modern cities together? The unspoken creed of densely packed urban dwellers is that we will give each other space and respect; that, even though I may not understand your language or your way of looking at things or particularly care about your culture, I'll make room for you, and maybe something new will come of our being here together.

The success of that concept is evident everywhere. Hong Kong, Budapest, Mexico City, and, yes, London; all modern cities have adopted the template. Put another way, New York's defining features signify what it means to be a modern city. It has turned out to be a recipe for innovation, for the fruitful churn of ideas. Even cities that are less than modern due to politics or religion— Moscow, Riyadh, Beijing—still try to look the part. It remains to be seen how the rise of remote working and the fear of pandemics will transform the very idea of urbanness, but the values inherent in the creation of New York have become self-evident.

And there is something else worth noting about the fact that the clash over control of Manhattan Island did not become a military battle, though the leaders on both sides went right to the precipice of violence. Despite the tensions, the ranks of cannons pointed at one another ready to unleash horror, not a single person died. For all the bluster and saber-rattling, the story is one of reason and pragmatism prevailing, resulting in the creation of something new. If today, amid all the anxiety and uncertainty about our future, we are looking for lessons in our history, that's not a bad one.

James Stuart may have bequeathed his title to New York, but others who lived through the period this story covers gave far more of themselves to the creation of the city.

Dorothea Angola died in about 1689. She had known life as a child in an African village, then experienced the horror of being ripped from home and family and subjected to the infamous ordeal of the Middle Passage, crossing the Atlantic as a captive on a slave ship. She became one of the earliest settlers of New Amsterdam, albeit an enslaved one, married twice, bore children, watched some of them die, adopted the son of a friend. She had lived in slavery, had won freedom, and ultimately had become a New Yorker. She had owned land, which had given her after much suffering a semblance of stability. She had known Manhattan in the most intimate way, through its soil, producing the food that sustained her family; she had known the island as a place of pain and cruelty and occasional joy. As she became an elderly matriarch, she enjoyed the satisfaction of living surrounded by friends and family, of watching the seasons change, seeing new generations find their way. She lived to see her adopted son, Anthony, set up in life on a farm next to hers and to have Richard Nicolls formally confirm that her land, her son's, and that of her Black neighbors was indeed theirs and would remain so forever under English rule.

But she had lived too through the first signs that that promise might be false. In 1671, when she was perhaps in her early sixties, she heard that two of her neighbors, Domingo and Manuel Angola, who were, like her, free Black residents of New York, had been brought before the city magistrates. Everyone knew that the two men hosted evening gatherings where people—mostly Black, some white, a mix of enslaved and free—drank and sang and laughed and forgot their troubles for a time. But there had been complaints—not about the noise but about the inconvenience to owners of enslaved people who sometimes didn't return home until late or until the next day, missing a day or more of work. This had caused "great damage" to the enslavers. The court cautioned the men not to host such parties again. A mere warning would have been a very mild punishment, but it was coupled with the most ominous of threats: "on pain of forfeiting their freedom." The two men were ordered as well to go around to each of "the other remaining free Negroes" and tell them that the same threat applied to them.

That was the first indication that things were about to change. It surely caused Dorothea Angola anxiety. Still, when she died, it was with the comfort of having land that she could pass on to her children.

About seven years after her death a white man named Wolfert Webber bought up her family farm as well as those of her neighbors, Anthony Portuguese, Manuel de Gerrit de Reus, and her adopted son. Together, these properties comprised thirty-two acres of lower Manhattan. Webber later referred collectively to this parcel as "the Negroes' farm." We don't know the circumstances of the buyout, but it's hard to imagine anything other than that the Black landowners were coerced to sell. New York was a city on the move, with a population of five thousand, about seven hundred of whom were enslaved. The city was pushing northward up the island, turning farmland into intersections and fields into houses and shops. These were wild times: anti-Catholic mobs caroused; dandyish pirates ran the town—men who made their fortunes by sailing from New York Harbor to the Caribbean to capture French trading ships on a license issued by London, then invested their profits in the city. The slave codes came into being, one of which outlawed the enslavement of whites and Native people. As slavery grew into an industry, skin color became a marker. More and more, Black meant simply "slave."

Catalina Trico died in 1689, at the age of eighty-four, surrounded by family, on her farm overlooking Wallabout Bay and, across the East River, lower Manhattan. Eight years earlier a missionary named Jasper Danckaerts who was traveling through the region happened to spend time with her and to record the visit in his diary. He described crossing from New York by boat to meet the aunt of a friend, who by this time was something of a local celebrity as the only resident who had been there from the very beginning of the Dutch colony and as the mother of "the first born Christian daughter" in the colony.

Danckaerts was charmed by the woman and described her as "worldly-minded" and "living with her whole heart." Her property went on, acre after acre of rolling farmland. Danckaerts recorded that there were 145 of Trico's extended family members living on her land, with 5 of the women pregnant, so that the number "soon will reach 150." He found it remarkable that despite—or maybe because of—the presence of so much family, Trico preferred her independence: "She lives alone by herself, a little apart from the others, having her little garden, and other conveniences, with which she helped herself."

A year before her death a justice of the peace named William Morris rowed across the river and paid a visit to Trico in her little farm dwelling. He was collecting statements from the earliest European settlers of the area. At his prompting Trico summoned her memories of arrival, sixty-four years earlier. The ship was called *Unity*. She remembered the captain's name and how, on arrival, he had ordered the handful of married couples and the small group of soldiers out across the vast landscape. How she and her new husband, Joris Rapalje, had spent their first years in the north. How cold and forbidding it was but how young they were, ready for anything. How they had tamed the land, befriended Native people, learned to differentiate their tribes and tongues. She recalled the crude bark huts the settlers had constructed to keep themselves sheltered from the cold. How she had given birth to Sarah in that wilderness. How they spent three long years there, then moved south, to Manhattan, and started all over again.

Catalina and Joris had worked, invested in, and helped to build with their own hands first New Amsterdam and then New York. Then they populated it. Their eleven children, together with their spouses and extensive progeny, created the core of the population of Wallabout, turning the couple's farm into a village, which in time merged with Brooklyn. Their descendants today are said to number in the millions.

Asser Levy, the leader of New Amsterdam's Jewish community, died in 1682. After the English takeover, he signed the oath of allegiance to the Duke of York. He and his wife, Miriam, seem not to have had children, but they continued to prosper in their lives as New Yorkers.

In addition to his numerous other business activities and to leading the Jews in what we would call civil rights cases, Levy assumed the position of "sworn butcher" for the city (and won an exemption from having to slaughter hogs). He opened a butcher shop at the corner of Wall and Pearl Streets. It may not be too much of a stretch to call it New York's first Jewish deli. He is remembered today in the naming of Asser Levy Park, on Coney Island, and the Asser Levy Recreation Center, on East 23rd Street.

Quashawam, the Montaukett sunksquaw, or female chief, who allied herself with English settlers after Stuyvesant rejected the offer to join forces with the Natives of Long Island, seems to have died in 1666, probably of smallpox. She lived only into her mid-twenties, but she accomplished much in a heroic effort to keep her people relevant in the swiftly changing political landscape. Encroachment was the dominant theme of her lifetime. By the time of her death nearly all of the land comprising the five boroughs of the present-day city of New York was in European hands. After Manhattan in 1626, Dutch buyers made deals for Staten Island in 1630, for parts of Brooklyn starting in 1636, and for a corner of the Bronx beginning in 1639.

Thus started a lurching process of hollowing out the Lenape homeland. In 1666, Philip Carteret, a relation of the onetime governor of the island of Jersey, to whom the Duke of York had given a portion of his territory, arrived to begin turning that gift into a functioning colony. That entailed first making real estate deals. The Hackensack sachem Pierwim resisted Carteret's entreaties for a time but finally succumbed and signed what became known as the Newark Tract, the first of dozens of property buyouts that would eventually constitute the state of New Jersey.

A Lenape contemporary of Quashawam, a sachem named Wassackarous, personified the step-by-step sell-off. Faced with drastic population decline due to smallpox, he first agreed to sell a portion of tribal land in present-day Brooklyn, whereupon he and his remaining people moved across the harbor to a spot on Sandy Hook Bay. Then in 1675 he sold that parcel, and they moved again, farther south and west. In 1681 a newly arrived Englishman named William Markham introduced himself. He was a cousin of William Penn, who, like Carteret and Berkeley, had recently been granted a large swath of North America by the English crown. As Penn's representative, Markham began making offers for land. In 1683, Wassackarous agreed for the third time to sell his people's land. It was among the first in a blizzard of sales constituting what would become Pennsylvania.

The continued Lenape migration paralleled the westward movement of white settlers, with the twist that they had always been here and were being pushed out of rather than pulled toward a home. As with people whose places of origin were Ireland or Germany, they had to deal with the loss of many traditions along the way. Lenape migrants found themselves thrown together with people of Oneida, Ojibwe, and Shawnee heritage. Intermarrying led to learning new customs and languages. Everywhere they faced the resistance of white people. The Lenape story is a variation of the American immigrant story but with more hardship, discrimination, and poverty.

Today there are significant Lenape-Munsee-Delaware settlements in Oklahoma, Kansas, Wisconsin, and Ontario. The chiefs of the widely scattered groups hold Zoom meetings to maintain continuity. They discuss legal issues, public health, education, and of course history. When it comes to the latter, the five thousand or so members of the Ramapough Lunaape of New Jersey have an advantage over their more dispersed brethren. If they want a sense of what once was, they can simply get in their car, drive over the George Washington Bridge into Manhattan, and head south down Broadway, following more or less the trail their forebears cut through the wilderness. They can take it all the way to the tip of the island.

This advantageous wedge of land—jutting into the harbor and flanked by rivers—was once a meeting place of Native tribes, where people from all around this ornate waterscape might pause in their peregrinations to come together and exchange goods. The Dutch made it their capital, New Amsterdam, at the heart of which stood Fort Amsterdam. The fort was meant above all as a refuge: in the event of attack by Indigenous tribes, such as happened during Kieft's War in the 1640s, it would be the one place on the island of Manhattan where the Europeans would be safe, where there would be no trace of an "Indian" presence.

The site of the fort is now occupied by the Alexander Hamilton US Custom House. As evidence that the universe has a sense of irony, the building is today the New York home of the Smithsonian Institution's National Museum of the American Indian. Like many museums, this one strives to be respectful of cultures the subjugation of which paved the way for a society that prides itself on such sensitivity.

Should the Lenape visitors from across the river choose to stop in, they might tour the museum's permanent exhibit, which is called "Native New York." From it they would learn about the original inhabitants of the island, how they lived, what they believed in. Then they could get in their cars again and be back home by dinnertime, leaving them free to spend the evening pondering how museums, like books, can impart worlds of information yet still not penetrate the mystery of who we are and of the past that lives on within us all.

Acknowledgments

Of all the people who helped me during the writing of this book, I would like to thank Charles Gehring first and foremost. Besides essentially creating the field of New Netherland studies, Charly pulled me into it with his passion and unparalleled knowledge. Throughout the period in which I worked on the book Charly and I had a weekly phone call in which he answered questions, provided translations, and offered guidance and suggestions. He has been my mentor and friend for twenty-five years.

I also especially want to thank Dennis Maika: for many long and enjoyable conversations on all things New Netherland, for sharing his work and insights, and for serving as a model of what a historian should be. My understanding of the uniqueness of the city of New Amsterdam in its later years is due in large part to his work.

I have been pleased to be associated with the New Netherland Institute for many years. I'm grateful for many forms of assistance from the NNI. I am particularly thankful to the members of the board for affording me a grant to write the proposal for this book: Phoebe Bender, Marilyn Douglas, Richard Kiger, Thomas Ruller, James Schermerhorn, Melissa Thompson-Flynn, Mike Vande Woude, Rett Zabriskie, and Ellen Zunon. I would also like to thank Jeanne Hawkey, Chelsea Teale, and Bonnie Urso. Deborah

Hamer, director of the NNI, offered advice, commiserated, traded war stories, and in ways large and small contributed to my understanding of the topic.

I'm very grateful for the support of the New-York Historical Society. Louise Mirrer, president and CEO, allowed me to create the New Amsterdam Project, which has served as a base not only for bringing history into the public sphere but for continuing my own exploration of New York's earliest period. Valerie Paley and Margi Hofer supported my idea to mount the exhibition "New York Before New York," on which I worked while researching this book and the research for which informed the book, and they advised me as I curated it. Nicole Mahoney assisted me at the New Amsterdam Project with keen intelligence. I would also like to acknowledge Gerhard Schlansky, Sofia Lin, Ivan Skrtic, Saray Vazquez, Jessica Kowal, Luke Johnson, Ryan Lentini, Alex Kreuger, Rebecca Klassen, and Eleanor Gillers.

I'm grateful to Huntley Gill and the crew of the *John J. Harvey*, who took me out for a day on New York Harbor, recreating what transpired in the late summer of 1664 and giving me a chance to approach Manhattan Island in something like the way Richard Nicolls would have experienced it.

Kevan Fadden, of the Archaeological and Local History Society of Ampthill, Bedfordshire, sent me books, offered insights, and gave me a thoughtful personal tour of the town where Richard Nicolls was born.

I would like to thank Chief Vincent Mann of the Turtle Clan of the Ramapough Lunaape Nation for sharing his knowledge, insights, and passion. Thanks also to Michaeline Picaro Mann and Brent Stonefish for helping me to appreciate the Lenape perspective on this history and to Beatrice Glow for sharing her knowledge and connections.

I'm grateful to many people at the New York State Library, Archives, and Museum, especially Jim Folts, Michael Lucas, Mark Schaming, and Susan Winchell-Sweeney.

People at the Dutch Consulate in New York helped in various ways during the time in which I worked on this book, including Ahmed Dadou, Monique Ruhe, and Sophie van Doornmalen.

Thank you to the New Amsterdam History Center for collaborating to produce a digital version of the Castello Plan, from which I came to see New Amsterdam in a new way. Thanks to Esme Berg, Toya Dubin, and especially Eduard van Dijk.

I'm grateful to Len Tantillo, whose work and dedication to his craft are a constant inspiration, and to Janny Venema for her translations and transcriptions. Jaap Jacobs gave me his insights into Petrus Stuyvesant. Lana Holden generously shared her research on Catalina Trico. Steve McErleane fed me digital files in the early stages.

A huge thank-you to Robert Cwiklik, Charles Gehring, Elizabeth Hines, Dennis Maika, Michael Martin, Jurriaan Ruys, and Pamela Twigg, all of whom read the manuscript and offered deep and constructive criticism, which improved it mightily.

Nina Forsythe fact-checked the manuscript with incisiveness and grace (though of course any remaining errors are mine alone).

I am grateful to the people at the Leiden Collection, including Sara Smith, Elizabeth Nogrady, Arthur Wheelock, Caroline van Cauwenberge, and Annie Correll. I also want to thank Tom Kaplan for his generosity and his insights into Dutch art history.

My thanks to Jeroen Dewulf, Martine Gosselink, Brandon Jacoby, Barbaro Martinez-Ruiz, Lavada Nahon, Ross Perlin, Jason Przewoznik, Susanah Shaw Romney, Lou Roper, Eva Shorto, and Isabella Watson.

Thank you to the Bedfordshire Archives, the Bodleian Library at Oxford University, the British National Archives, the Dutch National Archives, the Massachusetts Historical Society, and the Stadsarchief Amsterdam.

Thank you to Ambo-Anthos Uitgevers, especially my editor, Laurens Ubbink.

Thank you to my wife, Pamela, for being my greatest cheerleader.

I want to express my gratitude to everyone at W. W. Norton for supporting my work. Once again Julia Reidhead took time away from running the company to edit this book. She artfully guided me from the early idea phase through all the manuscript stages. Knowing that she was with me was especially reassuring in the early going. I also want to thank Louise Brockett, Caroline Adams, Meredith McGinnis, and Kyle Radler.

Finally, Anne Edelstein has been my agent since the neolithic period, aka the early 1990s, but she is much more than an agent. She has been there for all eight of my books: as sounding board, critic, reader, adviser, and an intelligent and cheerful champion, but above all as a friend.

Notes

A NOTE ON SOURCES

A major corpus of records that I relied on in writing this book is the official papers of the New Netherland colony. These documents, twelve thousand pages in all, give us a rich picture of what the Dutch built on Manhattan and in the wider colony. In particular, the records of the colony's later period allow us to appreciate why the English found the Dutch settlement so desirable. That said, anyone seeking to mine those records has a bit of a task. Some of the material remains untranslated and unpublished. Volumes that have been published are spread across different series and have different titles and translators. In the notes that follow, I have taken advantage of the fact that the nineteenth-century translator Edmund O'Callaghan, who sowed confusion by pulling apart the original volumes, nevertheless imposed some order on the material by dividing it into new volumes and assigning each a number. The first time I reference a volume, I give its full citation, including its number in the series. In subsequent notes referencing the same volume, I abbreviate it as NND, for New Netherland Documents, plus the volume number. I hope this will provide some clarity for anyone seeking to explore these records.

Most of the English records that I have relied on are found in three places: among the Clarendon State Papers at Oxford University, among the Colonial Office State Papers at the British National Archives, and in the New York State Archives. Many of these have been published (e.g., in the somewhat cryptically named *Books of General Entries of the Colony of New York*). These sources include information on Richard Nicolls's life in exile with the Duke of York, much of his correspondence during the standoff over the Dutch colony, and records of his time as the first (acting) governor of New York. Nicolls's will and his remarkable tombstone provided further biographical details.

PROLOGUE: THE VIEW FROM THE MOUNTAINTOP

3 **at least six centuries:** Grumet, Robert S. *The Munsee Indians: A History.* Norman: University of Oklahoma Press, 2009, 29.

4 **He gestures for me:** My interview with Chief Mann was conducted on July 16, 2023. Zimmer, David M. "NYU Researchers Study Toxic Ford Site, Ramapough-Lenape's Health." Northjersey.com, Aug. 30, 2017; Boburg, Shawn. "Donald Trump's Long History of Clashes with Native Americans." *Washington Post,* July 25, 2016; Illick-Frank, Emma. "NJ Superfund Lawsuit Offers Tribal Land a Path from Contamination to Cultural Restoration." Gothamist.com, June 28, 2022.

5 **The lack of federal:** Fallon, Scott. "Ramapoughs' Anger at Donald Trump Endures." Northjersey.com, July 4, 2016; Boburg, "Donald Trump's Long History."

6 **In fact, New York:** New York City Department of Health and Mental Hygiene. "Health of Indigenous Peoples of the Americas Living in New York City." *EPI Research Report,* Dec. 2021; Sandoval, Gabriel. "Native American New Yorkers Grow in Number, Latest Census Shows." Thecity. nyc, Oct. 10, 2021.

8 **We can track:** Huygens Instituut. "5 Million Scans VOC Archives Online and Searchable." Huygens.knaw.nl, Oct. 2, 2023.

8 **From "incidental" efforts:** Slavevoyages.org; Van Welie, Rik. "Slave Trading and Slavery in the Dutch Colonial Empire: A Global Comparison." *NWIG: New West-Indian Guide/Nieuwe West-Indische Gids* 82 (2008): 53.

CHAPTER 1: THE INVADER

15 **If the coastline:** I am referring here to what is officially called the New York–New Jersey Harbor Estuary or sometimes the Hudson Raritan Estuary. The most authoritative study of the length of the coastline that I know of was done by the US Treasury in 1910, which came up with a figure of 771 miles, but it described a smaller area than the New York–New Jersey Harbor Estuary as it is defined today. My calculation of the additional coastline comes to 125 miles, for a total of 896 miles. The California coastline is 840 miles long. Sources: email exchange with John Waldman; Lopate, Philip. *Waterfront: A Walk around Manhattan.* New York: Knopf Doubleday, 2005, 51; Yozzo, David, Pace Wilber, and Robert J. Will. "Beneficial Use of Dredged Material for Habitat Creation, Enhancement, and Restoration in New York–New Jersey Harbor." *Journal of Environmental Management* 73, no. 1 (Nov. 2004): 39–52; Hudson River Foundation. "NY/NJ Harbor & Estuary Program." Hudsonriver.org, accessed Apr. 3, 2022.

16 **Consider that 40 percent:** National Park Service. "Fact Sheet: Ellis Island—Statue of Liberty NM." NPS.gov, accessed Apr. 7, 2022.

16 **Consider that for a portion:** New York State Canal Corporation. "Canal History." Canals.ny.gov, accessed Oct. 10, 2022.

16 **"We sing this":** Sung by Grandmother Clara Soaring Hawk at "Future 400," National Museum of the American Indian, Mar. 27, 2024. A video of this version of the water song is viewable at singthewatersong.com.

18 **"exceedingly well fitted":** Stokes, I. N. Phelps. *The Iconography of Manhattan Island.* 6 vols. New York: Dodd, 1915–1928, vol. 4, 240.

18 **The packing of the holds:** Public Records Office. *Calendar of State Papers, Colonial, America and West Indies, Vol. 5, 1661–1668.* London, 1880, 189–90.

19 **"The woods are so":** Smith, John. *Adverts for Unexperienced Planters.* London, 1631, 6.

19 **"a desert Wildernesse":** Johnson, Edward. *Johnson's Wonder-Working Providence, 1628–1651.* Boston, 1825, 21.

20 **Sanhican. Naraticon. Canomaker:** All taken from Visscher, Nicolaes. "Novi Belgii Novaeque Angliae: Nec non partis Virginiae tabula multis in locis emendate." Amsterdam, 1685, loc.gov, accessed May 2022.

20 **They were going to dig:** Smith, John. *The Generall Historie of Virginia, New-England, and the Summer Isles.* London, 1624, 53; "Scuppet." Historicjamestown.org, accessed Jan. 2022.

20 **Their first interaction:** Philbrick, Nathaniel. *Mayflower: Voyage, Community, War.* New York: Penguin, 2007, 64.

21 **"informe all men":** O'Callaghan, E. B., and Berthold Fernow, trans. *Documents Relative to the Colonial History of the State of New York* (hereafter cited as *Docs. Rel.*). 15 vols. Albany: Weed, Parsons, 1856–1887, vol. 3, 57–58.

22 **"Our trusty and well beloved":** *Docs. Rel.*, 3: 51, 54.

22 **In order to defend:** Israel, Jonathan. *The Dutch Republic: Its Rise, Greatness, and Fall—1477–1806.* Oxford: Oxford University Press, 1995, 766.

23 **"hand grenades, fire works":** Sells, A. Lytton, trans. *The Memoirs of James II: His Campaigns as Duke of York, 1652–1660.* Bloomington: Indiana University Press, 1962, 146.

23 **In the same action:** Sells, *Memoirs of James II*, 145.

24 **In a battle at Étampes:** Sells, *Memoirs of James II*, 65–70.

24 **known to post:** Van Laer, Arnold J. F., trans. *New York Historical Manuscripts: Dutch* vol. 4. *Council Minutes 1638–1649.* Baltimore: Genealogical Publishing, 1974 (hereafter cited as NND, 4): 524–26.

24 **Claes Verbraech:** *Docs. Rel.*, 2: 410; Gehring, Charles T., trans. and ed. *Delaware Papers, Dutch Period, 1648–1664.* New Netherland Documents Series, vols. 18–19. Baltimore: Genealogical Publishing, 1981, 283. An English record, which was translated into Dutch then retranslated into English, lists the skipper as Claes Verkaech. There is no known person of that name in any of the records of the Dutch colony. My assumption is that the name Verbraech was miscopied. (My thanks to Dennis Maika for suggesting this and for noting Verbraech's connection to the South River.)

25 **for making bows:** Goddard, Ives. "The Origin and Meaning of the Name 'Manhattan.'" *New York History* 92, no. 4 (2010): 277–93.

25 **thirty-six cannons and a crack team:** Brodhead, John Romeyn. *The History of the State of New York, 1609–1691.* 2 vols. New York: Harper & Brothers, 1871, vol. 2, 20.

25 **Most of the wealth:** Nicolls, Richard. "Will of Richard Nicolls, Gentleman," July 14, 1670. National Archives, Kew. Ref no. PROB 11/333/329.

CHAPTER 2: THE DEFENDER

27 **"How They Were First":** Shorto, Russell. *The Island at the Center of the World: The Epic Story of Dutch Manhattan and the Forgotten Colony That Shaped America.* New York: Doubleday, 2004, 319.

30 **thirty-four people as witches:** Woodward, Walter. *Prospero's America.* Chapel Hill: University of North Carolina Press, 2013, 210.

30 **visiting Jesuit priest:** Jameson, J. F. *Narratives of New Netherland, 1609–1664.* New York: Charles Scribner's Sons, 1909; repr. New York: Barnes and Noble, 1937, 259.

30 **twenty-five languages:** Perlin, Ross. "Were 18 Languages Spoken in New Amsterdam?" Zoom talk. New Amsterdam History Center, New York, Oct. 11, 2022. Perlin estimates that twenty-six languages were spoken.

31 **"resolved by the Court":** Fernow, Berthold, ed. *The Records of New Amsterdam, from 1653 to 1674* (hereafter cited as RNA). 7 vols. New York: Knickerbocker, 1897, vol. 5, 104.

31 **"At this conjuncture":** RNA, 5: 105.

31 **about 150 in total:** RNA, 5: 115–16.

32 **He is a man:** I base this study of Stuyvesant's visage on the portrait, painted circa 1660, in the New-York Historical Society.

33 **laces his speech:** O'Callaghan, E. B., ed. and trans. *Remonstrance of New Netherland, and the Occurrences There, Addressed to the High and Mighty Lords States General of the United Netherlands.* Albany: Weed, Parsons, 1856, 47.

34 **"He believed he was":** Jacobs, Jaap. Conversation with the author, Oct. 7, 2021.

35 **"prayed to his God":** Venema, Janny, trans. and ed. *Correspondence 1663–1664.* New Netherland Documents Series, vol. 15. Unpublished (hereafter cited as NND, 15): 125.

35 **"All that has happened":** NND, 15: 125(2)v.

36 **Meanwhile, 150 miles:** Sources for this council: NND, 15: 129–30; *Docs. Rel.*, 13: 380–81; Bruchac, Margaret. "Revisiting Pocumtuck History in Deerfield." *Historical Journal of Massachusetts* 39, no. 1–2 (Summer 2011): 30–77; Bruchac, Margaret, and Peter Thomas. "Locating 'Wissatinnewag' in John Pynchon's Letter of 1663." *Historical Journal of Massachusetts* 34, no. 1 (Winter 2006): 56–82; O'Callaghan, E. B.

History of New Netherland, or New York under the Dutch. New York: Appleton, 1848, 518–19; *Docs. Rel.*, 2: 297–98.

36 **"Let them send us":** NND, 15: 129; *Docs. Rel.*, 13: 381.

37 **a man named Saheda:** Van Laer, A. J. F., trans. and ed. *Correspondence of Jeremias van Rensselaer.* Albany: University of the State of New York, 1932, 358.

38 **"The neat picture":** Richter, Daniel. "Cultural Brokers and Intercultural Politics: New York–Iroquois Relations, 1664–1701." *Journal of American History* 75, no. 1 (June 1988): 40–67.

38 **We might go even further:** Otterbein, Keith. "Huron vs. Iroquois: A Case Study in Inter-Tribal Warfare." *Ethnohistory* 26, no. 2 (Spring 1979): 141–52; Richter, Daniel. "War and Culture: The Iroquois Experience." *William and Mary Quarterly* 40, no. 4 (Oct. 1983): 528–59.

40 **Abraham Staets:** *Docs. Rel.*, 13: 116.

40 **flames, bloody murder:** NND, 15: 135.

41 **above the gate:** The provincial secretary's office was in this location. Charles Gehring offered in conversation his opinion that this would also have been Stuyvesant's office.

41 **"Our last letters":** NND, 15: 138.

43 **"from skippers and passengers":** NND, 15: 138(5–6).

43 **"introduce bishops":** NND, 15: 138(4).

44 **"in order to make":** NND, 15: 138(9).

45 **"an experiment with":** Venema, Janny, trans. and ed. *Correspondence 1659–1660.* New Netherland Documents Series, vol. 13. Syracuse: Syracuse University Press, 2022 (hereafter cited as NND, 13): 201.

45 **"Turks and Heathens":** Udemans, Godefridus. *'T Geestelijck roer van 't Coopmansschip.* Dordrecht, 1640, 363; quoted in Maika, Dennis. "Slavery, Race, and Culture in Early New York." *De Halve Maen* 73, no. 2 (Summer 2000): 29.

46 **"a very poor lot":** NND, 15: 139.

46 **the young man:** Some sources give his birth year as 1630. Blom, F., and H. Looijesteijn. "A Land of Milk and Honey: Colonial Propaganda and the City of Amsterdam, 1656–1664." *De Halve Maen* 85, no. 3 (2012): 47–56.

CHAPTER 3: ENEMY WATERS

48 **Nicolls was sailing:** Shurtleff, Nathaniel, ed. *Records of the Governor and Company of the Massachusetts Bay in New England.* Boston, 1854, vol. 4, pt. 2, 157–68.

49 **Houses were spread:** Cummings, Abbott Lowell. "The Domestic Architecture of Boston, 1660–1725." *Archives of American Art Journal* 9, no. 4 (1971): 1–2.

49 **"full of good shopps":** Maverick, Samuel. *A Briefe Discription of New England and the Severall Townes Therein.* Boston, 1885, 15.

49 **making them pay "tribute"**: Peterson, Mark. *The City-State of Boston.* Princeton: Princeton University Press, 2019, 51–54.
49 **"courteously enterteyned"**: Shurtleff, *Records of the Governor and Company,* vol. 4, pt. 2, 157.
50 **"words and carriages""**: Shurtleff, *Records of the Governor and Company,* vol. 4, pt. 2, 168.
51 **"terming it a badge"**: Maverick, *Briefe Discription,* 17–20.
51 **On top of all this**: Maverick, *Briefe Discription,* 8.
52 **"given a good example"**: Shurtleff, *Records of the Governor and Company,* vol. 4, pt. 2, 158–60.
54 **"a little above"**: Lamb, Martha. *History of the City of New York.* New York, 1877, vol. 1, 219.
55 **"make an act"**: Shurtleff, *Records of the Governor and Company,* vol. 4, pt. 2, 163.
55 **"many more things"**: Shurtleff, *Records of the Governor and Company,* vol. 4, pt. 2, 164.

CHAPTER 4: STUYVESANT'S ERROR
56 **a cluster of dusty streets**: Venema, Janny. *Beverwijck: A Dutch Village on the American Frontier, 1652–1664.* Albany: State University of New York Press, 2003. Venema says that while New Amsterdam's houses were brick, most of those in Beverwijck were of wood (73).
57 **La Montagne was**: Van Laer, Arnold J. F., trans. *New York Historical Manuscripts: Dutch,* vol. 1. *Register of the Provincial Secretary, 1638–1642.* Baltimore: Genealogical Publishing, 1974 (hereafter cited as NND, 1): 59, 122, 192; Van Laer, Arnold J. F., trans. *New York Historical Manuscripts: Dutch,* vol. 2. *Register of the Provincial Secretary, 1642–1647.* Baltimore: Genealogical Publishing, 1974 (hereafter cited as NND, 2): 32, 60; NND, 4: 1, 18, 94, 196, 265; Gehring, Charles T., trans. and ed. *New York Historical Manuscripts: Dutch,* vol. 5. *Council Minutes, 1652–1654.* Baltimore: Genealogical Publishing, 1983 (hereafter cited as NND, 5): 444; Gehring, Charles T., and Janny Venema, trans. and eds. New Netherland Documents Series, vol. 8. *Council Minutes: 1656–1658.* Syracuse: Syracuse University Press, 2018 (hereafter cited as NND, 8): 148, 904; NND, 13: 114; New Netherland Documents Series, vol. 14. *Correspondence, 1661–1662.* New York State Archives. Unpublished, 40; NND, 15: 94, 124, 133.
58 **"indisposition"**: NND, 15: 140.
59 **It came from one**: New Netherland Documents Series, vols. 10.1, 10.2, 10.3. *Council Minutes, 1661–1664.* New York State Archives. Unpublished (hereafter cited as NND, 10.1, 10.2, or 10.3), 10:3: 7–8; *Docs. Rel.,* 14: 540–41; Romney, Susanah Shaw. *New Netherland Connections.* Chapel Hill: University of North Carolina Press, 2014, 269–86.
59 **"the great Sunk squa"**: *The Second Book of Records of the Town of*

Southampton. Sag Harbor, NY, 1877. Thehamptons.com, accessed Oct. 2023.

60 **"Three ships would come":** NND, 10.3: 7–8.
60 **A month later:** *Second Book of Records of Southampton,* 10; NND, 10.3: 7–8; *Docs. Rel.,* 14: 540–41; Romney, *New Netherland Connections,* 269–86.
61 **"Whereas we are of":** RNA, 5: 105–6.
62 **"not only granted":** RNA, 5: 106.
62 **"the English general":** *Docs. Rel.,* 2: 410.
64 **"a deceitful race":** Oppenheim, Samuel. *American Jewish Historical Society Publications.* Vol. 18, 1909, 5.
64 **sold off to work:** Maika, Dennis. "To 'Experiment with a Parcel of Negroes': Incentive, Collaboration, and Competition in New Amsterdam's Slave Trade.'" *Journal of Early American History* 10 (2020): 66.

CHAPTER 5: RABBITS ON AN ANTHILL
70 **"We saw an immense":** Underwood, Andrew. *17th Century Ampthill and Hugh Reeve Its True and Lawful Parson.* Ampthill, Bedfordshire, UK: Merry Printers, 2000, 11.
70 **"Breeding, Rearing":** Moubray, Bonington. *A Practical Treatise on the Breeding, Rearing, and Fattening All Kinds of Domestic Poultry, Pheasants, Pigeons, and Rabbits.* London, 1830, 174.
70 **The central stream:** Underwood, *17th Century Ampthill,* 13, 33.
70 **There was a church:** Underwood, Andrew. *Ampthill Parish Church.* Ampthill, Bedfordshire, UK: Merry Printers, 2007, 6.
70 **The present building:** Underwood, *Ampthill Parish Church,* 7.
70 **In Shakespeare's *Henry VIII*:** Shakespeare, William. *Henry VIII,* Act 4, scene 1.
71 **Anglo-Saxon origin:** University of Nottingham. "Bedfordshire/Ampthill." Key to English Place Names, http://kepn.nottingham.ac.uk.
71 **part of his courtship:** Underwood, *17th Century Ampthill,* 22.
71 **"To the Kingdom":** Stained-glass window in Ampthill Parish Church.
72 **"And it is well known":** Norton, Rictor. "Queen James and His Courtiers." Gay History and Literature, http://rictornorton.co.uk/jamesi.htm.
72 **when James got a look:** Underwood, *17th Century Ampthill,* 25.
72 **"for the exercise":** Underwood, *17th Century Ampthill,* 73.
73 **six children, was born:** Underwood, *17th Century Ampthill,* 77.
73 **His mother retained:** Underwood, *17th Century Ampthill,* 77.
73 **And whenever he did:** Underwood, *17th Century Ampthill,* 24.
74 **a title James:** Sells, *Memoirs of James II,* 2.
74 **"bold and intrepid":** Nicholls, Walter. *Sergeant Francis Nicholls.* New York: Grafton, 1909, 12.
74 **ten grand bedrooms:** Underwood, *17th Century Ampthill,* 24–25.
74 **An illustration exists:** Ferguson, Lydia. "Tennis: 'The Game of Kings.'"

Research Collections at Trinity, Trinity College Dublin, June 30, 2016. Accessed Apr. 21, 2024.

74 **a crack tennis player:** Oxford University, Bodleian Libraries. Clarendon State Papers, vol. 83, no. 217 (hereafter cited as MSS. Clarendon).

75 **"princes are not bound":** Gardiner, Samuel Rawson, ed. *Constitutional Documents of the Puritan Revolution.* Oxford: Clarendon, 1906, 16.

76 **"only under me":** Gardiner, *Constitutional Documents,* 9.

76 **"conserve and maintain":** Gardiner, *Constitutional Documents,* 9–10.

76 **"Popish superstition":** Gardiner, *Constitutional Documents,* 14.

76 **"sundry new ceremonies":** Gardiner, *Constitutional Documents,* 14.

76 **"very great and imminent":** Gardiner, *Constitutional Documents,* 13.

77 **"Devil give you":** "Jenny Geddes." Stgilescathedral.org.uk, accessed Apr. 21, 2024.

78 **"bullet of a great":** Spencer, Charles. *To Catch a King: Charles II's Great Escape.* New York: Harper Collins, 2023, 4.

79 **where a wall painting:** Panel accompanying the painting in the White Hart Tavern, Amtphill, text by John Hele.

79 **"I serve":** Panel accompanying the painting in the White Hart Tavern, Amtphill, text by John Hele.

79 **In October of that year:** "Sir Lewis Dyve." Bedford Borough Council, Bedfordshire Archives. Bedford.gov.uk, accessed Apr. 21, 2024.

79 **"commanded a troop of horse":** Nicolls, Richard. Richard Nicolls's tombstone, St. Andrew's Church, Ampthill, Bedfordshire, UK.

80 **A troop such as Nicolls:** Nicholls, *Sergeant Francis Nicholls,* 12.

80 **"unboy" his eldest:** Spencer, *To Catch a King,* 4.

CHAPTER 6: THE TRAILBLAZER

85 **four million pounds:** Shorto, Russell. *Amsterdam: A History of the World's Most Liberal City.* New York: Doubleday, 2013, 116.

85 **Trico herself tells:** O'Callaghan, E. B. *The Documentary History of the State of New York.* 4 vols. Albany: Weed, Parsons, 1849–1851, vol. 3, 32–33.

85 **still holds services:** DeWaalseKerk.nl.

86 **they made marks:** Gemeente Amsterdam Stadsarchief. "Catharina Triko." Betrothal Register, archive no. 5001, inventory no. 428, p. 328.

86 **a landscape of wide:** Jameson, *Narratives of New Netherland,* 54–56.

87 **So two couples:** Zabriskie, George Olin, and Alice P. Kenney. "The Founding of New Amsterdam: Fact and Fiction: Part 1." *De Halve Maen* 51 (July 1976): 15; O'Callaghan, *Documentary History,* vol. 3, 32–33.

87 **"some huts of Bark":** Zabriskie and Kenney, "Founding of New Amsterdam," 12.

87 **"jet black, quite sleek":** Van der Donck, Adriaen. *A Description of New Netherland.* Lincoln: University of Nebraska Press, 2008, 73–74.

87 **all members of the:** O'Callaghan, *Documentary History,* vol. 3, 51.

87 "came & made Covenants": O'Callaghan, *Documentary History*, vol. 3, 51.

88 "yᵉ sᵈ Indians were": O'Callaghan, *Documentary History*, vol. 3, 51.

90 pregnant with their: Zabriskie, George Olin. "The Founding Families of New Netherland." *De Halve Maen* 46, no. 4 (1972): 14.

90 "Peace or war with neighbors": Van der Donck, *Description*, 90.

91 they marked important: Grumet, *Munsee Indians*, 83–87.

92 has argued that: Grumet, *Munsee Indians*, 52.

92 "all the Old Dutch records": Paltsits, Victor, ed. *Minutes of the Executive Council of the Province of New York*. Administration of Francis Lovelace, 1668–1673, vol. 1, 43–47. This entry mostly concerns Staten Island, but the paragraph on p. 47 shifts to Manhattan.

92 "they had all their grain": Newnetherlandinstitute.org, accessed Apr. 22, 2024.

94 Among the last: "The Walking Purchase." Delawaretribe.org, accessed Apr. 23, 2024; "Walking Purchase." Buckscounty.gov, accessed Apr. 23, 2024; Harper, Steven. "Making History: Documenting the 1737 Walking Purchase." *Pennsylvania History* (Spring 2010): 217–33.

95 "Nothing must be left": Van der Donck, *Description*, 91.

96 When Sarah was grown: Zabriskie, "Founding Families of New Netherland," pt. 3, 11.

96 first official school opened: Stokes, *Iconography*, vol. 1, 19.

97 Kieft issued edicts: Stokes, *Iconography*, vol. 1, 19.

97 illegal furs crowded out: Jacobs, Jaap. *New Netherland: A Dutch Colony in Seventeenth Century America*. Leiden: Brill, 2005, 205.

97 In the early years: Jacobs, *New Netherland,* 198.

98 Similar stories played out: NND, 1: 5, 6, 50, 76, 78, 79, 80, 89.

98 with descendants who: "Vita Brevis." Americanancestors.org, accessed Apr. 22, 2024.

98 I've made it elsewhere: Shorto, *Amsterdam*, chaps. 2 and 7.

99 herring to soap: Shorto, *Amsterdam*, 34–37.

99 an experiment got under way: Shorto, *Island*, 105–6.

100 The toleration that the Dutch: There is a long literature on the development of religious toleration in the Dutch Republic. For one-stop shopping it is chronicled in Israel, *Dutch Republic,* 490–645. One instance of its spread is detailed in Israel, Jonathan, and Stuart Schwartz. *The Expansion of Tolerance: Religion in Dutch Brazil (1624–1654)*. Amsterdam: Amsterdam University Press, 2007.

100 "that each person": "The Union of Utrecht, January 23, 1579." Constitution.org, accessed June 26, 2024.

101 "betook himself": *Docs. Rel.*, 1: 305.

102 The ancestors of: Gelfand, Noah. "A Transatlantic Approach to Understanding the Formation of a Jewish Community in New Netherland and New York." *New York History* 89, no. 4 (Fall 2008): 375–95;

Maybaum, Ignaz. "Sephardim and Ashkenazim." *European Judaism: A Journal for the New Europe* 4, no. 1 (Summer 1969): 29–33.

103 **Sixteen ships left:** Hershkowitz, Leo. "By Chance or Choice: Jews in New Amsterdam 1654." American Jewish Archives, Cincinnati, 2005, 3.

103 **He made for New Amsterdam:** Gelfand, "Transatlantic Approach," 377.

104 **Then the government:** *Docs Rel.*, 12: 96.

104 **"depart whenever":** New York State Archives. New Netherland, Council. Dutch Colonial Council Minutes, 1638–1665, series A1809, vol. 6.

105 **Scholarly estimates:** Grumet, *Munsee Indians*, 16.

105 **Waves of infectious:** Starna, William A. "From Homeland to New Land: A History of the Mahican Indians, 1600–1830." Northeast Region NAGPRA Program, National Parks Service, 2011, 42.

106 **"none of the chiefs":** Gehring, Charles, and William Starna. *A Journey into Mohawk and Oneida Country*. Syracuse: Syracuse University Press, 2013, 4.

106 **"numbers have dwindled":** Van der Donck, *Description,* 69.

106 **"there is now":** Gehring, Charles T., and Robert S. Grumet. "Observations of the Indians from Jasper Danckaerts's Journal 1679–1680." *William and Mary Quarterly* 44, no. 1 (Jan. 1987): 107.

106 **"were nothing short":** Grumet, *Munsee Indians*, 65.

106 **six hundred deeds:** Grumet, Robert. *First Manhattans*. Norman: University of Oklahoma Press, 2011, 60.

106 **One day two Lenape:** Jameson, *Narratives of New Netherland*, 213.

107 **"in the presence of":** NND, 4: 232–33.

109 **Adam Roelantsen:** NND, 2: 152c and 152d.

109 **"a whore and a wampum thief":** NND, 2: 139e.

109 **They bought land:** O'Callaghan, Edmund. *Calendar of Dutch Historical Manuscripts in the Office of the Secretary of State*. Albany: Weed, Parsons, 1865; repr. Gregg Press, 1968, 367; wikitree.com, accessed Apr. 22, 2024.

CHAPTER 7: THE EXILE

111 **"a true and faithfull":** "Will of Richard Nicolls, Gentleman."

111 **"preferred Exile":** Nicholls, *Sergeant Francis Nicholls*, 12.

112 **Within days of his arrival:** Routledge, F. J., et al. *Calendar of Clarendon State Papers Preserved in the Bodleian Library*. 5 vols. Oxford: Clarendon, 1869–1970, vol. 1, 421.

112 **by the name of Robert Moray:** Robertson, Alexander. *The Life of Sir Robert Moray: Soldier, Statesman and Man of Science (1608–1673)*. London: Longmans, Green, 1922, 58–59.

113 **"a sad, poor condition":** Pepys, Samuel. *The Diary of Samuel Pepys*. London, 1893, entry for May 16, 1660.

113 **"At this time I have":** Lister, T. H. *The Life and Administration of Edward, First Earl of Clarendon*. London, 1838, vol. 1, 375.

114 **"Parliament was victorious"**: Kishlansky, Mark. *A Monarchy Transformed: Britain 1603–1714*. London: Penguin, 1996, 161.

114 **"a most splenetick"**: Harris, William. *An Historical Account of the Lives and Writings of James I and Charles I and of the Lives of Oliver Cromwell and Charles II*. London, 1814, vol. 3, 13.

114 **"did Laugh so"**: Howell, Roger, Jr. "Cromwell's Personality: The Problems and Promises of a Psychohistorical Approach." *Biography* 1, no. 1 (Winter 1978): 50.

115 **no more than eight men**: Sells, *Memoirs of James II*, 58.

115 **fought door to door**: Sells, *Memoirs of James II*, 112.

117 **"communicating with the King's"**: Routledge et al., *Calendar of Clarendon State Papers*, vol. 3, no. 166.

117 **Or he might have**: Routledge et al., *Calendar of Clarendon State Papers*, vol. 3, no. 176.

118 **The leaders crossed**: Firth, C. H. "Cromwell and the Insurrection of 1655." *English Historical Review* 4, no. 14 (Apr. 1889): 325.

118 **"The writer saw"**: Routledge et al., *Calendar of Clarendon State Papers*, vol. 3, no. 176.

118 **He may have been confined**: *West Stow Parish Registers, 1558 to 1850, and Wordwell Parish Registers, 1580–1850, with Sundry Notes*. Woodbridge, England: George Booth, 1903, 203.

119 **wrote a poem**: Denham, Sir John. *The Poetical Works of Sir John Denham*. New Haven: Yale University Press, 1928, 135–41; MSS. Clarendon, vol. 2, no. 217.

120 **"His most serene"**: *New Englander and Yale Review, 1886*. Vol. 9, new series, 985.

121 **He lived a long**: Ramsey, Robert. "Richard Cromwell, Protector of England." *American Historical Review* 42, no. 2 (Jan. 1937): 302–3.

122 **"The whole design"**: Routledge et al., *Calendar of Clarendon State Papers*, vol. 3, 353.

122 **"Nicolls arrived safe"**: MSS. Clarendon, vol. 64, no. 133.

123 **telling him to go to Amiens**: Turner, F. C. *James II*. London, 1948, 58.

123 **hundred-mile journey**: MSS. Clarendon, vol. 64, no. 236–37.

124 **1,200 infantrymen**: Turner, *James II*, 58.

124 **"Receiving the dukes"**: MSS. Clarendon, vol. 64, no. 236–37.

124 **"I have communicated"**: MSS. Clarendon, vol. 64, no. 236–37.

124 **"I promised to inform you"**: MSS. Clarendon, vol. 65, no. 143–44.

125 **"very earnest"**: MSS. Clarendon, vol. 67, no. 299. (Note this is in Routledge et al., *Calendar of Clarendon State Papers*, vol. 66, p. 435.)

125 **"Mr Nicholls is to be"**: MSS. Clarendon, vol. 66, no. 312–13.

125 **authorized his agents**: Routledge et al., *Calendar of Clarendon State Papers*, vol. 4, 101; Abernathy, George. "The English Presbyterians and the Stuart Restoration: 1648–1663." *Transactions of the American Philosophical Society* 55, no. 2 (1965): 33.

125 **Charles sweetened:** Routledge et al., *Calendar of Clarendon State Papers*, vol. 4, 268–69.

125 **"free and general":** *Journal of the House of Lords: Vol. 11, 1660–1666.* London, 1767–1830, 7–8.

126 **"Your sentence is":** Brewer, J. S. *Letters and Papers, Foreign and Domestic, of the Reign of Henry VIII.* London, 1867, vol. 3, pt. 1, cxxxiv.

126 **"We do declare":** Charles II, King of England. "King Charles II. His declaration to all his loving subjects of the kingdom of England. Dated from his Court at Breda in Holland, the 4/14 of April." Reprinted by Christopher Higgins in Harts Close, over against the Trone-Church, 1660.

126 **Of the three Nicolls:** "Will of Richard Nicolls, Gentleman."

127 **They strolled along:** Pepys, *Diary*, Monday, May 14, 1660, to Tuesday, May 22, 1660.

127 **"seems to be a very":** Pepys, *Diary*, Thursday, May 17, 1660.

128 **women dressed:** Royal Collection Trust. *"The Embarkation of Charles II at Scheveningen*—Description." Rct.uk, accessed Apr. 22, 2024.

128 **"In the morning came":** Pepys, *Diary*, Wednesday, May 23, 1660.

CHAPTER 8: DOROTHEA ANGOLA

130 **"like a father":** *Docs. Rel.*, 1: 446.

130 **"Peacock like":** *Docs. Rel.*, 1: 310.

130 **They brandished:** *Docs. Rel.*, 1: 195–99.

130 **"Was it ever heard":** NND, 4: 291.

131 **"slaughtered . . . like sheep":** *Docs. Rel.*, X: 205–9; NND, 4: 313.

131 **"I think it's likely":** Jacobs, Jaap. Conversation with author on July 28, 2021.

131 **"It looks as if":** *Docs. Rel.*, 14: 126.

133 **Stuyvesant sent a letter:** Stuyvesant's letter is lost, but the directors of the West India Company refer to it in Gehring, Charles T., trans. and ed. New Netherland Documents Series, vol. 11. *Correspondence 1647–1653.* Syracuse: Syracuse University Press, 2000 (hereafter cited as NND, 11): 149.

134 **For one terribly:** RNA, 1: 2–5.

134 **"a bench of justice":** NND, 11: 149.

134 **Historian Dennis Maika:** This paragraph relies on Part 1 of Dennis Maika's forthcoming book *Merchants of Manhattan: Private Entrepreneurs and Their City Government in 17th Century New Netherland and New York.*

135 **Maika highlights:** Maika, *Merchants of Manhattan*, part 1. On the Varlets I have also consulted Snabel, Cor, and Elizabeth Johnson, *The Varlet Family of Amsterdam, and Their Associated Families in the American Colonies and in the Netherlands.* Varletfamilypbworks.com, accessed Apr. 22, 2024.

135 **Allard Antonides:** Gehring, Charles T., trans. and ed. New Netherland Documents Series, vol. 6. *Council Minutes: 1655–1656.* Syracuse: Syracuse University Press, 1995 (hereafter cited as NND, 6): 114b.

135 **Margaret Hardenbroeck:** Sources on Margaret Hardenbroeck include NND, 8: 691; 10.1: 176; 10.2: 421; 10.3: 175; Danckaerts, Jasper. *Journal of Jasper Danckaerts, 1679–1680.* New York: Charles Scribner's Sons, 1913; Koot, Christian. *Empire at the Periphery: British Colonists, Anglo-Dutch Trade, and the Development of the British Atlantic, 1621–1713.* New York: New York University Press, 2011, 161–62; Jacobs, *New Netherland,* 337–38; "The Philipse Family." Philipsemanorhall.com, accessed Apr. 22, 2024; Dann, Leslie, and Guido Jiminéz-Cruz, directors. "A Colonial Trading Woman: Margaret Hardenbroeck Philipse" (documentary). Hudsonvalley.org, Film and Video, accessed Apr. 22, 2024.

136 **"excessive covetousness":** Danckaerts, *Journal,* 40.

137 **"These new resident":** Maika, *Merchants of Manhattan.* The quote is from chapter 2 of an as-yet-unpublished manuscript.

137 **"We know he had":** Jacobs, Jaap. Personal conversation with author, July 28, 2021.

138 **In May 1660:** NND, 13: 74–74(4)v.

139 **"As the cultivation":** NND, 13: 74(3)v. I'm relying on Maika, "To 'Experiment with a Parcel of Negros,'" 33–69.

139 **It consisted of five children:** NND, 13: 70, 70(1), 70(2).

140 **"very stout and strong":** NND, 13: 185.

140 **"in dry and good condition":** Quoted in Maika, "To 'Experiment with a Parcel of Negros,'" 34.

140 **"Thus it was":** Gehring, Charles T., and J. A. Schiltkamp, trans. and eds. New Netherland Documents Series, vol. 17. *Curaçao Papers, 1640–1665.* Interlaken, NY: Heart of the Lakes Publishing, 1987, 172.

140 **"devising speculative":** Maika, "To 'Experiment with a Parcel of Negros,'" 33.

141 **We don't know:** Jacobs, Jaap. "The First Arrival of Enslaved Africans in New Amsterdam." *New York History* 104, no. 1 (Summer 2023): 96.

141 **The Portuguese were:** De Laet, Joannes. *Iaerlyck verhael van de verrichtinghen der Geoctroyeerde West-Indische compagnie.* The Hague: M. Nijhoff, 1931, 117; Jacobs, "First Arrival," 110.

141 **Portuguese middlemen:** Newson, Linda, and Susie Minchin. *From Capture to Sale: The Portuguese Slave Trade to Spanish South America in the Early Seventeenth Century.* Leiden: Brill, 2007, 32–33.

142 **People from other:** Dewulf, Jeroen. "Iberian Linguistic Elements among the Black Population in New Netherland (1614–1664)." *Journal of Pidgin and Creole Languages* 34, no. 1 (2019): 56–57.

142 **"As for the names":** Dewulf, Jeroen. Email exchange with author, Oct. 27, 2022.

143 **"there are many churches"**: Quoted in Mosterman, Andrea. *Spaces of Enslavement: A History of Slavery and Resistance in Dutch New York.* Ithaca: Cornell University Press, 2021, 42.

143 **born and baptized**: Dewulf, Jeroen. *Afro-Atlantic Catholics: America's First Black Christians.* Notre Dame, IN: University of Notre Dame Press, 2022, introduction.

143 **shared a common language**: Dewulf, "Iberian Linguistic Elements," 58.

144 **"were spacing their children"**: Romney, Susana Shaw. "Reytory Angola, Seventeenth-Century Manhattan (US)." In *As If She Were Free: A Collective Biography of Women and Emancipation in the Americas,* ed. Erica Ball et al. New York: Cambridge University Press, 2020, 68.

144 **An *mpungu* like this**: Cantwell, Anne-Marie, and Diana Dizerega Wall. "Looking for Africans in Seventeenth Century New Amsterdam." In *The Archaeology of Race in the Northeast,* ed. Christopher Matthews and Allison Manfra McGovern. Gainesville: University of Florida Press, 2015. *Mpungu* and *bilongo*: Barbaro Martinez-Ruiz. Interview with author, Sept. 14, 2023.

145 **Black people tended**: Mosterman, *Spaces of Enslavement*, 35–37.

146 **we have records**: Mosterman, *Spaces of Enslavement*, 45.

146 **In Amsterdam itself**: Ponte, Mark. "Blacks in Amsterdam around 1650." In *Blacks in Rembrandt's Time*, ed. Elmer Kolfin et al. Amsterdam: Rembrandt House Museum, 2020.

147 **"setting them free"**: NND, 4: 183.

147 **There is no evidence**: Mosterman, *Spaces of Enslavement*, 28.

147 **model of ancient Rome**: Mosterman, *Spaces of Enslavement*, 28.

148 **a six-acre tract**: New York State Archives. Letters Patent 12953-78, vol. 2, 128–29; references in Romney, "Reytory Angola," 69.

149 **"in order thus"**: Scott, Kenneth, and Kenn Stryker-Rodda, eds. *The Register of Salomon LaChaire.* Baltimore: Genealogical Publishing, 1978, 22.

150 **"The matter being"**: New Netherland Documents Series, vol. 9. *Council Minutes, 1660–1661.* New York State Archives. Unpublished, 557.

CHAPTER 9: RESTORATION LONDON

151 **"a heap of Houses"**: Sorbiere, M. *A Voyage to England.* London, 1709, 16.

153 **"Pimp statesmen"**: Sackville, Charles. *The Poems of Charles Sackville, Sixth Earl of Dorset.* New York: Garland, 1979, 137.

153 **"should have no more"**: Bickley, Francis, ed. *An English Letter Book.* London, n.d., 65.

153 **"I do not believe"**: Turner, *James II*, 61.

154 **It stayed there**: Kishlansky, *Monarchy Transformed*, 223.

155 **Charles was a man**: Kishlansky, *Monarchy Transformed*, 222–23.

155 **He was a passionate hunter**: Turner, *James II*, 62.

156 **may have had an affair**: Turner, *James II*, 69.

156 "has not the King's": Turner, *James II*, 64.

156 For the first year: Bucholz, Robert, project director. The Database of Court Officers, 1660–1837. "Household of James Duke of York (1660–1685)." Courtofficers.ctsdh.luc.edu, accessed Apr. 22, 2024.

157 "the Duke of York hath": Pepys, *Diary*, Oct. 7, 1660.

158 "the variation of the needle": Robertson, *Life of Sir Robert Moray*, 160.

158 deeply interested in: *Proceedings of the Massachusetts Historical Society* 16 (1878): 225–29.

158 "advice on how best": Turner, *James II*, 70.

159 Some historians consider: Scott, Jonathan. "'Good Night, Amsterdam': Sir George Downing and Anglo-Dutch Statebuilding." *English Historical Review* 118, no. 476 (2003): 356.

159 "the most unscrupulous": Scott, "Good Night, Amsterdam," 356.

159 "a perfidious rogue": Pepys, *Diary*, Mar. 12, 1661/62, and June 28, 1660.

160 He had a unique: Scott, "Good Night, Amsterdam," 337–38, 349–56.

160 In the summer of: Roper, L. H. "The Fall of New Netherland and Seventeenth-Century Anglo-American Imperial Formation, 1654–1676." *New England Quarterly* 87, no. 4 (Dec. 2014): 683.

161 "in all humilitie": New-York Historical Society. *Collections of the New-York Historical Society for the Year 1869*. New York, 1870, 19–57.

162 "the severall Colonies": *Docs. Rel.*, 3: 34–35.

162 "The King to all Captains": Public Records Office, *Calendar of State Papers, Vol. 5*, 132, 139, 144, 146, 161, 169, 170, 171, 172, 174, 176.

164 "looke on themselves": *Collections of New-York Historical Society for 1869*, 16–19.

164 What's more, Maverick: *Collections of New-York Historical Society for 1869*, 20.

165 "the mystery of this state": Scott, "Good Night, Amsterdam," 349.

166 "the wrongs inflicted": Rommelse, Gijs. "The Role of Mercantilism in Anglo-Dutch Political Relations, 1650–74." *Economic History Review* 63, no. 3 (Aug. 2010): 603.

166 "I am now sending": Rommelse, "Role of Mercantilism," 603.

167 "one Mr. Nicolls": Public Records Office, *Calendar of State Papers, Vol. 5*, 127.

167 "the Dutch have of late": Public Records Office, *Calendar of State Papers, Vol. 5*, 147, 157.

168 "Hudsons river": *Collections of New-York Historical Society for 1869*, 20.

168 Having "discoursed with": Public Records Office, *Calendar of State Papers, Vol. 5*, 183–84.

169 "for a voyage": Public Records Office, *Calendar of State Papers, Vol. 5*, 189.

169 "500 firelocks": Public Records Office, *Calendar of State Papers, Vol. 5*, 189–90.

169 **Clerk of the Signet:** Public Records Office, *Calendar of State Papers, Vol. 5,* 189.

170 **"Justices of the peace":** Public Records Office, *Calendar of State Papers, Vol. 5,* 192.

170 **"CHARLES the second":** Christoph, Peter, and Florence Christoph, eds. *Books of General Entries of the Colony of New York, 1664–1673.* Baltimore: Genealogical Publishing, 1982, 1–4.

172 **The "first" in the Doctrine:** Miller, Robert. "The Doctrine of Discovery: The International Law of Colonialism." *Indigenous Peoples' Journal of Law, Culture & Resistance* 5, no. 1 (2019): 35–42.

172 **"his Deputy":** Public Records Office, *Calendar of State Papers, Vol. 5,* 196.

173 **"to visite our Colony":** *Docs. Rel.,* 3: 51.

173 **"Though the maine end":** *Docs. Rel.,* 3: 57–59.

174 **"the possessing Long Island":** *Docs. Rel.,* 3: 57.

175 **"to an entyre submission":** *Docs. Rel.,* 3: 57.

175 **"wee cannot tell":** *Docs. Rel.,* 3: 60.

CHAPTER 10: DOPPELGANGER

180 **"My mast and rigging":** Ollard, Richard. *Man of War: Sir Robert Holmes and the Restoration Navy.* London: Phoenix, 1969, 93.

180 **The battered English:** Ollard, *Man of War,* 92–93.

180 **The Dutch company was:** Irwin, Douglas. "Mercantilism as Strategic Trade Policy: The Anglo-Dutch Rivalry for the East India Trade." *Journal of Political Economy* 99, no. 6 (Dec. 1999): 1300.

181 **"the Apple of its time":** Petram, Lodewijk. "Was the VOC the Most Valuable Company Ever? (Answer: NO!)." Worldsfirststockexchange. com, accessed Apr. 22, 2024.

181 **"That done, they":** *A true relation of the unjust, cruel, and barbarous proceedings against the English, at Amboyna in the East-Indies, by the Netherlandish Governour & Council there.* London, 1651, 17–18.

183 **"all the Court":** Pepys, *Diary,* Feb. 22, 1664.

184 **some past historians:** Schuyler Van Rensselaer, Mariana. *History of the City of New York in the Seventeenth Century.* New York: Macmillan, 1909, vol. 2, 1; Wilson, C. H. "Who Captured New Amsterdam?" *English Historical Review* 72, no. 284 (July 1957): 469–74.

184 **"protecting and promoting":** Ollard, *Man of War,* 86.

185 **made for Gorée Island:** Ollard, *Man of War,* 89–90.

185 **"If I goe":** Ollard, *Man of War,* 94.

185 **This led the Africans:** Ollard, *Man of War,* 117–18.

186 **"the King do joy":** Pepys, *Diary,* Sept. 29, 1664.

186 **Historian Lou Roper has:** Roper, "Fall of New Netherland," passim.

187 **"It is not possible":** Burns, E. Bradford, *A History of Brazil.* New York: Columbia University Press, 1993, 45.

188 **73 died en route:** Mosterman, Andrea. "Reconstructing a Slave Ship Voyage: The *Gideon* and the Dutch Slave Trade into New Amsterdam." Paper presented at 129th Annual Meeting of the American Historical Association, New York, Jan. 2015, p. 7.

188 **"You have now all":** Ollard, *Man of War*, 94.

CHAPTER 11: GRAVESEND

189 **"straw and clapboard":** Jacobs, Jaap. *Dutch Colonial Fortifications in North America, 1614–1676*. Amsterdam: New Holland Foundation, 2015, 14–16.

189 **"six old soldiers":** Jacobs, *Dutch Colonial Fortifications*, 14–16.

190 **The messenger would likely:** My thanks to Jaap Jacobs for his insights on Dutch communications in the region.

190 **"not a little frightened":** *Docs. Rel.*, 13: 393.

191 **"an obstruction to":** NND, 10.3: 297.

191 **"By effective resistance":** Jameson, *Narratives of New Netherland*, 464.

194 **supplied the lumber:** RNA, 1: 73.

194 **turned pirate:** NND, 5: 186.

194 **first migration of Puritans:** Baxter, Frances. *The Baxter Family*. New York, 1913, 8–9.

194 **He was at Stuyvesant's:** Baxter, *Baxter Family*, 15–16.

195 **Baxter reacted:** Baxter, *Baxter Family*, 16–17; O'Callaghan, *History of New Netherland*, vol. 2, 238–39, 243–46.

195 **Stuyvesant had him arrested:** NND, 6: 178a.

195 **He eventually made:** NND 6: 239–40.

CHAPTER 12: THE ALCHEMIST

197 **about one-fifth:** Cummins, Neil, Morgan Kelly, and Cormac Ó Gráda. "Living Standards and Plague in London, 1560–1665." *Economic History Review* 69 (2016): 4.

197 **"Many shall run":** Daniel 12:4, New International Version Bible.

198 **His fellow colonists:** "When Gov. John Winthrop Jr. Doctored the Connecticut Colony: For Free." Newenglandhistoricalsociety.com, accessed Apr. 22, 2024.

199 **"The power of His":** Henneton, Lauric. "A Matter Too Hard for Man to Comprehend: John Winthrop Jr. and the 'Leaping' Hill of Southern Maine." *New England Quarterly* 79, no. 3 (Sept. 2006): 465–67.

199 **Scholars of American:** Roper, "Fall of New Netherland," 667–69.

200 **Besides nearly exterminating:** Peterson, *City-State of Boston*, 51–52.

201 **This moderate alchemist:** Woodward, *Prospero's America*, 121–24; Winslow, Edward. *New-Englands salamander, discovered by an irreligious and scornefull pamphlet, called New-Englands Jonas cast up at London, &c. Owned by Major Iohn Childe, but not probable to be written by him*. London, 1647.

201 "city on a hill": Winthrop, John. "A City upon a Hill," 1630. Gilderlehrman. org, accessed July 1, 2024.

201 Winthrop's closeness with: Chaplin, Joyce. *Subject Matter: Technology, the Body, and Science on the Anglo-American Frontier, 1500–1676.* Cambridge, MA: Harvard University Press, 2001, 180–87.

201 They didn't kill: Woodward, *Prospero's America*, 116.

202 "powder of sea-horse": Black, Robert. *The Younger John Winthrop.* New York: Columbia University Press, 1968, 193.

204 Thanks to Winthrop: Woodward, *Prospero's America*, 210–15.

204 Charles Stuart rode in procession: "Venice: June 1660." In *Calendar of State Papers Relating to English Affairs in the Archives of Venice, Vol. 32, 1659–1661,* ed. Allen B. Hinds. London, 1931, 150–63; British History Online. "Venice: June 1660." British-history.ac.uk, accessed Dec. 19, 2022.

204 "who gave Judgement": Great Britain Record Commission. "Charles II, 1660: An Act of Free and Generall Pardon Indempnity and Oblivion." *Statutes of the Realm,* vol. 5, 1625–80. London, 1819.

204 "were entertained by": Hutchinson, Thomas. *A Collection of original papers relative to the history of the colony of Massachusets-Bay.* Boston, 1769, 419.

205 he penned an extravagant: Trumbull, J. H. *The Public Records of the Colony of Connecticut, 1636–1776.* Hartford, 1850–1890, vol. 1, 582–83.

206 "cast the skirt": Black, *Younger John Winthrop*, 209.

206 "I was wholly disappointed": *Collections of the Massachusetts Historical Society,* series 4, vol. 7, 548–49.

207 "privilidges wee inioy": *Collections of the Massachusetts Historical Society,* series 5, vol. 1, 369–70.

207 "peopled by the scrapings": *Docs. Rel.,* 13: 205.

208 stirred his interest: *Proceedings of the Massachusetts Historical Society* 16 (1878): 230–31, 234.

208 "I did speacke": *Collections of the Massachusetts Historical Society,* series 5, vol. 1, 391.

210 "I heartily thank you": *Proceedings of the Massachusetts Historical Society* 16 (1878): 212, 213.

210 "by reason of the late": Public Records Office, *Calendar of State Papers, Vol. 5,* 74.

210 He had thought: Public Records Office, *Calendar of State Papers, Vol. 5,* 74–75.

211 "the South Sea": Public Records Office, *Calendar of State Papers, Vol. 5,* 86–88.

212 in one go: Woodward, Walter. "From the State Historian: The Map That Wasn't a Map." Connecticuthistory.org, accessed Apr. 22, 2024.

213 It had been a year: Winthrop left London in June 1663.

214 "we intend with": Christoph and Christoph, *General Entries,* 24.

214 "It is no small satisfaction": *Proceedings of the Massachusetts Historical Society* 16 (1878): 222–23.

215 "I am not a litle proud": *Proceedings of the Massachusetts Historical Society* 16 (1878): 224; Black, *Younger John Winthrop*, 273.

215 "I do much applaud": *Proceedings of the Massachusetts Historical Society* 16 (1878): 226.

CHAPTER 13: THE DELEGATION

218 "could not leave": *Docs. Rel.*, 2: 410.

218 "the very distressed": *Docs. Rel.*, 13: 392.

218 "The Sergeant must be": Here and elsewhere, on the advice of translator Charles Gehring, I have substituted "native" for "savage," which was used in nineteenth-century translations but is a harsher and more loaded word than the Dutch *wild* (which literally means "person of the wilderness").

218 "Difficult, on account": NND, 15: 140.

220 "A Proclamation": Christoph and Christoph, *General Entries*, 24.

221 "Ordinances to be": Christoph and Christoph, *General Entries*, 25.

222 "a young man": Gehring, Charles T., trans. and ed. New Netherland Documents Series, vol. 12. *Correspondence: 1654–1658*. Syracuse: Syracuse University Press, 2003, 46.

223 "by what order": Christoph and Christoph, *General Entries*, 25–26.

CHAPTER 14: THE EFFUSION OF CHRISTIAN BLOOD

226 A gibbous moon: Nextfullmoon.org, accessed Apr. 22, 2024.

226 "A great end": *Docs. Rel.*, 3: 57.

227 "Col. Nicolls his": Christoph and Christoph, *General Entries*, 26–27.

230 "some principal burghers": NND, 15: 143; for their respective offices, see RNA, 7: 81.

231 At some point: NND, 10.3: 303.

233 "These to the Honorable": Christoph and Christoph, *General Entries*, 27.

233 "claimed this place": NND, 15: 144.

234 drinking was forbidden: Venema, *Beverwijck*, 135–37.

235 a short note to Nicolls: Christoph and Christoph, *General Entries*, 30.

236 "As the bearer": NND, 15: 141.

237 Stuyvesant, seeing this: O'Callaghan, *Calendar of Dutch Historical Manuscripts*, 269.

238 "would not be taken": NND, 15: 144.

CHAPTER 15: WHITE FLAG

240 "Honorable Sir": *Docs. Rel.*, 2: 411.

240 "purchase of the lands": *Docs. Rel.*, 2: 411–14.

240 "that his Majesty hath": Christoph and Christoph, *General Entries*, 31.

241 "Moreover it is": Christoph and Christoph, *General Entries*, 31–33.

241 "did not enter": NND, 15: 144(3), 144(4); *Docs. Rel.*, 2: 414.

242 "if a white": NND, 15: 144 (3), 144(4); *Docs. Rel.*, 2: 414.

243 "liberty to beate": Christoph and Christoph, *General Entries*, 29.

243 Soldiers loaded: Deposition of two soldiers. Archief van de Notarissen ter Standplaats Amsterdam. Stadsarchief Amsterdam. Notary Hendrick Outgers, Scan KLAB04497000096 and KLAB04497000097, Mar. 4, 1667. Translations by Simon Hart and Charles Gehring.

243 "to prosecute": Christoph and Christoph, *General Entries*, 34.

244 "They had put": *Docs. Rel.*, 13: 393.

245 "Poorly armed": Deposition of two soldiers.

245 "I shall precede": Deposition of two soldiers.

245 De Sille echoed: Stadsarchief Amsterdam. NA3016/1309, Notary Hendrick Venkel, Oct. 27, 1664.

245 a white flag: *Collections of the Massachusetts Historical Society*, series 4, vol. 6, 527–29.

246 "as if he wanted": Stokes, *Iconography*, vol. 4, 243.

246 "Now the lousy": Deposition of two soldiers.

248 "the like reall": *Collections of the Massachusetts Historical Society*, series 4, vol. 6, 526.

249 tavern of Hans Dreper: Stokes, *Iconography*, vol. 2, 269; Stuyvesant (*Docs. Rel.*, 2: 444) says they went to "the nearest tavern."

249 "from any mischief": *Docs. Rel.*, 2: 444.

250 he handed Stuyvesant: *Collections of the Massachusetts Historical Society*, series 4, vol. 6, 527–29.

251 "for reasons": *Docs. Rel.*, 2: 444.

251 "it was resolved": *Docs. Rel.*, 2: 445.

CHAPTER 16: "THE TOWN OF MANHATANS"
253 two hundred thousand years: Graham, J. L., L. Lawrence, W. H. Requejo. *Inventive Negotiation*. New York: Palgrave Macmillan, 2014, chap. 1.

255 "the just right": Christoph and Christoph, *General Entries*, 29.

255 Through time immemorial: Mnookin, Robert. *Bargaining with the Devil: When to Negotiate, When to Fight*. New York: Simon & Schuster, 2010, 27–28.

256 "misery, sorrow": *Docs. Rel.*, 2: 248.

257 "However, in regard": Christoph and Christoph, *General Entries*, 29.

258 "You may easily": Christoph and Christoph, *General Entries*, 30.

258 "honor shot": Deposition of soldiers. Stadsarchief Amsterdam, NA3016/1309. Notary Hendrick Venkel, Oct. 27, 1664.

258 Throughout history: LeoGrand, William, and Peter Kornbluh. *Back Channel to Cuba: The Hidden History of Negotiations between Washington and Havana*. Chapel Hill: University of North Carolina Press, 2015, passim.

260 "arrival of the English": NND, 10.3: 317. Note that the names of the "half slaves" are listed in O'Callaghan, *Calendar of Dutch Historical Manuscripts*, on p. 269, but the names are not listed in the corresponding record.

261 "true freedom": Secretan, Catherine. "'True Freedom' and the Dutch Tradition of Republicanism." *Republics of Letters* 2, no. 1 (2010). Arcade.stanford.edu, accessed Apr. 22, 2024.

263 The document they: I'm grateful to Dennis Maika for developing this argument in many articles and in conversations.

263 "free Denizens": Christoph and Christoph, *General Entries*, 35–37.

264 "if at any time": Christoph and Christoph, *General Entries*, 35–37.

266 "tobacco frenzy": Maika, Dennis. *Commerce and Community: Manhattan Merchants in the Seventeenth Century*. PhD dissertation, New York University, 1995, 118.

267 Just in the few: Maika, Dennis. "New Light on an Old Story: Re-examining the English Invasions of New Amsterdam, 1660–1664." Presentation at the New Netherland Seminar, Rotterdam Junction, NY, Sept. 13, 2012. For the ships, Maika is referencing *Docs. Rel.*, 2: 464–66.

267 "not once": *Docs. Rel.*, 2: 472.

267 Everyone in the colony: *Docs. Rel.*, 2: 472.

268 "The story goes": Maika, "New Light on an Old Story."

269 "come here from": Stokes, *Iconography*, vol. 4, 244.

269 It set the city: See Maika, Dennis. "'We Shall Bloom and Grow Like the Cedar on Lebanon': Dutch Merchants in English New York City, 1664–1672." *De Halve Maen* 74, no. 1 (Spring 2001): 9.

270 "To all People": Christoph and Christoph, *General Entries*, 41–42.

270 If the mood: Deposition of soldiers.

271 "the Towne of Manhatans": Christoph and Christoph, *General Entries*, 37.

271 "comprehend all": *Docs. Rel.*, 3: 105.

CHAPTER 17: REMAINING ENGLISH

276 He wrote the first: Ciecka, James. "The First Mathematically Correct Life Annuity." *Journal of Legal Economics* 15, no. 1 (2008): 59–63.

277 "Honorable and Strict": Dutch National Archives, collection 3.01.17, inv. nr. 1008. Nationaalarchief.nl, accessed Apr. 22, 2024. Translation by Jaap Jacobs is in note 4, Nationaalarchief.nl, accessed Apr. 22, 2024.

279 tending his garden: Fox, Frank. *The Four Days' Battle of 1666*. Andover, MA: Docema, 2009, 134.

280 "I hear fully": Pepys, *Diary*, Dec. 22, 1664.

280 Willem Doeckles: RNA, 5: 108.

280 Geleyn Verplanck: RNA, 5: 113.

280 Pieter Claessen: RNA, 5: 112.

280 Albert the Trumpeter: RNA, 5: 117.

280 "whence they came": Stokes, *Iconography*, vol. 4, 248.

280 "De Ruither being": *Docs. Rel.*, 3: 85.

281 "We, your Honors' loyal": RNA, 5: 114–15.

282 Mayor Willet put forth: RNA, 5: 269.

283 "the greatest sea fight": Fox, *Four Days' Battle*.

286 "we did not have": Van Laer, *Correspondence of Jeremias van Rensselaer*, 403.

CHAPTER 18: MERGER

288 "and I will obey": RNA, 5: 143.

289 "Whereas there is": Christoph and Christoph, *General Entries*, 54.

289 "conformable to": RNA, 5: 143.

289 "Democracy hath": *Collections of New-York Historical Society for 1869*, 119.

289 The Dutch ministers: Van Rensselaer, *History of the City of New York in the Seventeenth Century*, vol. 2, 20.

290 "may freely and": Christoph and Christoph, *General Entries*, 67.

290 "a Generall Liberty": *Collections of New-York Historical Society for 1869*, 118.

290 Nicolls understood: Christoph, Peter, ed. *New Netherland Historical Manuscripts: English*, vol. 22. *Administrative Papers of Governors Richard Nicolls and Francis Lovelace, 1664–1673*. Baltimore: Genealogical Publishing, 1980, 3–5.

290 The agreement established: Grumet, *Munsee Indians*, 113.

291 It was important: Christoph and Christoph, *General Entries*, 47–48.

291 Such a strong: Grumet, *Munsee Indians*, 147–48.

292 "Goods or Beaver": Maika, "To 'Experiment with a Parcel of Negros,'" 66; Christoph and Christoph, *General Entries*, 57.

293 "The Negroe is": Christoph and Christoph, *General Entries*, 52.

293 Nicolls obliged: Christoph and Christoph, *General Entries*, 53.

293 quietly forged: Christoph, Peter. "The Freedmen of New Amsterdam." In *A Beautiful and Fruitful Place: Selected Rensselaerswijck Seminar Papers*, ed. Nancy Zeller. Albany: New Netherland Publications, 1991, 164.

294 "welfare and mutual": *Docs. Rel.*, 3: 143–44.

294 He confirmed: Stokes, *Iconography*, vol. 6, 76; Christoph, "Freedmen of New Amsterdam," 164.

295 "judged thereunto": Wiecek, William. "The Statutory Law of Slavery and Race in the Thirteen Mainland Colonies of British America." *William and Mary Quarterly* 34, no. 2 (Apr. 1977): 261; *Memoirs of the Historical Society of Pennsylvania*, vol. 7. Philadelphia, 1860, 102.

295 "slave code": New York State. Acts of Assembly, passed in the Province of New York, from 1691 to 1718. London, 1719, 58.

296 fee of 200 pounds: Mosterman, *Spaces of Enslavement*, 56–57.

296 **42 percent of families:** Sylviane Diouf. "New York City's Slave Market." Nypl.org, blog, June 29, 2015, accessed Apr. 22, 2024.

296 **The act freed no one:** Benton, Ned. "Slavery and the New York State Legislature." New York Slavery Records Index. Nyslavery.commons. gc.cuny.edu, accessed Apr. 22, 2024.

296 **Ten years after:** Mosterman, *Spaces of Enslavement*, 57.

296 **"Slave catchers":** Berlin, Ira, and Leslie Harris, eds. *Slavery in New York*. New York: New Press, 2005, 23–26.

296 **"almost as dependent":** Wright, Gavin. "Slavery and the Rise of the Nineteenth Century American Economy." *Journal of Economic Perspectives* 36, no. 2 (Spring 2022): 139–41.

297 **"forc't Obedience":** Ritchie, Robert. *The Duke's Province: A Study of New York Politics and Society, 1664–1691*. Chapel Hill: University of North Carolina Press, 1977, 68; New York State Library. *History Bulletin.* Albany, NY, 1898, 59.

297 **"beget a prejudice":** Schoonmaker, Marius. *The History of Kingston, New York*. New York, 1888, 51.

297 **"wee cannot expect":** Ritchie, *Duke's Province*, 68.

297 **heresy or witchcraft:** Van Rensselaer, *History of the City of New York in the Seventeenth Century*, vol. 2, 31.

298 **"fortunate that his Highness":** RNA, 5: 160.

298 **"proove better subjects":** Docs. Rel., vol. 3, 114.

299 **congenial settlement:** Christoph and Christoph, *General Entries*, 66–67.

299 **Later the two:** Van Rensselaer, *History of the City of New York in the Seventeenth Century*, vol. 2, 23–24.

299 **"the summe of":** New Jersey Historical Society. *Documents Relating to the Colonial History of the State of New Jersey*. Newark, 1880, vol. 1, 8–9.

299 **informing him:** Docs. Rel., 3: 105.

300 **"late Indenture":** *Collections of New-York Historical Society for 1869*, 75–77.

302 **"in all which we":** National Archives (UK). Calendar of State Papers, Colonial Office, 1/19, folio 66.

302 **"that all administration":** Docs. Rel., 3: 97.

303 **"orthodox in matters":** *Collections of New-York Historical Society for 1869*, 84.

303 **"They have put":** Maine Historical Society. *Documentary History of the State of Maine*. Portland, 1889, vol. 4, 292.

CHAPTER 19: GOING DUTCH

305 **a scathing rebuttal:** Docs. Rel., 2: 419–23.

305 **Stuyvesant served up:** Docs. Rel., 2: 363–488.

306 **a lone pear tree:** "The Stuyvesant Pear Tree." *Harper's New Monthly Magazine*, May 1862; *New York Times*, Feb. 27, 1867; New-York Historical Society, object file, accession no. 1867.439.

307 **"every kind of minerall":** *Proceedings of the Massachusetts Historical Society* 16 (1878), 225–29.

307 **"to consorte & cooperate":** *Proceedings of the Massachusetts Historical Society* 16 (1878), 231.

307 **was still icebound:** *Collections of New-York Historical Society for 1869,* 113.

308 **"shuffling sort of":** *Collections of New-York Historical Society for 1869,* 113.

309 **2,000 pounds:** *Collections of New-York Historical Society for 1869,* 114.

309 **$500,000:** Bankofengland.co.uk, accessed Apr. 24, 2024.

309 **He made a last:** *Collections of New-York Historical Society for 1869,* 126.

309 **"I hope your Lordship":** *Collections of New-York Historical Society for 1869,* 126.

309 **"Elizabeth Bennet":** "Will of Richard Nicolls, Gentleman"; National Archives, Kew—Prerogative Court of Canterbury. July 14, 1670. PROB 11/333/329.

310 **"people not only":** *Proceedings of the Massachusetts Historical Society* 16 (1878), 232.

310 **"the best of all":** *Docs. Rel.,* 3: 106.

311 **"There is good":** *Docs. Rel.,* 3: 182–85.

311 **The duke's flagship:** Turner, *James II,* 103–4.

312 **"In the year 1664":** As translated in Underwood, *Ampthill Parish Church,* 45.

315 **The Dutch government:** Van Rensselaer, *History of the City of New York in the Seventeenth Century,* vol. 2, 106.

315 **The fleet had been sent:** Van Rensselaer, *History of the City of New York in the Seventeenth Century,* vol. 2, 98–99.

315 **Its commander:** Van Rensselaer, *History of the City of New York in the Seventeenth Century,* vol. 2, 99.

315 **He seems to have:** My characterization of the retaking of New York comes in part from Artyom Anikin's as-yet-unpublished introduction to New Netherland Document Series, vol. 23. *Colve Papers, 1673–1674.* New York State Archives. Unpublished.

315 **The Royal African Company:** Pettigrew, William. *Freedom's Debt.* Chapel Hill: University of North Carolina Press, 2013, 11.

316 **subjected to being:** Newman, Simon P. *Freedom Seekers.* London: University of London Press, 2022, 188.

317 **"one of the greatest":** Israel, Jonathan, ed. *The Anglo-Dutch Moment: Essays on the Glorious Revolution and Its World Impact.* Cambridge: Cambridge University Press, 2003, 14.

317 **"overturned the Religion":** British History Online. "Prince of Orange's Declaration: 19 December 1688." In *Journal of the House of Commons, Vol. 10, 1688–1693.* London, 1802, 1–6. British-history.ac.uk.

317 **more than four hundred:** Israel, *Dutch Republic,* 849–50.

318 **When the Bank of England:** Jardine, Lisa. *Going Dutch: How England Plundered Holland's Glory.* New York: Harper, 2009, 346–48.

318 **The success of:** Scott, "Good Night Amsterdam," 355.

318 **"an invasion":** Jardine, *Going Dutch,* 349.

CHAPTER 20: THE MYSTERY

321 **When the Puritans:** Here is a selection of sources on the Puritan strain in American politics: Wood, Gordon. "Struggle over the Puritans." *New York Review of Books,* Nov. 9, 1989; Heike, Paul. *The Myths That Made America.* New York: Columbia University Press, 2014, esp. chap. 3, "Pilgrims and Puritans and the Myth of the Promised Land"; Cherry, Conrad, ed. *God's New Israel: Religious Interpretations of American Destiny.* Chapel Hill: University of North Carolina Press, 1998; Grosby, Steven. "America: The Israel of Our Time." Law and Liberty, June 25, 2018.

321 **"Is it a coincidence":** Jackson, Kenneth T., and David S. Dunbar, eds. *Empire City: New York through the Centuries.* New York: Columbia University Press, 2002, 2.

322 **"They have as many":** Maxwell, William, ed. *The Virginia Historical Register and Literary Advertiser,* vol. 1. Richmond, 1848, 208.

322 **"our chiefest":** "New York in 1692. Letter from Charles Lodwick, to Mr. Francis Lodwick and Mr. Hooker, dated May 20, 1692. Read before the Royal Society of London." New York, 1848, 244.

323 **Dorothea Angola died:** Romney, "Reytory Angola," 78.

324 **"on pain of forfeiting":** RNA, 6: 286.

324 **"the Negroes' farm":** Stokes, *Iconography,* vol. 6, 70, 76.

324 **coerced to sell:** Goodfriend, Joyce. *Before the Melting Pot.* Princeton: Princeton University Press, 1994, 116.

324 **seven hundred of whom:** Berlin and Harris, *Slavery in New York,* 63.

325 **dandyish pirates:** Burrows, Edwin G., and Mike Wallace. *Gotham: A History of New York City to 1898.* New York: Oxford University Press, 1999, 105–7.

325 **outlawed the enslavement:** Berlin and Harris, *Slavery in New York,* 60–61.

325 **"the first born Christian":** Danckaerts, *Journal,* 235–36.

325 **A year before:** O'Callaghan, *Documentary History,* 32.

327 **first Jewish deli:** Hershkowitz, Leo. "Asser Levy and the Inventories of Early New York Jews." *American Jewish History* 80, no. 1 (Autumn 1990): 26 and passim.

327 **Dutch buyers made:** Grumet, *Munsee Indians,* 53.

328 **The Hackensack sachem:** Grumet, *Munsee Indians,* 123.

328 **In 1683, Wassackarous:** Grumet, *Munsee Indians,* 159–60.

Selected Bibliography

**LETTERS, JOURNALS, MINUTES, WILLS, MAPS, AND OTHER
PRIMARY SOURCES**

Bickley, Francis, ed. *An English Letter Book*. London, 1925.

Brewer, J. S. *Letters and Papers, Foreign and Domestic, of the Reign of Henry VIII*. 3 vols. London, 1867.

British History Online. "Prince of Orange's Declaration: 19 December 1688." In *Journal of the House of Commons, Vol. 10, 1688–1693*. London, 1802.

Bucholz, Robert, project director. The Database of Court Officers, 1660–1837. "Household of James Duke of York (1660–1685)." Courtofficers.ctsdh.luc. edu, accessed Apr. 22, 2024.

Charles II, King of England. "King Charles II. His declaration to all his loving subjects of the kingdom of England. Dated from his Court at Breda in Holland, the 4/14 of April." Reprinted by Christopher Higgins in Harts Close, over against the Trone-Church, 1660.

Charles II, King of England. "The King's Declaration." *Journal of the House of Lords: Vol. 11, 1660–1666*. London, 1767–1830.

Christoph, Peter, ed. *New Netherland Historical Manuscripts: English*, vol. 22. *Administrative Papers of Governors Richard Nicolls and Francis Lovelace, 1664–1673*. Baltimore: Genealogical Publishing, 1980.

Christoph, Peter, and Florence Christoph, eds. *Books of General Entries of the Colony of New York, 1664–1673*. Baltimore: Genealogical Publishing, 1982.

Clarendon State Papers. Manuscripts and Archives, Bodleian Libraries, Oxford University.

Danckaerts, Jasper. *Journal of Jasper Danckaerts, 1679–1680*. New York: Charles Scribner's Sons, 1913.

De Laet, Joannes. *Iaerlyck verhael van de verrichtinghen der Geoctroyeerde West-Indische compagnie*. The Hague: M. Nijhoff, 1931.

Denham, Sir John. *The Poetical Works of Sir John Denham*. New Haven: Yale University Press, 1928.

Dutch National Archives. Collection 3.01.17, inv. nr. 1008. Nationaalarchief.nl.

Fernow, Berthold, ed. *The Records of New Amsterdam, from 1653 to 1674*. 7 vols. New York: Knickerbocker, 1897.

Gardiner, Samuel Rawson, ed. *Constitutional Documents of the Puritan Revolution*. Oxford: Clarendon, 1906.

Gehring, Charles T., trans. and ed. *Delaware Papers, Dutch Period, 1648–1664*. New Netherland Documents Series, vols. 18–19. Baltimore: Genealogical Publishing, 1981.

Gehring, Charles T., trans. and ed. New Netherland Documents Series, vol. 6. *Council Minutes: 1655–1656*. Syracuse: Syracuse University Press, 1995.

Gehring, Charles T., trans. and ed. New Netherland Documents Series, vol. 11. *Correspondence 1647–1653*. Syracuse: Syracuse University Press, 2000.

Gehring, Charles T., trans. and ed. New Netherland Documents Series, vol. 12. *Correspondence: 1654–1658*. Syracuse: Syracuse University Press, 2003.

Gehring, Charles T., trans. and ed. *New York Historical Manuscripts: Dutch*, vol. 5. *Council Minutes, 1652–1654*. Baltimore: Genealogical Publishing, 1983.

Gehring, Charles T., and J. A. Schiltkamp, trans. and eds. New Netherland Documents Series, vol. 17. *Curaçao Papers, 1640–1665*. Interlaken, NY: Heart of the Lakes Publishing, 1987.

Gehring, Charles, and William Starna. *A Journey into Mohawk and Oneida Country*. Syracuse: Syracuse University Press, 2013.

Gehring, Charles T., and Janny Venema, trans. and eds. New Netherland Documents Series, vol. 8. *Council Minutes: 1656–1658*. Syracuse: Syracuse University Press, 2018.

Great Britain Record Commission. "Charles II, 1660: An Act of Free and Generall Pardon Indemnity and Oblivion." *Statutes of the Realm*, vol. 5, 1625–80. London, 1819.

Hutchinson, Thomas. *A Collection of original papers relative to the history of the colony of Massachusets-Bay*. Boston, 1769.

Huygens Instituut. "5 Million Scans VOC Archives Online and Searchable." Huygens.knaw.nl, accessed Oct. 2, 2023.

Jameson, J. F. *Narratives of New Netherland, 1609–1664*. New York: Charles Scribner's Sons, 1909; repr. New York: Barnes and Noble, 1937.

Johnson, Edward. *Johnson's Wonder-Working Providence, 1628–1651*. Boston, 1825.

Lodwick, Charles. "New York in 1692: Letter from Charles Lodwick, to Mr. Francis Lodwick and Mr. Hooker, dated May 20, 1692. Read before the Royal Society of London." New York, 1848.

Maine Historical Society. *Documentary History of the State of Maine*, vol. 4. Portland, 1889.

Massachusetts Historical Society. *Proceedings of the Massachusetts Historical Society* 16 (1878).

Maverick, Samuel. *A Briefe Discription of New England and the Severall Townes Therein*. Boston, 1885.

Maxwell, William, ed. *The Virginia Historical Register and Literary Advertiser*, vol. 1. Richmond, 1848.

National Archives (UK). Colonial Office. CO 1: America and West Indies, Colonial Papers 1574–1757; CO 5: America and West Indies, Original Correspondence 1606–1822; CO 389: Board of Trade, Entry Books 1660–1803.

New Jersey Historical Society. *Documents Relating to the Colonial History of the State of New Jersey*. Newark, 1880.

New Netherland Documents Series, vol. 9. *Council Minutes, 1660–1661*. New York State Archives. Unpublished.

New Netherland Documents Series, vols. 10.1, 10.2, 10.3. *Council Minutes, 1661–1664*. New York State Archives. Unpublished.

New Netherland Documents Series, vol. 14. *Correspondence, 1661–1662*. New York State Archives. Unpublished.

New Netherland Documents Series, vol. 23. *Colve Papers, 1673–1674*. New York State Archives. Unpublished.

New-York Historical Society. *Collections of the New-York Historical Society for the Year 1869*. New York, 1870.

New York State Archives. Letters Patent 12953-78, vol. 2, I28–29.

New York State Archives. New Netherland, Council. *Dutch Colonial Council Minutes, 1638–1665*, series A1809, vol. 6.

Nicolls, Richard. Richard Nicolls's tombstone, St. Andrew's Church, Ampthill, Bedfordshire, UK.

Nicolls, Richard. "Will of Richard Nicolls, Gentleman," July 14, 1670. National Archives, Kew—Prerogative Court of Canterbury. Ref no. PROB 11/333/329.

O'Callaghan, Edmund. *Calendar of Dutch Historical Manuscripts in the Office of the Secretary of State*. Albany: Weed, Parsons, 1865; repr. Upper Saddle River, NJ: Gregg Press, 1968.

O'Callaghan, E. B. *The Documentary History of the State of New York*. 4 vols. Albany: Weed, Parsons, 1849–1851.

O'Callaghan, E. B., ed. and trans. *Remonstrance of New Netherland, and the Occurrences There, Addressed to the High and Mighty Lords States General of the United Netherlands*. Albany: Weed, Parsons, 1856.

O'Callaghan, E. B, and Berthold Fernow, trans. *Documents Relative to the Colonial History of the State of New York*. 15 vols. Albany: Weed, Parsons, 1856–1887.

Paltsits, Victor, ed. *Minutes of the Executive Council of the Province of New York*. Administration of Francis Lovelace, 1668–1673, vol. 1. Albany, 1910.

Pepys, Samuel. *The Diary of Samuel Pepys*. London, 1893. Accessed at pepysdiary.com.

Routledge, F. J., et al. *Calendar of Clarendon State Papers Preserved in the Bodleian Library.* 5 vols. Oxford: Clarendon, 1869–1970.

Royal Collection Trust. *"The Embarkation of Charles II at Scheveningen—Description."* Rct.uk, accessed Apr. 22, 2024.

Sackville, Charles. *The Poems of Charles Sackville, Sixth Earl of Dorset.* New York: Garland, 1979.

Scott, Kenneth, and Kenn Stryker-Rodda, eds. *The Register of Salomon LaChaire.* Baltimore: Genealogical Publishing, 1978.

The Second Book of Records of the Town of Southampton. Sag Harbor, NY, 1877.

Sells, A. Lytton, trans. *The Memoirs of James II: His Campaigns as Duke of York, 1652–1660.* Bloomington: Indiana University Press, 1962.

Shurtleff, Nathaniel, ed. *Records of the Governor and Company of the Massachusetts Bay in New England.* Boston, 1854.

Smith, John. *Adverts for Unexperienced Planters.* London, 1631.

Smith, John. *The Generall Historie of Virginia, New-England, and the Summer Isles.* London, 1624.

Sorbiere, M. *A Voyage to England.* London, 1709.

Stadsarchief Amsterdam. "Catharina Triko." Betrothal Register, archive no. 5001, inventory no. 428, p. 328.

Stadsarchief Amsterdam. Deposition of two soldiers. Archief van de Notarissen ter Standplaats Amsterdam. Notary Hendrick Outgers, Scan KLAB04497000096 and KLAB04497000097, Mar. 4, 1667. Translations by Simon Hart and Charles Gehring.

Stadsarchief Amsterdam. NA3016/1309, Notary Hendrick Venkel, Oct. 27, 1664.

A true relation of the unjust, cruel, and barbarous proceedings against the English, at Amboyna in the East-Indies, by the Netherlandish Governour & Council there. London, 1651.

Trumbull, J. H. *The Public Records of the Colony of Connecticut, 1636–1776.* Hartford, 1850–1890.

Udemans, Godefridus. *'T Geestelijck roer van 't Coopmansschip.* Dordrecht, 1640.

"The Union of Utrecht, January 23, 1579." Constitution.org, accessed June 26, 2024.

Van der Donck, Adriaen. *A Description of New Netherland.* Lincoln: University of Nebraska Press, 2008.

Van Laer, Arnold J. F., trans. and ed. *Correspondence of Jeremias van Rensselaer.* Albany: University of the State of New York, 1932.

Van Laer, Arnold J. F., trans. *New York Historical Manuscripts: Dutch,* vol. 1. *Register of the Provincial Secretary, 1638–1642.* Baltimore: Genealogical Publishing, 1974.

Van Laer, Arnold J. F., trans. *New York Historical Manuscripts: Dutch,* vol. 2. *Register of the Provincial Secretary, 1642–1647.* Baltimore: Genealogical Publishing, 1974.

Van Laer, Arnold J. F., trans. *New York Historical Manuscripts: Dutch*, vol. 4. *Council Minutes, 1638–1649*. Baltimore: Genealogical Publishing, 1974.

Venema, Janny, trans. and ed. *Correspondence 1659–1660*. New Netherland Documents Series, vol. 13. Syracuse: Syracuse University Press, 2022.

Venema, Janny, trans. and ed. *Correspondence 1663–1664*. New Netherland Documents Series, vol. 15. Unpublished.

Visscher, Nicolaes. "Novi Belgii Novaeque Angliae: Nec non partis Virginiae tabula multis in locis emendate." Amsterdam, 1685. Accessed at loc.gov.

West Stow Parish Registers, 1558 to 1850, and Wordwell Parish Registers, 1580–1850, with Sundry Notes. Woodbridge, England: George Booth, 1903.

Winslow, Edward. *New-Englands salamander, discovered by an irreligious and scornefull pamphlet, called New-Englands Jonas cast up at London, &c. Owned by Major Iohn Childe, but not probable to be written by him*. London, 1647.

Winthrop, John. "A City upon a Hill," 1630. Gilderlehrman.org, accessed July 1, 2024.

SECONDARY SOURCES

Abernathy, George. "The English Presbyterians and the Stuart Restoration: 1648–1663." *Transactions of the American Philosophical Society* 55, no. 2 (1965): 1–101.

Baxter, Frances. *The Baxter Family*. New York, 1913.

Benton, Ned. "Slavery and the New York State Legislature." New York Slavery Records Index. Nyslavery.commons.gc.cuny.edu, accessed Apr. 22, 2024.

Berlin, Ira, and Leslie Harris, eds. *Slavery in New York*. New York: New Press, 2005.

Black, Robert. *The Younger John Winthrop*. New York: Columbia University Press, 1968.

Blom, F., and H. Looijesteijn. "A Land of Milk and Honey: Colonial Propaganda and the City of Amsterdam, 1656–1664." *De Halve Maen* 85, no. 3 (2012): 47–56.

Brodhead, John Romeyn. *The History of the State of New York, 1609–1691*. 2 vols. New York: Harper & Brothers, 1871.

Bruchac, Margaret. "Revisiting Pocumtuck History in Deerfield." *Historical Journal of Massachusetts* 39, no. 1–2 (Summer 2011): 30–77.

Bruchac, Margaret, and Peter Thomas. "Locating 'Wissatinnewag' in John Pynchon's Letter of 1663." *Historical Journal of Massachusetts* 34, no. 1 (Winter 2006): 56–82.

Burrows, Edwin G., and Mike Wallace. *Gotham: A History of New York City to 1898*. New York: Oxford University Press, 1999.

Cantwell, Anne-Marie, and Diana Dizerega Wall. "Looking for Africans in Seventeenth Century New Amsterdam." In *The Archaeology of Race in the Northeast*. Edited by Christopher Matthews and Allison Manfra McGovern, 29–55. Gainesville: University of Florida Press, 2015.

Chaplin, Joyce. *Subject Matter: Technology, the Body, and Science on the Anglo-American Frontier, 1500–1676*. Cambridge, MA: Harvard University Press, 2001.

Cherry, Conrad, ed. *God's New Israel: Religious Interpretations of American Destiny*. Chapel Hill: University of North Carolina Press, 1998.

Christoph, Peter. "The Freedmen of New Amsterdam." In *A Beautiful and Fruitful Place: Selected Rensselaerswijck Seminar Papers*. Edited by Nancy Zeller, 157–70. Albany: New Netherland Publications, 1991.

Ciecka, James. "The First Mathematically Correct Life Annuity." *Journal of Legal Economics* 15, no. 1 (2008): 59–63.

Cummings, Abbott Lowell. "The Domestic Architecture of Boston, 1660–1725." *Archives of American Art Journal* 9, no. 4 (1971): 1–16.

Cummins, Neil, Morgan Kelly, and Cormac Ó Gráda. "Living Standards and Plague in London, 1560–1665." *Economic History Review* 69 (2016): 3–34.

Dann, Leslie, and Guido Jiminéz-Cruz, directors. "A Colonial Trading Woman: Margaret Hardenbroeck Philipse." Hudsonvalley.org, accessed Apr. 22, 2024.

Dewulf, Jeroen. *Afro-Atlantic Catholics: America's First Black Christians*. Notre Dame, IN: University of Notre Dame Press, 2022.

Dewulf, Jeroen. "Iberian Linguistic Elements among the Black Population in New Netherland (1614–1664)." *Journal of Pidgin and Creole Languages* 34, no. 1 (2019): 49–82.

Diouf, Sylviane. "New York City's Slave Market." Nypl.org, blog, June 29, 2015.

Ferguson, Lydia. "Tennis: 'The Game of Kings.'" Research Collections at Trinity, Trinity College Dublin, June 30, 2016, accessed Apr. 21, 2024.

Firth, C. H. "Cromwell and the Insurrection of 1655." *English Historical Review* 4, no. 14 (Apr. 1889).

Fox, Frank. *The Four Days' Battle of 1666*. Andover, MA: Docema, 2009.

Gehring, Charles T., and Robert S. Grumet. "Observations of the Indians from Jasper Danckaerts's Journal 1679–1680." *William and Mary Quarterly* 44, no. 1 (Jan. 1987): 104–20.

Gelfand, Noah. "A Transatlantic Approach to Understanding the Formation of a Jewish Community in New Netherland and New York." *New York History* 89, no. 4 (Fall 2008): 375–95.

Goddard, Ives. "The Origin and Meaning of the Name 'Manhattan.'" *New York History* 92, no. 4 (2010): 277–93.

Goodfriend, Joyce. *Before the Melting Pot*. Princeton: Princeton University Press, 1994.

Graham, J. L., L. Lawrence, and W. H. Requejo. *Inventive Negotiation*. New York: Palgrave Macmillan, 2014.

Grosby, Steven. "America: The Israel of Our Time." Law and Liberty, June 25, 2018.

Grumet, Robert. *First Manhattans*. Norman: University of Oklahoma Press, 2011.

Grumet, Robert S. *The Munsee Indians: A History*. Norman: University of Oklahoma Press, 2009.

Harper, Steven. "Making History: Documenting the 1737 Walking Purchase." *Pennsylvania History* (Spring 2010): 217–33.

Harris, William. *An Historical Account of the Lives and Writings of James I and Charles I and of the Lives of Oliver Cromwell and Charles II*. 3 vols. London, 1814.

Heike, Paul. *The Myths That Made America*. New York: Columbia University Press, 2014.

Henneton, Lauric. "A Matter Too Hard for Man to Comprehend: John Winthrop Jr. and the 'Leaping' Hill of Southern Maine." *New England Quarterly* 79, no. 3 (Sept. 2006): 461–72.

Hershkowitz, Leo. "Asser Levy and the Inventories of Early New York Jews." *American Jewish History* 80, no. 1 (Autumn 1990): 21–55.

Hershkowitz, Leo. "By Chance or Choice: Jews in New Amsterdam, 1654." American Jewish Archives, Cincinnati, 2005.

Howell, Roger, Jr. "Cromwell's Personality: The Problems and Promises of a Psychohistorical Approach." *Biography* 1, no. 1 (Winter 1978).

Hudson River Foundation. "NY/NJ Harbor & Estuary Program." Hudsonriver.org, accessed Apr. 3, 2022.

Irwin, Douglas. "Mercantilism as Strategic Trade Policy: The Anglo-Dutch Rivalry for the East India Trade." *Journal of Political Economy* 99, no. 6 (Dec. 1999): 1296–1314.

Israel, Jonathan, ed. *The Anglo-Dutch Moment: Essays on the Glorious Revolution and Its World Impact*. Cambridge: Cambridge University Press, 2003.

Israel, Jonathan. *The Dutch Republic: Its Rise, Greatness, and Fall—1477–1806*. Oxford: Oxford University Press, 1995.

Israel, Jonathan, and Stuart Schwartz. *The Expansion of Tolerance: Religion in Dutch Brazil (1624–1654)*. Amsterdam: Amsterdam University Press, 2007.

Jackson, Kenneth T., and David S. Dunbar, eds. *Empire City: New York through the Centuries*. New York: Columbia University Press, 2002.

Jacobs, Jaap. *Dutch Colonial Fortifications in North America, 1614–1676*. Amsterdam: New Holland Foundation, 2015.

Jacobs, Jaap. "The First Arrival of Enslaved Africans in New Amsterdam." *New York History* 104, no. 1 (Summer 2023): 96–114.

Jacobs, Jaap. *New Netherland: A Dutch Colony in Seventeenth Century America*. Leiden: Brill, 2005.

Jardine, Lisa. *Going Dutch: How England Plundered Holland's Glory*. New York: Harper, 2009.

Kishlansky, Mark. *A Monarchy Transformed: Britain 1603–1714*. London: Penguin, 1996.

Koot, Christian. *Empire at the Periphery: British Colonists, Anglo-Dutch*

Trade, and the Development of the British Atlantic, 1621–1713. New York: New York University Press, 2011.

Lamb, Martha. *History of the City of New York*. New York, 1877.

LeoGrand, William, and Peter Kornbluh. *Back Channel to Cuba: The Hidden History of Negotiations between Washington and Havana*. Chapel Hill: University of North Carolina Press, 2015.

Lister, T. H. *The Life and Administration of Edward, First Earl of Clarendon*. London, 1838.

Lopate, Philip. *Waterfront: A Walk around Manhattan*. New York: Knopf Doubleday, 2005.

Maika, Dennis J. *Commerce and Community: Manhattan Merchants in the Seventeenth Century*. PhD dissertation, New York University, 1995.

Maika, Dennis J. *Merchants of Manhattan: Private Entrepreneurs and Their City Government in 17th Century New Netherland and New York*. Forthcoming.

Maika, Dennis J. "New Light on an Old Story: Re-examining the English Invasions of New Amsterdam, 1660–1664." Presentation at the New Netherland Seminar, Rotterdam Junction, NY, Sept. 13, 2012.

Maika, Dennis J. "Slavery, Race, and Culture in Early New York." *De Halve Maen* 73, no. 2 (Summer 2000): 27–33.

Maika, Dennis J. "To 'Experiment with a Parcel of Negroes': Incentive, Collaboration, and Competition in New Amsterdam's Slave Trade.'" *Journal of Early American History* 10 (2020): 33–69.

Maika, Dennis J. "'We Shall Bloom and Grow Like the Cedar on Lebanon': Dutch Merchants in English New York City, 1664–1672." *De Halve Maen* 74, no. 1 (Spring 2001): 7–14.

Maybaum, Ignaz. "Sephardim and Ashkenazim." *European Judaism: A Journal for the New Europe* 4, no. 1 (Summer 1969): 29–33.

Miller, Robert. "The Doctrine of Discovery: The International Law of Colonialism." *Indigenous Peoples' Journal of Law, Culture & Resistance* 5, no. 1 (2019): 35–42.

Mnookin, Robert. *Bargaining with the Devil: When to Negotiate, When to Fight*. New York: Simon & Schuster, 2010.

Mosterman, Andrea. "Reconstructing a Slave Ship Voyage: The *Gideon* and the Dutch Slave Trade into New Amsterdam." Paper presented at 129th Annual Meeting of the American Historical Association, New York, Jan. 2015.

Mosterman, Andrea. *Spaces of Enslavement: A History of Slavery and Resistance in Dutch New York*. Ithaca: Cornell University Press, 2021.

Moubray, Bonington. *A Practical Treatise on the Breeding, Rearing, and Fattening all Kinds of Domestic Poultry, Pheasants, Pigeons, and Rabbits*. London, 1830.

National Park Service. "Fact Sheet: Ellis Island—Statue of Liberty NM." NPS. gov, accessed Apr. 7, 2022.

New York City Department of Health and Mental Hygiene. "Health of

Indigenous Peoples of the Americas Living in New York City." *EPI Research Report*, Dec. 2021.

New York State Canal Corporation. "Canal History." Canals.ny.gov, accessed Oct. 10, 2022.

Newman, Simon P. *Freedom Seekers*. London: University of London Press, 2022.

Newson, Linda, and Susie Minchin. *From Capture to Sale: The Portuguese Slave Trade to Spanish South America in the Early Seventeenth Century*. Leiden: Brill, 2007.

Nicholls, Walter. *Sergeant Francis Nicholls*. New York: Grafton, 1909.

Norton, Rictor. "Queen James and His Courtiers." Gay History and Literature, http://rictornorton.co.uk/jamesi.htm.

O'Callaghan, E. B. *History of New Netherland, or New York under the Dutch*. New York: Appleton, 1848.

Ollard, Richard. *Man of War: Sir Robert Holmes and the Restoration Navy*. London: Phoenix, 1969.

Oppenheim, Samuel. "The Early History of the Jews in New York, 1654–1664." *American Jewish Historical Society Publications*. Vol. 18, 1909.

Otterbein, Keith. "Huron vs. Iroquois: A Case Study in Inter-Tribal Warfare." *Ethnohistory* 26, no. 2 (Spring 1979): 141–52.

Perlin, Ross. "Were 18 Languages Spoken in New Amsterdam?" Zoom talk. New Amsterdam History Center, New York, Oct. 11, 2022.

Peterson, Mark. *The City-State of Boston*. Princeton: Princeton University Press, 2019.

Petram, Lodewijk. "Was the VOC the Most Valuable Company Ever? (Answer: NO!)." Worldsfirststockexchange.com, accessed Apr. 22, 2024.

Pettigrew, William. *Freedom's Debt*. Chapel Hill: University of North Carolina Press, 2013.

Philbrick, Nathaniel. *Mayflower: Voyage, Community, War*. New York: Penguin, 2007.

Ponte, Mark. "Blacks in Amsterdam around 1650." In *Blacks in Rembrandt's Time*. Edited by Elmer Kolfin et al., 56–61. Amsterdam: Rembrandt House Museum, 2020.

Public Records Office. *Calendar of State Papers, Colonial, America and West Indies, Vol. 5, 1661–1668*. London, 1880.

Ramsey, Robert. "Richard Cromwell, Protector of England." *American Historical Review* 42, no. 2 (Jan. 1937): 302–3.

Richter, Daniel. "Cultural Brokers and Intercultural Politics: New York–Iroquois Relations, 1664–1701. *Journal of American History* 75, no. 1 (June 1988): 40–67.

Richter, Daniel. "War and Culture: The Iroquois Experience." *William and Mary Quarterly* 40, no. 4 (Oct. 1983): 528–59.

Ritchie, Robert. *The Duke's Province: A Study of New York Politics and Society, 1664–1691*. Chapel Hill: University of North Carolina Press, 1977.

Robertson, Alexander. *The Life of Sir Robert Moray: Soldier, Statesman and Man of Science (1608–1673)*. London: Longmans, Green, 1922.

Rommelse, Gijs. "The Role of Mercantilism in Anglo-Dutch Political Relations, 1650–74." *Economic History Review* 63, no. 3 (Aug. 2010): 591–611.

Romney, Susanah Shaw. *New Netherland Connections*. Chapel Hill: University of North Carolina Press, 2014.

Romney, Susana Shaw. "Reytory Angola, Seventeenth-Century Manhattan (US)." In *As If She Were Free: A Collective Biography of Women and Emancipation in the Americas*. Edited by Erica Ball et al., 58–78. New York: Cambridge University Press, 2020.

Roper, L. H. "The Fall of New Netherland and Seventeenth-Century Anglo-American Imperial Formation, 1654–1676." *New England Quarterly* 87, no. 4 (Dec. 2014): 666–708.

Sandoval, Gabriel. "Native American New Yorkers Grow in Number, Latest Census Shows." Thecity.nyc, accessed Oct. 10, 2021.

Schoonmaker, Marius. *The History of Kingston, New York*. New York, 1888.

Schuyler Van Rensselaer, Mariana. *History of the City of New York in the Seventeenth Century*. 2 vols. New York: Macmillan, 1909.

Scott, Jonathan. "'Good Night, Amsterdam': Sir George Downing and Anglo-Dutch Statebuilding." *English Historical Review* 118, no. 476 (2003): 334–56.

Shorto, Russell. *Amsterdam: A History of the World's Most Liberal City*. New York: Doubleday, 2013.

Shorto, Russell. *The Island at the Center of the World: The Epic Story of Dutch Manhattan and the Forgotten Colony That Shaped America*. New York: Doubleday, 2004.

Snabel, Cor, and Elizabeth Johnson. *The Varlet Family of Amsterdam, and Their Associated Families in the American Colonies and in the Netherlands*. Varletfamilypbworks.com, accessed Apr. 22, 2024.

Spencer, Charles. *To Catch a King: Charles II's Great Escape*. New York: Harper Collins, 2023.

Starna, William A. "From Homeland to New Land: A History of the Mahican Indians, 1600–1830." Northeast Region NAGPRA Program, National Parks Service, 2011.

Stokes, I. N. Phelps. *The Iconography of Manhattan Island*. 6 vols. New York: Dodd, 1915–1928.

"The Stuyvesant Pear Tree." *Harper's New Monthly Magazine*, May 1862.

Turner, F. C. *James II*. London, 1948.

Underwood, Andrew. *17th Century Ampthill and Hugh Reeve Its True and Lawful Parson*. Ampthill, Bedfordshire, UK: Merry Printers, 2000.

Underwood, Andrew. *Ampthill Parish Church*. Ampthill, Bedfordshire, UK: Merry Printers, 2007.

Van Welie, Rik. "Slave Trading and Slavery in the Dutch Colonial Empire:

A Global Comparison." *NWIG: New West-Indian Guide/Nieuwe West-Indische Gids* 82 (2008): 47–96.

Venema, Janny. *Beverwijck: A Dutch Village on the American Frontier, 1652–1664*. Albany: State University of New York Press, 2003.

"Walking Purchase." Buckscounty.gov, accessed Apr. 23, 2024.

"The Walking Purchase." Delawaretribe.org, accessed Apr. 23, 2024.

"When Gov. John Winthrop Jr. Doctored the Connecticut Colony: For Free." Newenglandhistoricalsociety.com, accessed Apr. 22, 2024.

Wiecek, William. "The Statutory Law of Slavery and Race in the Thirteen Mainland Colonies of British America." *William and Mary Quarterly* 34, no. 2 (Apr. 1977): 258–80.

Wilson, C. H. "Who Captured New Amsterdam?" *English Historical Review* 72, no. 284 (July 1957): 469–74.

Wood, Gordon. "Struggle over the Puritans." *New York Review of Books*, Nov. 9, 1989.

Woodward, Walter. "From the State Historian: The Map That Wasn't a Map." Connecticuthistory.org, accessed Apr. 22, 2024.

Woodward, Walter. *Prospero's America*. Chapel Hill: University of North Carolina Press, 2013.

Wright, Gavin. "Slavery and the Rise of the Nineteenth Century American Economy." *Journal of Economic Perspectives* 36, no. 2 (Spring 2022): 123–48.

Yozzo, David, Pace Wilber, and Robert J. Will. "Beneficial Use of Dredged Material for Habitat Creation, Enhancement, and Restoration in New York–New Jersey Harbor." *Journal of Environmental Management* 73, no. 1 (Nov. 2004): 39–52.

Zabriskie, George Olin. "The Founding Families of New Netherland." *De Halve Maen* 46, no. 4; 47, nos. 1 and 2 (1972).

Illustration Credits

Index

Page numbers in *italics* refer to illustrations and accompanying captions.